DO NEW LEADERS MAKE A DIFFERENCE?

D0077264

"In the Soviet Union there are no normal procedures for regularly replacing the country's political leadership. Changes have always taken place during crises, and have therefore inevitably been unhealthy, confronting the nation with sudden 'fait accomplis' of an ominous kind."
—*Roy Medvedev* (*On Socialist Democracy*, 1977:37)

DO NEW LEADERS MAKE A DIFFERENCE?

Executive Succession and Public Policy under Capitalism and Socialism

V ALERIE B UNCE

PRINCETON UNIVERSITY PRESS
PRINCETON, NEW JERSEY

Publication of this book has been aided by the Whitney
Darrow Publication Fund of Princeton University Press

This book has been composed in Linotron Baskerville

Clothbound editions of Princeton University Press books
are printed on acid-free paper, and binding materials are
chosen for strength and durability

Printed in the United States of America by Princeton
University Press, Princeton, New Jersey

To My Parents and to Gerry:

You Have Always Been There
When I Needed You

Contents

List of Tables

Acknowledgments

In the course of writing this book I have benefited from the advice and support of a number of people. While in the final analysis this work is my own, it represents the culmination of years of personal and intellectual exchanges with scores of colleagues—in graduate school at the University of Michigan, and in the years that followed as an assistant professor at Lake Forest College and Northwestern University.

I should mention, first, Bill Zimmerman, who chaired my dissertation committee and pulled me kicking and screaming through graduate school. While at the time of writing the dissertation, I never dreamed that so many more revisions were ahead of me—indeed, I thought his standards were too harsh, if not idiosyncratic—I can now say, years later, that his comments were very helpful and fair and greatly improved the quality of this work. I should also add that Bill's influence went beyond that of a chairman. His common-sense approach to Soviet politics, as a topic which went beyond idiosyncratic and draconian power struggles, influenced me a great deal. Finally, that he never laughed at what in 1972 was a bizarre argument—that Soviet successions may be functional processes (and in fact encouraged me in developing that thought)—is something for which I will always be grateful. I suppose that in a way I am now saying: yes, you were right about many things and, yes, I'm sorry for how long it took me to realize it.

I would also like to thank other scholars who influenced me at the University of Michigan. In particular, I should mention Bob Putnam, who opened my eyes as an undergraduate to elite analysis and comparative inquiry, and whose enthusiasm for political science reminded me of a child opening presents on Christmas morning. In a discipline where the tendency is to attack all previous work and to avoid learning much that is positive—indeed, while physicists stand on each other's shoulders, political scientists stand on each other's faces—Bob's approach was an important influence on me. I can only hope, to harken back to one of my favorite stories about him, that this book represents a step up from "our pre-paradigmatic state."

I would also like to thank Sam Eldersveld, Zvi Gitelman, Jack Walker, and Al Meyer, all of whom contributed time, ideas, and support for this project. Zvi in particular provided many useful criticisms throughout graduate school, and Al's skepticism about much of the discipline has been, especially in recent years, very influential on my thinking. Jack's concern with innovation has also affected me, as did Sam's course on political parties.

However, as any graduate student or assistant professor knows, much of one's ideas are developed through exchanges with those who shared the excruciating experience of moving through graduate school and into that peculiar world known as "professional life." The contacts made during this rite of passage were and are emotionally and intellectually important. I would like to thank, in particular, Sharon Wolchik, Fritz Gaenslen, Bruce Cameron, Michael McKuen, Barbara Farah, Gretchen Sandles, and David and Stephanie Cameron. I would also like to thank more recent colleagues, especially Ron Herring, and, as well, Joe Carens, Jean Hardisty, Alex Hicks, Phil Schrodt, Susan Clarke, Sarah Maza, and Ted Gurr. While it would be hard to pinpoint each of their contributions, the point remains that they all have contributed in their own ways to my intellectual development.

Of course, ideas come not just from discussion, but also from the work of others. As is obvious throughout this book, I owe a great deal to Jerry Hough. As a graduate student first discovering his work, I felt uncomfortable, yet intrigued. In the years since that time, I have become in many ways a fellow-traveler. I should also mention the influence of Merle Fainsod, whose work has withstood the test of time and which can always be reexamined with profit. Finally, I would like to thank George Breslauer for the good work he does and for his comments on this project.

Mention should also be made of my editor at Princeton, Sandy Thatcher, and the high quality of the reviews I received in the process of turning the dissertation into a book. While I felt at times that Princeton University Press loved nothing more than sending me back repeatedly to square one, I have to admit that the criticisms did substantially refine the quality of the arguments presented here. Ann Larson is also to be commended for drudging through all the revisions and for typing the final copy of the manuscript.

Finally, I would like to thank John Echols, who, far more than anyone, provided the support and the ideas that turned what was a quirky idea into a book. It would not be an exaggeration to say that this book reflects his efforts and his endurance as much as my own.

July 1980 VALERIE BUNCE

DO NEW LEADERS MAKE A DIFFERENCE?

Introduction

Do new leaders make a difference? This question lies at the heart of much of the discipline of political science. For political theorists, conceptions of the ideal polity presuppose that certain types of leaders are optimal, if one is to maximize fairness, democracy, political stability, or government efficiency. Implicit in such arguments is the assumption that leaders do matter, that the ways in which they are recruited and the constraints under which they operate will affect how well the system functions and how responsive it is to various groups. Thus, the importance of leaders and their succession to office are central concerns in political theory.

Similarly, much of the work on elites, decision-making, and political development is concerned with the role of leaders in the political system. Whether one speaks of corporatism or incrementalism, the circulation of elites, or their control over the policy process, one fundamental issue remains the same. "Who governs" is seen to have an important effect on what happens in public policy and in the system at large.

Similar kinds of concerns underline area studies as well. The central motif in analyses of the American Presidency and the Soviet First Secretary, for example, is the nature of their power, and the degree to which different men do and can do different things. Even analyses which deal with structural differences between types of systems focus on the leadership question. To what extent, for instance, is the Soviet polity more leader-dependent than its polyarchical counterparts?

Indeed, many of the debates that go on within the social sciences as a whole are concerned with this issue, which

Fred Greenstein (1969) has called "actor dispensability."
Did Lenin "make" the Russian Revolution in 1917, or is
Theda Skocpol (1978) correct in her structuralist interpretation? Is public policy in advanced industrial societies insulated from elite influence, as the incremental model
would suggest, or is that influence decisive, as many case
studies seem to indicate? Will Indira Gandhi's return to
power, or Tito's death, lead to important changes in their
respective countries, or will politics go on essentially as before?

The list of such questions could go on indefinitely, but
the essential point remains, whether one looks at utopian
schemes or succession crises, revolutions or routine policy-
making. That point is that many of the questions we ask
as political scientists have to do with the role of leaders in
the policy process. Indeed, our very paradigms diverge on
this issue. A structural approach downgrades the importance of particular elites and places more emphasis on the
interaction between institutional and socioeconomic forces
in shaping various results. Leadership is important only
insofar as it transmits this complex interaction. By contrast,
middle-range behavioralist approaches based on positivist
assumptions tend to treat elites, when they are involved in
the issue at hand, as an important influence on what happens. Thus, elite and policy studies which come out of the
structuralist tradition understand elites as a tool or reflection of the prevailing socioeconomic structure and hence
of minimal independent influence, while such analyses,
when done by more mainstream political scientists, tend to
allow for some—and sometimes a great deal of—impact by
the ruling stratum.

Given all this concern with evaluating the importance of
political leadership and the diverse stances taken on this
topic, it would indeed be surprising if a large literature had
not developed around the impact of political leadership on
public policy. Such, however, is not the case. Assumptions
abound, yet evidence eludes us. While there is a great deal

of work that suggests the impact of elites, an equally sizeable body of inquiry would seem to indicate that elites matter very little. On the one hand, the proliferation in recent years of middle-range elite background and recruitment studies would seem to corroborate the "importance of elites" view. After all, why go to the trouble of analyzing such matters unless one feels that recruitment, values, and policy arrangements affect the political system in important ways?

On the other hand, there is a great deal of support for the position that leaders do not have much effect. Much of the work on policy-making in advanced industrial societies—with their corporatist tendencies, bureaucratization, and sheer complexity—would lead one to downgrade a pivotal role for political leadership. In fact, a similar argument could be made with respect to Third World nations as well, given the general thrust of the dependency research.

But all of these studies share one basic problem: they do not directly confront the issue of the impact of elites. It remains an assumption, supporting a particular approach, or a position that one can with difficulty extrapolate from the analysis at hand. Even those studies which purport to deal with this issue more directly do not provide convincing and entirely relevant evidence. For example, a number of recent studies have focused on the impact of politics on macro-economic policy (Tufte, 1978; Hibbs, 1977), but have not really shown how, how much, and which participants shape what appear to be certain politically advantageous and/or ideologically motivated economic policy outcomes. Even those studies which seek to identify the effects of party rule cannot—because of their research designs—really disentangle the influences of individual leaders versus their contexts. It may matter less who rules, for example, than the varying conditions under which different leaders rule.

All of this is to say, then, that while we know the issue

to be important, we have little sense of how it is resolved in the real world. We do not know how much influence leaders have and whether exchanging one for another has any impact. We have endless studies of elections, coups d'état, and succession processes in socialist and bourgeois democratic states, but almost all focus on the process by which power is transferred. In those rare cases where the impact of succession is considered, and hence the importance of leaders, the dependent variable is invariably system stability. Linking succession to public policy and generalizing from that to the role of political leadership are tasks that still await rigorous scrutiny.

THE GOALS OF THE STUDY

In this book I will begin to fill in this gap by assessing the policy impact of chief executive turnover in the Soviet and Western bloc states in the postwar era. My goals are several. First, in keeping with the discussion above concerning the ambiguities present in elite analysis, I will be concerned with trying to disentangle the relative effects of leadership and policy environment on the evolution of public policy. Towards that end I will examine the linkages between political leadership, policy-making, and policy outputs under varying conditions—when the leadership stratum is stable and when there is turnover, and where there are polyarchical governments and where there are one-party socialist states. Thus, by looking at the policy process and the priorities that result under diverse circumstances, I hope to be able to assess how much and under what conditions political leaders actually shape public policies. As a result, I hope to get some sense of both the parameters of elite influence under bourgeois democracy and under "developed socialism," and the different policy processes that operate in both system types when leadership is in flux and when the stratum at the apex is stable.

A second concern is more directly focused on the succession process. However, in contrast to most such analyses, this study will not treat succession as a dependent variable, as a process whose primary importance lies in sorting through the field of candidates. I will be less concerned with the "who" question and its resulting emphases on primaries and power struggles than on the "so what?" question. Given that certain people win because of certain attributes of the system and of the particular candidates, how does this affect the policy process? Second, in treating succession as an independent variable that influences decision-making, I will not reduce the analysis to a simple formula of, say, elite changeover yields this much policy change. Rather, I treat succession as a complex process that sets in motion certain changes in the policy environment—obviously, in the actual decision-makers involved, but also in the demands that surface, the values and interests of the principal players, the policy agenda and its contraints, and ultimately, the types of priorities that evolve. The linkage, then, between new leaders and new policies cannot be mapped out without paying attention to the "who?" the "how?" and the "so what?" questions of leadership succession. And the parameters and regularities of those linkages cannot be set without consideration of the effects of varying succession rites and policy contexts.

The final goal of this study is implicit in the objectives noted above: that is, to expand our understanding of comparative politics by examining an important issue—indeed, one which applies to all political systems—within a cross-national and cross-system-type framework. I will not belabor the common observation that, as a field of study, comparative politics has all too often fallen short of what one could call genuine comparative inquiry. It is sufficient to say that this study is prefaced on several key assumptions and, one could say, intellectual commitments. First, it is important to emphasize that it does not reduce politics to a particular variable or to a particular context: for example, political institutions, elite background, or policy outputs in a group of similar countries. Rather, I will be concerned with, first, processes rather than just players and political arrangements, and, second, with linkages rather than simple correlations in diverse political economies. I will examine, then, what is a functionally equivalent and central issue for all political systems: the relationship between the manner in which leaders are circulated and the ways in which policy is made.

Second, if we are to establish the existence of regularized patterns in the political process and to explain their causes, we need to build similarities (or controls) and variance into our studies. In addition, we need to understand, not just regularities, but also deviations, for the latter define what is possible. Thus, to be comparative, in my view, is to be able to make generalizations and to be able to note their limitations. It is for these reasons that I have focused on decision and succession processes and have extended the analysis to encompass a number of countries, some of which are bourgeois democratic and some of which are communist party states.

It is, of course, no secret that if the history of similar system-type studies is problematic, then the comparatively briefer history of "different systems" analysis is even more jagged and fraught with great dangers. Clearly, in the latter case scholars are often caught between the Scylla of trivial comparisons and the Charybdis of functional inequivalence. The Central Committee of the Soviet Union, for example, is far different in form and functioning from the American Congress; voting hardly means the same thing in Los Angeles versus Leningrad; and the background of members of the British Cabinet versus the Politburo may be suspect as a point of comparison, both because the two bodies play different roles and because such characteristics in and of themselves may have few political consequences. However, such problems are less burdensome when one can argue for the importance and comparability of the issue at hand. Certainly, every polity must confront the issue of replacing its leadership, and every polity provides for certain arrangements whereby major decisions are made at the apex of the system. Moreover, in every political system, the acquisition of power is linked—sometimes directly and sometimes indirectly—to the determination of public policy, and that linkage tells us about who rules and how decisions are made. Insofar as succession, decision-making, and their interactions are common to all systems, one can talk of functional equivalence and one can safely extend the study to different systems.

Going beyond these obvious similarities, of course, one enters the thicket of what Giovanni Sartori (1968) has called "concept stretching": that is, the obvious point that certain concepts and variables imply very different things when observed or applied in different political environments. This is always a problem, even when one compares politics within one nation. However, to the degree that one sticks to central processes and allows for diversity in the ways these processes proceed, one can avoid such problems. This book does not equate Prime Ministers with First Secretaries or Soviet electorates with their American counterparts. What it does do is to argue that policy is made in all countries (albeit in different ways), succession is something for which all systems provide, and the linkage between these two processes can tell us something about the impact of leaders and their environments and the rhythms of policy change as systems move from leadership stability to leadership flux. Whether new leaders make a difference, then, can be assessed only if we look at the relationship between changes in leadership and the policy process in a range of political contexts.

THE DESIGN OF THE STUDY

In Chapter One, I lay out a series of arguments concerning the degree to which and the conditions under which succession should usher in changes in the policy process and in the priorities that evolve in socialist and capitalist states. Put briefly, I hypothesize—extrapolating from existing evidence—that new leaders in the Soviet bloc and in the West will be innovative early in their terms and then settle somewhat into fairly stable priorities until the next succession. Thus, I expect to find a policy cycle, calibrated by succession, in which more innovative priorities will alternate with more incremental modes of decision-making. This follows from what I perceive to be the ebb and flow in the incentives and capacity of chief executives to put through new public policies, an ebb and flow which reflects the distinction between politics as usual and honeymoon policy-making.

In the second chapter, I deal with methodological issues, having to do with the logic behind my decisions to combine a case study with an aggregate data approach and to look at electoral, as well as "selectoral," modes of succession. In Chapter Three, the quantitative results concerning the impact of chief executive turnover on budgetary outlays in Western national and subnational contexts is presented, along with a discussion of the linkages involved. These linkages are expanded into a more explicit model of policy innovation in Chapter Four, where I combine the statistical results with a study of changes in American welfare policy in the postwar era. In Chapter Five I assess the effects of succession on budgetary, investment, and macro-economic policy in the Soviet Union and in Eastern Europe. As with the Western portion of the study, the results of that analysis are refined and elaborated in Chapter Six through a more contextual analysis of one policy area—Soviet agricultural policy in the post-Stalinist era. Here, the emphasis is once again on developing two models of policy-making: one which applies to the succession period and one which describes decision-making during periods of stability in the leadership stratum. The final chapter is concerned with drawing the results together, and then addressing some broader issues—primarily having to do with the implications of this book for comparative elite and policy analysis.

For example, the conclusion of this study—that succession functions as a mechanism for policy *innovation*, East and West, is an argument that goes against much of the common wisdom in these two areas of study. Thus, in the concluding chapter, I challenge, among other things, the tendency to treat socialist successions as dysfunctional processes and Western elections as processes which merely maintain prevailing priorities. Rather, in both cases succession has remarkably similar effects, in that it sets in motion a distinct policy cycle which is repeated each time one governing team succeeds another. In this sense, leadership succession calibrates the policy process East and West.

ONE

Changing Leaders and Changing Policies

It is widely presumed . . . that important system developments
. . . are connected with changes in the political elite.
—*John Nagle* (1977)

Students of Soviet and American politics have tended to study
[their] own system as an end in itself. The esoteric cult of
Kremlinology on the one hand has been matched by the worship
of American uniqueness on the other.
—*Samuel Huntington and Zbigniew Brzezinski* (1963)

INTRODUCTION

In the fall of 1976 the United States was entering the final
stretch of that quadrennial "marathon" (Witcover, 1977)
known as the Presidential election. The nominee of the
Democratic Party, Jimmy Carter, had in the space of two
years moved from virtual nonentity (Jimmy "who?") to become the leading contender for the office of President. An
endless round of primaries and numerous public appear-
ances had seemingly convinced the electorate that Carter
was the best the Democrats had to offer and the man most
suited to occupying the Oval Office for the next four years.

However, despite their continuous exposure to the candidate, the electorate and the stalwarts of the Democratic
Party seemed to have some misgivings about Jimmy Carter.
The main source of discomfort revolved around the question of predictability. What would Carter do once he was
elected? The fact that he was an "outsider," an untested
political amateur, made him at the same time exciting and
yet suspect. While he was not "tainted" by a long career in

[12]

Washington—a definite asset in 1976—he was at the same time unpredictable and inexperienced—a decided liability.

By contrast, his opponent, Gerald Ford, was a familiar and experienced politician. This meant, in his case as well, a number of trade-offs in terms of his appeal to the electorate. While some voters saw his political experience as good because it implied that he was competent and predictable, others felt that such a background would lead to stagnation in public policy.

Thus, while in some respects the 1976 Presidential election could be characterized as unusual, in this one aspect— the tension between wanting a known quantity, yet desiring "politics as unusual"—the election was in fact typical. As in past elections, the voters had to decide between a stable transfer of power and a more uncertain succession, between continuity or change in personnel and public policies, and, finally, between a more experienced leader as opposed to a political novice. The decisive issue in the 1976 election, then, was an issue that had dominated previous elections as well: how much policy change would the electorate tolerate for the next four years?

A similar issue underscored a very different succession going on at the same time halfway around the globe: the battle for the mantle of Mao Zedong, who had died in September, 1976. As with the American case, in the Chinese succession political routines were held in suspension while various contenders jockeyed for position. The rhetoric in the political arena took on much the same cast as it had in the American marathon; discussions of specific government actions were interspersed with broader philosophical exchanges about the proper nature of public policy in a socialist state and the overall performance of China since 1949. As with Carter and Ford, so Chinese contenders for power argued their cases in terms of continuity and of change in public policy in the future—the amount they felt China needed and the amount they felt the people wanted. And, in both successions, the answers to these questions

influenced which successor eventually won and the amount
of policy change that occurred after the transfer of power.

SUCCESSION AND POLICY CHANGE

The fact that both the Chinese and the American successions—despite their very different contexts and processes—
revolved around the issue of policy innovation says a great
deal about the extent to which all changes in leadership,
wherever they occur, are thought to involve as well changes
in public policy. This, of course, is something that citizens
and politicians know very well. Indeed, they both monitor
succession closely precisely because of its implications for
change in the system and in policy priorities. What counts
in succession, then, is not so much the appearance of new
faces, but rather the fact that these new faces may do new
things.

Ironically enough, this rather obvious point has been lost
on political scientists. They have worked from the assumption that succession somehow "matters" and have, as a result, focused most of their research efforts on detailing the
actual struggle for power—what the Soviets call "kto-kogo"
(who over whom) (see, for example, Butler and Stokes,
1974; Keech and Matthews, 1976; Burling, 1974; Polsby
and Wildavsky, 1971; Rush, 1968). To take one typical
example, Nelson Polsby and Aaron Wildavsky (1971) have
written a 332-page book concerned with Presidential elections, yet they devoted a mere 6 pages to what they perceive
to be the policy ramifications of the electoral process. Scholars have, therefore, reduced succession to the status of a
dependent variable, a process that needs to be described
and explained rather than one which acts on the political
environment. Political scientists can speak authoritatively
about voting behavior, elite·recruitment, campaigns, and
general patterns of elite turnover, but they have considerably less to say about the amount of policy change that

resulted from these processes.[1] Such a truncated notion of succession—emphasizing the "who" and the "how"—has meant little concern for what is an equally, if not more important question: so what?

It is precisely with this issue—the impact of succession in East and West—that this book is concerned. What difference does it actually make when one leader succeeds another? Is this merely a personnel shift that occurs within the context of an ongoing policy process—as many have argued with respect to Western elections—or does succession have important policy ramifications beyond a simple transfer of political power—as is often asserted by communist area specialists? To what extent and how does succession affect policy priorities in West and East? Do they march on as before, unencumbered by the transition to new decision-makers, or do new priorities evolve in response to the new governing team? In short, is leadership succession, through elections or coups d'état, a crisis with dramatic policy effects, an institutionalized mechanism that periodically readjusts policies to new needs and demands, or is it a process that merely continues previous practices, essentially placing old priorities in new bottles?[2]

It is with these issues, then, having to do, not with the

---

[1] It should be emphasized that a variety of studies have dealt with this issue, but only tangentially. One kind examines how different various parties are in their policy priorities (for example, Fried, 1971; Fried, 1976; Kornberg and Frasure, 1971; Hibbs, 1977; Cameron, 1978); a second cluster of studies examines how an upcoming election affects policy priorities (Tufte, 1978; Frey, 1978); and, finally, a third assesses the effects of succession, but on a narrow range of policies (Lowi, 1963; Rosen, 1974). However, in none of these cases (or those cited in the text), does one find comparative, rigorous assessments of the impact of individual successions on public policy.

[2] Indeed, it is surprising that succession has generated such interest, given the fact that its importance for the political system is so debatable, or at best assumed. If elections are merely symbolic exercises, then one must wonder at their central place in the discipline.

mechanics of succession or the drama that unfolds as contestants vie for power, but rather with the policy shifts that
occur in its wake, that this work is concerned. In this sense,
I am interested here in answering what is the most obvious,
and indeed the most common, question that one can pose
about political leadership, a question which has been asked
by philosophers and queens since Aristotle's time. That
question is: do new leaders make a difference?

In seeking an answer to this question, I will deal with two
related issues. The first has to do with the linkage between
succession processes and policy-making: that is, the extent
to which the process by which leaders are circulated sets
in motion certain changes in the policy environment—in
its participants, agenda, clienteles, and pressures—which
in turn affect policy outcomes. I therefore do not conceptualize succession as a mere replacement of governing officials, but rather as a complex process which alters the
policy environment in certain ways and, perhaps, policy
priorities as well.

A second and related issue is one that has in recent years
become a point of contention among policy analysts and
among elite theorists. Indeed, it lies at the heart of competing paradigms within the social sciences as a whole. That
issue is the relative importance of individuals versus their
environments, or, in the terrain we are considering, leaders
versus their contexts. To what extent can we explain political phenomena, such as policy priorities, as resulting
from the impact of leaders as opposed to other forces em-
anating from the structure within which they make decisions? To paraphrase Fred Greenstein (1969:51-55), are
leaders "dispensable" actors and actresses, or do they shape
the decisions they oversee?

In the course of assessing the policy impact of succession,
this study will necessarily address this question. First, I can
say something about the importance of leaders, simply because I am speaking about the effects of new leaders and
hence establishing to some degree the parameters of elite

influence. Second, in order to establish those parameters, I focus on how the policy environment changes as it moves from a condition within which the leadership stratum is stable to a condition wherein leadership is in flux. In tracing these changes, I will assess how and to what degree leaders versus their environments shape policy priorities. Thus, in understanding the linkage between succession rites and policy processes, and in trying to provide some control cases where succession did not occur, I necessarily will face the issue of leader dispensability.

However, this is not to suggest that this book will in any way be definitive. As is always the case, one cannot easily disentangle the effects of what historians call "great people" versus "social forces." The problem is that leaders never operate in a vacuum, and this truism holds even when one looks at succession. As noted above, succession is not simply a circulation of elites; it is also a reorientation of the policy environment. Thus, while one can make logical arguments about the mix of leadership and environmental effects when routine policy-making is replaced by the politics of succession, one cannot be absolutely sure about the generalizations that are made.[3] However, given the degree to which the impact of succession does say something about the impact of leadership and environment and its variance under different conditions, I will at least be suggestive on this important issue.

The two major concerns in this book, then, will be to assess the effects of leadership succession on the policy process and the priorities that evolve, and to provide some

---

[3] However, it is important to note that, while leaders are never separable from the environment and that succession alters both leaders and their decision context, one can still separate these effects to some degree by looking at successions which returned incumbents to office. While this is hardly an optimal control—indeed, the real world rarely cooperates in such matters—it does help us, along with the theory and other evidence, to be able to say something about the effects of succession and leadership in general.

evidence on the relative effects of leaders and their environments on policy-making under conditions of elite flux and elite stability. I will examine both issues by looking at the general nature of the policy process and the changes it undergoes when one leader succeeds another in a variety of political contexts, primarily in the United States and the Soviet Union in the postwar period, but also, respectively, in other bourgeois democratic and socialist states. Thus, I hope to be able to answer, not just whether new leaders make a difference in East and West, but also what range and forms that impact takes around the world. On a general level, is succession more a force for policy change in socialist than in polyarchical states, and how does that affect the policy process in both contexts when the leadership stratum moves from stability to change? Within bourgeois democratic states, how does the linkage between elections and public policy vary according to, for example, differing types of party systems and policy arrangements? To what extent, when focussing on the socialist bloc, does one find variations in policy after succession, depending on how regularized the succession process is? It is these kinds of questions, specifying the particular parameters of succession as a mechanism of policy change, and the comparative influences of leaders versus their contexts on decision-making, that I will address in this book.

Just as a wide variety of systems and decisional contexts is necessary to get at the range of the effects that succession and elites can have, so a number of approaches is important to addressing these kinds of questions. This study is decidedly empirical, but that does not mean that it relies wholly on quantitative analysis. Rather, a variety of evidence is employed, ranging from numerical assessments to some case studies of particular leaders in particular times dealing with particular policies. The combination of case studies, illustrative examples, and quantitative analysis is necessary, in my view, if we are to go beyond simple correlations and deal with succession and decision-making as the complex processes they are. Correlations "hint" at linkages, but only theory and case studies can tell us about the nature of those linkages. It is hoped, then, that by combining quantitative analysis with case studies, I will be able to look at a variety of public policies and to understand the relationship between new leaders and the policy process.

THE IMPACT OF SUCCESSION: THE WESTERN DEMOCRACIES

Before one can begin to evaluate the effects of leadership turnover on public policy, it would be useful to set out some reasonable expectations concerning the linkage between succession and policy change in bourgeois democratic and socialist systems. How and how much *should* elite change-over affect policy priorities in these two types of polities, given what is known about the nature of the succession process, and the elites and their policy environment?

If we turn first to the Western case, a simple extrapolation from the literature on democratic political culture, campaigns, and decision-making in pluralist systems would lead one to hypothesize that elections would *not* result in new policy priorities. Indeed, in the few cases where scholars have engaged in such prognostications (but with little or no evidence), there seems to be a consensus—among mainstream social scientists as well as among critical theorists—that liberal democratic elections "contribute to the defense of things as they are" (Dolbeare, 1974:80, also see Edelman, 1964; Beglov, 1971). Thus, because of "the political culture of bargaining and consensus" (Braybrooke and Lindblom, 1965:73), the extent to which campaigns discourage the development of new issues and innovative candidates (Rosen,1974; Downs, 1957; Kirchheimer, 1966; Sartori, 1968; Anichkin, 1972), and the conflict and complexity embedded in the decision process (Braybrooke and Lindblom, 1969; Wildavsky, 1974, 1975), one would anticipate that executive succession should have little influence on the policy process. Incrementalism would seem to hold sway, even in the aftermath of an election.

Or would it? If one works from a different stream of the literature—that is, Presidential memoirs, policy case studies, detailed accounts of campaigns, and general theories of innovation—a rather different hypothesis suggests itself. It can be argued that one cannot generalize from all the literature on the "routines of politics" (see Sharkansky, 1970) to the nature of decision-making during a new chief executive's initial period in office. In fact, decision-making in the White House or Whitehall seems to follow a certain temporal rhythm, reflecting "differences of pace, attitudes, objectives and responses" (Hess, 1977:43). Just as one can compare different leaders, then, so one can compare how leaders, their power and their priorities, change as they move from the beginning to the end of their terms. There may not be a great deal of justification, therefore, for assuming that decision-making always adheres to the incremental model (with its implied overwhelming resource and political constraints), especially when the focus is on the honeymoon period.

The question then becomes, how does this temporal notion fit in with the concern here: the impact of elections on public policy? It would seem reasonable to suggest that the constraints on policy change so often noted would be less compelling in the honeymoon period than in the later stages of an administration. Indeed, it can be argued that the campaign experience, when combined with the unique politics of the honeymoon, produces an optimal environment for policy innovation. Specifically, the transition period (from the campaign through the first year in office) provides many of the conditions under which policy innovation could be said to flourish. The succession process may work, then, to enhance the *incentives* and *capacity* of newly elected chief executives to innovate.

The incentives portion of this equation comes from two

sources: the impact of the campaign experience on the candidate and the role of the honeymoon as an antechamber for new ideas. The first aspect, the campaign experience, is one which most analysts have tended to treat as a factor that works against policy innovation. However, in arguing that both competitive and non-competitive campaigns discourage the discussion of issues (but for different reasons) and hence minimize the amount of policy change after the election (King, 1969; Sartori, 1968; Kirchheimer, 1966; Arian and Barnes, 1974), scholars have made what appears to be a mistaken inference. There is in fact no logical reason why campaign issues (or their veritable absence, I should add) should structure decisions after the election; policy can change after all whether or not such changes were proposed during the campaign discourses.

Second, this disjuncture is all the more likely when one realizes the extent to which each campaign is really two campaigns: one for public consumption, in which "issues are treated as a political football" (Hess, 1974:46), and one which is concerned with the impact of the campaign on the candidate—what Barbara Hershey (1977) has called "the social learning process." It is the latter effect that would seem to work to enhance the candidate's desire for innovation. The logic behind this assertion is that the candidate is in a sea of uncertainty and needs information as well as power. Both come from various groups in the electorate and the staff to whom candidates are continually exposed as they go about the process of acquiring votes. On the one hand, there is steady pressure from ideologues—politicians, staff members, the opposition, and the like who have certain interests to push—to act and act in certain ways. On the other hand, the candidate is affected by the electorate— the issues that keep coming up, their objections to the status quo, and their support for the candidate (which is the primary input contenders receive from them).

As a result, Presidents and Prime Ministers, when running for office, get a sense of an agenda that needs attention; it may not be terribly specific, but it is there and it can be, and apparently is, construed as a forcing action (see, for example, Johnson, 1971:88-111; Wilson, 1976: Brandt, 1976:138-166). This in turn leads to the beginning of a picture that the candidates carry with them to keep the adrenalin flowing: what will be done once they are in office. Candidates have to believe they will win; the tortures of the campaign demand complete confidence, or the exhaustive schedule would prove too much. The pressures of the campaign, the ideas pressed repeatedly on candidates from all corners, and the sense that urgent action is required—all join to enhance the candidates' desire to be innovative once the campaign is over (Hess, 1974; Drew, 1975).

In this sense, issues do play a major role in the political campaign, and do work to heighten the desire of major contenders to make a mark once elected. Issues, and a mentality of doing something, are both byproducts of the campaign experience. Moreover, the candidate's desire for change is reinforced by the politics of the honeymoon period. Nothing is more striking about this critical time in office than the optimism that permeates the air—the sense of "can do," to borrow Lyndon Johnson's phrase. As Stephen Hess (1977:43-44) has explained:

> The new administration begins in a state of euphoria. Reporters are inclined to be kind. Congress is quiescent. There is not yet a record to defend. The President, for the only time, takes a broad-gauged look at existing policies. His popularity ratings in the polls will never again be as high. . . . You only have a year at most for new initiatives, a time when you can establish some programs of your own. . . .

This optimism flows from several sources. One is the glow that still lingers from the recent election victory, and another is the strong, indeed inflated, support that every new chief executive receives from the masses, as expressed in public opinion polls (Mueller, 1975; Stimson, 1976; Kernell, 1978). This affects the new leader a great deal, since he or she has just emerged from a two-year habit of estimating power and worth in terms of public support. Another source is the heady feeling that anything is possible, which comes from the fact that a whole new team is in office for the first time. There is no sense of prior commitments, there is much (often false) consensus, and there is the shared experience of having undergone a grueling campaign which paid off and must be justified in terms of creating an administration that is different from and better than its predecessors. Thus, new chief executives and their surrounding lieutenants think they can do a great deal and want to show their mettle (Pressman and Wildavsky, 1973). They are naive—one can cite, for example, Harry Truman's smug comments to Eisenhower about control in the Army versus the Presidency—but their optimism and sense of urgency flow naturally from the polls, their staff, their mandate, and their sense of newness.

This sense of desiring change is also aided by the degree to which the new chief executive is bombarded by ideas. Just as the campaign encouraged new thoughts on public policy, so the honeymoon carries this process further. Indeed, it is the victorious candidate's feeling in the first days after the election that he or she knows only voters, not policies, that opens up the newly elected head of state to any and all policy options. It is the irony of the campaign— that it encourages endurance, not reflection—that bodes well for innovation. While, as noted above, candidates get a general sense of what they will do, they become a sponge for ideas once in office. It is a feeling of desperation—now that I won, what do I do?—that opens up the policy process to new directions at this time.

All of this means that the transition is a time for entertaining new options, for filling in the victor's vague picture of what the new administration will do. This picture is filled in, first, by task forces (which is a peculiar American invention in lieu of any meaningful party program) and in both the European and American contexts by the bureaucracy, the Cabinet, and ideologues within the governing party (Christoph, 1975; Thomas, 1975; Yarmolinsky, 1969; Thomas and Wolman, 1968). All focus their efforts on providing the new leader with policy proposals and diagnoses of existing problems. All of this in turn is enhanced by the unusually clear power structure that characterizes new administrations; as one observer put it: "All the lines are cut for a few seconds and they will listen to you for a while" (Worth Bateman, quoted in Burke and Burke, 1974:39). There is a new pie which is to be divided, and each group wants a slice.

The honeymoon, therefore, is a peculiar blend of activism and inexperience, of mounting desires for innovation at precisely the time expertise is lacking. Yet that very lack, ironically, is what makes action so desirable; an experienced chief executive would be too enmeshed, too submerged by demands, and too immobilized by previous defeats and declining support, to make that experience work for him or her. Thus, when scholars talk about the honeymoon and equate inexperience with timidity, they miss the point; inexperience works to energize, not immobilize, the new leader. It provides a receptivity to new directions in public policy.

At the same time that a new executive feels a need to make a mark and is inundated with proposals, the structuring of power in the system is such as to facilitate the translation of at least some of these ideas into actual policies. First, as noted above, there is a great deal of consensus in new administrations, which reflects, among other things, the fact that executives surround themselves with familiar faces and have not yet made those decisions which inevitably factionalize their staff, their cabinet, the legislature, and the bureaucracy. Moreover, each group has a strong incentive to cooperate: the first concern is to get in with the new leader and then to worry about pet projects. Thus, the new executive and the surrounding assistants serve as a focal point for all those groups who have been out of power, and even those who have tasted power in the previous administration and who want to maintain their position at the apex of the system. This means that each group during the honeymoon period will try to carve out a role and ingratiate itself with the chief executive and his or her cronies. While some will use this opportunity to do their own thing, most will try to ally themselves closely with the new governing team.

Compliance, then, is the norm in the honeymoon period. For example, in all Western systems, legislatures, to quote Lyndon Johnson, "give a new man a little cooperation, a little breathing room" (quoted in Hess, 1974:43-44) to see what he or she wants and what he or she can do.[4] Having just undergone an election, and sensing public desire for decisive action, legislators tend to shy away from overt conflict with the new chief executive until later in the administration. Indeed, any tabulation of Congressional support scores reveals that Presidents get their way more often in the honeymoon than later in their administrations. In the case of the bureaucracy and the Cabinet, a similar process of "cozying up" takes place. This is most apparent, for example, in the cases of Germany and Britain, with the Nixon experience in 1969 being an important but unusual exception (Christoph, 1975; Gunther, 1970; Stanley, 1965; Aberbach and Rockman, 1976).

Thus, in focusing on the interaction between the campaign experience and the politics of the honeymoon period,

---

[4] It is reasonable, however, in view of Jimmy Carter's first year in office, to wonder about the accuracy of this point. However, Carter's batting average with Congress was high, despite impressions given by the media. That it was not higher can be explained as a function of: (1) his narrow mandate, combined with a large and thus independent democratic majority; (2) the fact that he followed two presidents—Nixon and Ford—with the lowest Congressional support scores in the postwar era; and (3) his campaign theme as an outsider, which undermined the efforts of an already inexperienced staff to deal with Congress.

one sees an optimal climate for innovation. The new leader's desire for change—enhanced by optimism, the mandate, and the influx of new ideas—is matched by a capacity to make change, which reflects the consensus of the new team, the clarity of the power structure, the compliance of other actors and actresses in the system, and the lack of any prior commitments that would divide loyalties and solidify factions. The familiar list of constraints on innovation in Western systems, then, seems to shorten considerably when the focus is on the honeymoon period. Time, resources, information, and power are all seen as sufficient, and this is met by a corresponding desire to make a mark, to prove that this administration is different and capable, and to go ahead with some long-cherished policy innovations. Thus, by any model of innovation (Wilson, 1966; Downs and Mohr, 1975), the honeymoon would seem to be a breeding ground for new public policies.

However, this does not mean that constraints do not operate. There is still the political culture, of which the elites are a part, which sees "radical change as suspect" (Brzezinski and Huntington, 1963:51). There is as well the fact that politicians are, even when amateurs, a product of a socialization process that emphasizes compromise and extolls the benefits—both psychological and political—of making small change at the margins (Putnam, 1976:Chapters 2-3; Matthews, 1973). Third, one must remember that constraints operate even during the honeymoon: resource constraints always exist to some degree; cabinets are often composed of either strangers or political enemies; the bureaucracy can opt for waiting out the new person and the political appointees that stand above it; the political appointees may have trouble controlling their underlings; the new executive may be immobilized by the bombardment of ideas, demands, and grievances; and the inexperience of the new government may prevent the development of either new policies or of a coherent set of proposals (Wildavsky, 1974 and 1975; Heclo and Wildavsky, 1974). Finally, there is the tension between groups lining up behind the new leader and yet becoming alienated rather quickly once a few decisions are made. The fact that in making a decision a President or a Prime Minister must necessarily choose among policies, positions, and clienteles means that the benefits of a honeymoon in terms of innovation may be short-lived, so short-lived that the actual policy ramifications may be negligible.

These considerations imply that the linkage between elections and policy innovation will be shaped both by the inevitable limitations built into decision-making in Western democracies, and by the unusually innovative nature of the honeymoon period. With this set of opposing influences in mind, I will test the following three hypotheses:

1. Elections will usher in changes in public policy, but these changes will not constitute dramatic departures from past practices. Rather, they will involve deviations that are somewhat greater than the annual deviations in priorities in the past administration.

2. I expect such changes to occur primarily in the honeymoon and to be more pronounced when a new leader is inaugurated (as opposed to a reelection), when that leader has a large mandate, when the more leftist party rules, and when there is an actual change in the party in power. These conditions are all predicated on the argument that newer teams will be more innovative, that leftist parties are more change-oriented than rightist ones, and that "innovations cannot be forced on slender majorities" (Thomas Jefferson, quoted in Schlesinger, 1969:137; also see Crossman, 1976).

3. Within administrations, policy change will be incremental; that is, it will represent marginal adjustments in the priorities advanced during the honeymoon period. This hypothesis is drawn from the argument that, once innovations are introduced, they become stuck as coalitions solidify around them, as leaders become enmeshed by new demands and depressed by policy failures, and as political

and resource constraints increasingly cut into the incentives
and the capacity of the chief executive to advocate new
priorities. Thus, just as innovation is both the most logical
and perhaps the most preferred strategy during the honeymoon, so incrementalism would seem to make the most
sense under conditions of limited resources and political
conflict (see Walker, 1973)—that is, in the interim between
successions.

Changing Leaders and Changing Policies: The Impact of Succession in Socialist States

The question, then, becomes, what impact would one expect new leaders to have in socialist states? Would there be
a similar cycle, as hypothesized for the West, or a different
linkage between succession and policy innovation?

I would argue that most of the hypotheses outlined for
the Western case would apply as well, for many of the same
reasons, to the Soviet bloc. This assertion is based on two
different lines of argument. The first has to do with the
nature of ideology, power, and succession in socialist systems, in general, and the second deals with the changes in
these three factors that have occurred as these systems have
moved from the mobilization stage to a period of developed
(*razvitoi*) socialism (Jowitt, 1975; Evans, 1977; Kukushkin,
1977). Turning to the first set of contentions, we can argue
that there is much about the policy context and the succession process in the Soviet bloc that would encourage innovation in the period immediately following the transfer
of power. First, there is the general role of ideology, a force
which legitimates radical change and which "may add to
the learning capacity of the regime" (Breslauer, 1973:304).[5]
Indeed, the very notion of an ideological value system im-

---

[5] Of course, the more common argument is that ideology breeds rigidity.
The problem with this notion is that there is little evidence to support it,
either in studies of elite political culture or the policy process (see Hough,
1972; Hough, 1976; Breslauer, 1976; Putnam, 1971).

plies that rapid and constant change is both desirable and viable:

> The value system of the Soviet Union might be characterized as one of ideological activism; that is, a self-conscious set of directives to change society in accordance with a generalized theoretical doctrine. This involves a constant scrutiny of canonical texts . . . [and] a constant specification of goals in order to spur the people to the ends set by the regime. Such a society has a high, built-in drive toward social change (Bell, 1970:105; also see *Materialy*, 1974:88-90).

Moreover, the prospects for radical change would seem to be, if anything, heightened by the very nature of socialist successions, which, in the Western view, are events of cataclysmic proportions. As Andrzej Korbonski (1976:5) expressed this notion, "any change in leadership (in communist states) is bound to result in a change in the political system as a whole." In direct contrast to scholarly views about Western elections, successions in socialist nations have generally been seen as irregular, quasi-legitimate processes that produce or at least reflect crises in the political system. Thus, the impact of succession is perceived to be negative, since in the view of most Western observers, "no political system can be considered healthy when it lacks an effective and sure means of circulating the political elite" (Wesson, 1976:187-188; also see Drakhovitch, 1964; Hodgson, 1976; Rush, 1974; for critical views, see Zimmerman, 1976).

One "unhealthy" consequence of such a disorderly procedure is, of course, policy change. As Robert Conquest (1967:11) has summarized, "It is impossible to speak of struggles for substantial power without the context of issues." In fact, poor policy performance serves as *the* rationale for beginning the process of changing political leadership in socialist nations (Hodnett, 1975; Rakowska-Harmstone, 1976:70). In contrast to the Presidential system, where the calendar determines whether an election occurs, and Parliamentary systems, where Prime-Minister-designated issues are virtually all that can bring down a government, in socialist states policy performance is directly and consistently linked to the onset, duration, and resolution of the succession struggle. For example, Khrushchev's fall from grace in 1964 is commonly attributed (given the advantage of hindsight, one should add) to his numerous failings in the policy arena, failings which purportedly forced his successors to respond with new policy initiatives:

> By 1964 Khrushchev's agricultural panaceas, from massive corn cultivation to the virgin lands campaign had turned out to be failures. The latest harvest was wretched, and flour was at a premium. His successive re-organizations in industry, agriculture, and the Party had come to grief. The widely hailed educational reform had been virtually aborted. The grandiose promises to overtake the United States in the production of meat and butter . . . did not seem to be forthcoming. The truce between the party and the intellectuals had been brutally disrupted in late 1962 and early 1963. . . . De-Stalinization, too, in its symbolic aspect, seemed to have come to a halt. . . . The Sino-Soviet conflict had produced not only a weakening of Moscow's hold over its one time empire, but a pluralism and dogged search for independence among the East European communist countries [and] . . . the non-bloc parties. . . . Under these circumstances, is it any wonder that Khrushchev's star had become lackluster? (Brumberg, 1971:6).

Thus, in producing "new leaders who are intent upon correcting their predecessor's errors" (Laird, 1970:115), socialist successions would necessarily produce new directions in public policy. This outcome is all the more likely when one considers the nature of the "selectorate" in these states (Hodnett, 1975). The party *apparatchiki* choose the new leader, and they would be too sophisticated to tolerate fuzziness on the big issues of the day. Competition in such a context would seem to enhance innovation, not imitation, in contrast to the dynamics of Western electioneering. This would seem, moreover, to be particularly the case when one considers the infrequency of socialist successions, an infrequency which would seem to create a serious backlog of important issues and needs. Thus, the "instability" of socialist successions implies not just that they are irregular and infrequent and can place the system itself in jeopardy, but also that they bring past policy priorities into question, and thereby generate new ideas. It follows, then, that the changing of the political guard under such circumstances may very well produce a concurrent and substantial change in public policy.[6]

The desire to change public policy—enhanced by the regime ideology and the nature of the succession process— is matched, some scholars would argue, by great power as well, such that socialist leaders can in fact translate the ideas they have bandied around during the succession crisis into concrete programs. At the core of this argument is the belief that the policy environment in the East is more malleable than it is in the West (see Welsh, 1975). Because of the purported "fluidity" of the policy process, changes in leadership could more easily alter the prevailing policy concerns than in Western nations, where policy-making is more constrained and less leader-dependent. The power of a socialist leader, then, in sitting on the top of a centralized party apparatus and a centralized polity, implies that his fall will

---

[6] It is important to point out that this linkage between succession and policy change is one that politicians in socialist states have noted as well. See, for example, *Zarya Vostoka*, November 3, 1973, 3, quoted in *Current Digest of the Soviet Press*, 25 (November 28, 1973), 4; Leonid Brezhnev (1971):118; Demichev (1971):21-59. Such dynamics seem to be the case even when a succession arises in response to the death of the First Secretary. Even then, a platform must be created and must necessarily evaluate past performance and pinpoint current problems.

affect the goals and the functioning of the whole political system.

However, there is a problem with these arguments, and that is that they may be dated and hence may overstate the power and radicalism of socialist leaders. It can be asserted, for example, that there is an "end of ideology" in the Second World: that is, a diminishing concern with radical goals and a growing emphasis, in its place, on leadership continuity, stable performance expectations, and incremental policy change. Zbigniew Brzezinski (1966:9), for example, has described a decline in the ideological temper of the Soviet elite over time, arguing that "the Soviet political system, initially led by an internationalist and ideologically motivated elite, has increasingly passed into the hands of a chauvinist, etatist, and bureaucratic political elite, inimical to social change and hostile to innovation."

This so-called petrification of the leadership stratum is evidenced, among other things, by the statements of the leaders themselves. Leonid Brezhnev (1973:3), for example, has reiterated on numerous occasions that "we must guard against extremes; we must proceed in a rational manner, taking into account all aspects and implications of each measure." The familiar chant of the Brezhnev regime—the need for a business-like approach (*praktichnyi podkhod*) to decision-making—can be construed as an opposition among the leadership to dramatic shifts in public policy, and a commitment to a more incremental approach to policy-making. In fact, in more recent Western studies of socialist policy-making, it has been argued that both the process and its outputs conform rather well to what we term incrementalism in the West (Cocks, 1977; Bunce and Echols, 1978).

However, it is not just that ideological fervor seems to be on the wane and that small change has become legitimate, if not desirable. It is also that there has been what appears to be a reduction in the power of the top leader as well, a decline in capability that would seem to portend ill for the policy impact of succession. In the place of the *vozhd'* (supreme leader), there now is a leader who seems to be constrained by other elites, interest groups, and even the masses (Hough, 1977; Bruce and Clawson, 1977; Bunce and Echols, 1978; Bunce, 1980a and 1980b). With the end of the cult of personality, scholars argue, it has become increasingly difficult for the First or General Secretary to achieve his policy objectives. Rather, just as with the American President, the power of the leader may very well be the power to persuade:

> The collective leader must thoroughly understand that a situation must not arise whereby any authority . . . can cease to heed . . . the opinions of those who have advanced him in office. . . . It is simply impossible to permit the inception and development of instances when the prestige of an individual may assume forms in which he fancies that everything is permissible for him and that he no longer has need of the collective (Khrushchev, 1964:200).

And persuasion and compromise, it can be easily argued, would tend to foster incremental, not radical policy change. In the Soviet context, this follows from the fact that:

> government by committee is never easy. It is hindered all the more difficult when each member of the group is engaged in a contest for ascendancy, and every position taken is weighed not merely for its contribution to the common weal, but for its effect on the power struggle (Fainsod, 1965:112).

Unlike a President or Prime Minister, then, the General Secretary cannot readily appoint his Cabinet or dismiss recalcitrant members.[7] He must, instead, live with the antagonists who surround him. He may be, in other words, as

[7] Of course, the "harmony" of Western Cabinets is certainly subject to many qualifications (see Hess, 1976; Crossman, 1976).

strapped as his Western counterparts are by the conflict imbedded in the policy process.

But the constraints that operate on socialist leaders also seem to come from outside the ruling stratum, and these constraints are a direct product of the modernization process. With decision-making becoming more complex and a greater number of demands being made on the political system, leaders at the apex increasingly have to rely on others for information when they make decisions and have to make tough choices about who is going to get what (Beliakov and Shvets, 1967; Gorskaia, 1975; Khromov, 1972; Cocks, 1977). Socialist leaders seem to be just as hemmed in by resource constraints as their counterparts in the West. Thus, the decline in elite power in socialist systems would seem to encourage a concomitant decline in policy innovation—before, during, and after succession—precisely because time, information, and monetary constraints and politics as a bargaining process imply incremental policy change.

Nor would this generalization be altered by the effects of the succession process, which in recent years has become more routinized as well. Changing leaders, purportedly, no longer engenders a crisis but, rather, functions as a comparatively regularized vehicle for changing personnel and systematically, though not substantially, adjusting policy priorities. In analyses of early successions in socialist states, the duration of the crisis, the ruthlessness of the participants, and the uncertainty of the outcome were all seen as indicators of an unstable, or at least destabilizing, process of leadership selection. However, as Andrzej Korbonski (1976:19-20) and others (Baumann, 1971; Rigby, 1970) have noted, this process has been undergoing some changes:

> Clearly, there was a difference between Stalin and Khrushchev, Rakosi and Kadar, or Novotny and Dubcek, and their respective influences on the political system.

However, as with a number of concepts, the importance
of leadership and personality should not be exaggerated.
It was most likely greater in the early stages of East European development when it formed an integral part of
the totalitarian syndrome, but its role today is not as easily
ascertained. . . . [Moreover], the notion of a "succession
crisis" may be a thing of the past, and one could assume
that eventually succession in communist systems might
not differ greatly from succession in other political systems.

Thus, there may be less need or desire for contenders in
the succession to espouse different or terribly imaginative
policy ideas. This may no longer be the way power is won
and maintained in the communist party states.

The question then becomes, how can these two lines of
argument be reconciled? One way to get around this seeming contradiction is to recognize that socialist states have
changed, and that succession has, as a result, ceased to be
the mechanism of policy change it once was. A second way
to jell this literature is to assert, as I did in the Western
case, that what may be happening is a two-stage process of
decision-making, wherein innovation within certain limits
is more likely in the honeymoon but declines as the leader
settles into office. It is reasonable to suggest that the dynamics of succession—combining a new team, a leader ea-
ger to prove his worth by introducing new policies and
attacking past practices, and a circle of colleagues who want
to line up behind the new man and at the same time improve the performance of the system—work to encourage
policy change. However, once the mandate is won, the costs
of change made apparent, the various supporters paid off,
and the appeals of incrementalism in a complex, conflictual
world made all too compelling, more routinized modes of
decision-making would seem to prevail until the next
succession crisis. Thus, just as the honeymoon in the West
frees the new leader to be innovative, in the East, because

campaigning is restricted to the inner circle and follows the acquisition of power, the honeymoon there works to *force* the new First Secretary to be innovative. In both cases, though, the incentives and capacity to reorder priorities would seem to expand in the aftermath of succession— reflecting a similarly supportive environment and strong incentives to be different—and contract once the new regime settles into middle age—when conflict and complexity rear their heads and the need to innovate to create a mandate withers away.

This cyclical notion of policy-making in the socialist states suggests four hypotheses regarding the impact of succession on public policy in these systems.

1. Successions in the Soviet bloc should, like elections, lead to changes in public policy, but these changes will not be of the magnitude implied by the term "crisis." This notion of similarity, East and West, is premised on the argument that, while succession is inherently more destabilizing in the Eastern case, this is offset by the nature of the "decision process," which is more centralized in socialist states and hence more complex and conflictual than in the West. This implies that the policy effects of succession would be similar—that is strong, but not dramatic—in both types of polities.

2. It follows from this that this impact should be immediate but declining, as in the West, for many of the same reasons. New policies once introduced develop supporting coalitions and, over time, other groups begin to demand their fair share at the trough, the costs of innovations rise, and the incentive to introduce them declines. The administration, therefore, once succession is resolved, increasingly succumbs to "politics as usual" and incremental decision-making becomes the norm.

3. There will be a decline over time in the impact of succession on public policy, reflecting the growing institutionalization of the process, and the rise of essentially

tactical issues in a complex, conflictual, and increasingly pragmatic policy environment.

4. The impact of succession will vary with the extent of the crisis that precipitated it. Thus, successions which occurred in response to the death of the leader will have the fewest policy ramifications, followed by those which involved an elite coup d'état. The most disruptive successions in terms of policy change should be those which mobilized discontented sectors of the population, and hence strongly pressured the new leader to change current practices.

CONCLUSION

These then are the hypotheses that will be examined in this book. To reiterate, I expect policy-making in socialist and bourgeois democratic states to be cyclical, moving from incrementalism, when the leadership stratum is stable, to innovation, when that stratum is in flux. Succession therefore is seen as a complex process that alters principal players and their policy environment in ways that reduce conflict, complexity, and cultural biases against change. The honeymoon period thus opens up the system and its leaders to new priorities, precisely because it enhances the incentives and capacity of new chief executives to make a mark. However, once the leader is ensconced in office, the opportunities and desire fade, and incrementalism returns until the next succession.

In the course of tracing the linkages between successions and policy-making, I will touch on a number of related issues. For example, what do these linkages tell us about policy processes during stable versus transitional leadership periods and the nature of succession rites in socialist and bourgeois democratic states? Are there any similarities between these two types of systems in terms of the relative impact of leaders versus their environments on public policy? How salient is the distinction between socialist and bourgeois democratic polities, when one examines policy cycles and their influence on political performance? Do socialist successions really amount to "crises," and are democratic elections really processes with few consequences, as much of the literature seems to suggest? Is succession in socialist and liberal democratic states in fact so different in how it affects the political system as a whole?

Thus, in the process of testing the impact of leadership turnover on public policy, I will touch on a number of key issues that have long concerned political observers. Does it matter how leaders get into power? How much power do leaders have? How and how often do they change policy priorities? How much difference is there in these respects between purportedly different types of political systems? All of these topics will be addressed in the course of answering the basic question of this study: do new leaders make a difference?

TWO

Methodology

A budget may be characterized as a series of goals with price tags attached.
—*Aaron Wildavsky* (1974)

Given our present state of knowledge in the social sciences, we cannot afford to tie one operationalization to one variable.
—*Hubert Blalock* (1964)

INTRODUCTION

Social scientists traditionally have employed two different approaches to specify and test relationships among variables: quantitative analyses and case studies. Both of these methodologies, as their practitioners are quick to admit, have their strengths and their weaknesses. Case studies, for example, are strong on contextual information but lacking in generalizability. By contrast, quantitative research is (or can be) strong on generalizability, but is often deficient in specifying processes and causal linkages. Thus, both methods—case studies and quantitative analyses—seem to provide some, but not all of the answers that political scientists need to engage in rigorous research.

In this book I decided against selecting one of these approaches to the neglect of the other (a practice that is quite common in studies of public policy, for example), but, rather, to test the impact of succession on public policy by employing *both* methodologies. By combining these two approaches, we can speak about processes, correlations, and causes, and be more confident in drawing concrete conclusions about the role of succession in generating policy innovation.

[39]

The differences between the two approaches, however, necessitates a discussion of the methodology. In this chapter I will dwell a bit on the logic behind the case studies and the quantitative approaches, discussing why certain variables and indicators were selected for study and how the hypotheses outlined in Chapter One will be tested.

THE QUANTITATIVE ANALYSIS

To briefly summarize: the quantitative analysis will assess the impact of succession on public policies by focusing primarily on the effects of *national*-level leadership change on shifts in policy priorities in a group of fourteen nations— seven liberal democratic and seven socialist—for the period 1950-1976.[1] In order to supplement this analysis, the policy effects of succession will be examined in two subnational contexts, the American states, 1950-1970, and the Soviet republics, 1955-1970.[2] The independent variable, leader-

[1] Unfortunately, due to data deficiencies, these time-points were not always possible to attain in the analysis.

[2] These time-points were chosen primarily because they were the longest span of reliable data available. The analysis focused on the twenty-three American states that had four-year governorships for the entire period (two-year administrations were rejected because of the difficulties involved in assessing impact). In the Soviet case, the RSFSR was excluded because of its unique administrative arrangements which make it incomparable to the other fourteen republics. For a discussion of similar and different systems designs, both of which are employed here, see Przeworski and Teune (1970: Chapter 2) and Teune (1975). In a different systems design, the most nagging problem is establishing functional equivalence, while in a similar systems design variance is often lacking. I have tried to take these and other issues into account by: (1) focussing on a universal process—succession and policy-making—without forcing equivalence among nations in the way these processes evolve; (2) matching where possible, so that variation can to some extent be explained; and (3) building in sufficient variation in order to test hypotheses, enhance generalizability, and deal with the parameters of relationships. I have therefore not equated chief executives or policy processes with one another, except insofar as they all deal with certain types of policies, confront roughly similar constraints, and are affected by succession. This study, then, seeks

ship change, will be defined in the analysis as all changes
or attempted changes in the top leadership posts of each
state. Thus, succession will refer to all changes in the President (the United States), the Prime Minister (Canada, Japan, Great Britain, Austria, and Sweden), the Chancellor
(the German Federal Republic), the Governor (the American states), and, finally, the First Secretary of the Soviet
bloc states and the Soviet republics. The dependent variable, policy priorities, will be operationalized in this portion
of the study as budgetary allocations (and capital investments for the socialist nations).[3] Thus, the quantitative analysis will concentrate primarily on the impact of changes in
the top leadership of each polity on budgetary priorities.

   I will assess this impact by measuring the immediate and
long-term disturbances in patterns of budgetary expenditures and investments brought on by leadership turnover.
In the first case, I will measure the extent to which budgetary priorities in the year following succession (that is, the
first year the newly elected chief executive had control over
the budget) are similar to those prior to succession.[4] The

---

to avoid the pitfalls of many previous studies of comparative public policy
and comparative elites: for example, too much variance with insufficient
controls (for instance, Brzezinski and Huntington, 1963); too much data
and too little contextual information; too little variation (as with single
nation studies); and too few cases to allow for generalizations (for example,
Heclo, 1974).
   [3] I looked at investment allocations along with budgetary expenditures
in socialist nations in order to test whether investment decisions are affected, as many scholars have hypothesized, by changes in political leadership. Instead of examining budgetary investment, though, I looked at
capital investment (*kapital'noe vlozhenie*) since this is a more all-inclusive
category than the sub-total that is reported in the budget.
   [4] By the phrase, "the year following succession," I mean the first year
that the new administration exerts control over budgetary expenditures.
In the case of the United States, for instance, this means two years after
succession (i.e., 1966 for the 1964 election), whereas in the Soviet Union
and Eastern Europe, this means the first year after the succession, since
in the latter case budgets are officially ratified in December of each year
and spending can be and usually is modified during the fiscal year.

second case, which is concerned with long-term effects, will compare budgetary priorities across the entire span of different administrations, and assess the extent to which whole administrations diverge from one another in their policy priorities. Thus, while the first method addresses the issue of short-term change—getting at the concept of the honeymoon period developed in Chapter One—the second tests the *permanence* of that change. If in fact budgetary priorities change in the first year of the new administration and then slip back to previous levels, the impact of succession would seem to be transitory and minimal. However, if both the short- and long-term measures indicate a reordering of priorities, then the impact of succession would be strong indeed.

The Selection of Countries

I have opted to focus the quantitative efforts (and the entire analysis, for that matter) on succession in industrial societies, because such a focus offers a number of theoretical and practical advantages. Developing nations, whether liberal democratic or authoritarian, have generally less reliable data than their more industrialized counterparts.[5] This

[5] On the issue of the reliability of the data for socialist states, one should cite Franklyn Holtzman's remarks (1974:48) on Soviet data: ". . . in the opinion of most Western scholars, there have been very few instances (if any) over the past 55 years of publication by the Soviets of deliberately falsified data, despite many examples of 'withholding,' 'misleading,' and so forth. The publication of falsified data would, it should be noted, serve an extremely dysfunctional role internally, since published data does serve as a basis for work done by most Soviet scholars" (also see Nove and Newth, 1967:11; Hunter, 1972).

There is, however, one possibly serious problem in this area that should be noted, and that is the effect of the economic reforms of the 1960's. One aspect of these reforms involved (in most countries, anyway) the removal of some economic investment expenditures from the budget; control over these was instead to be devolved to the individual enterprises. Thus, the scope of the budget was to change, since a lower share would

is particularly true of budgetary expenditures, where reliable time-series data are hard, if not impossible, to procure. Second, much of the scholarly work on succession and the related issues of elite power and constraints embedded in the policy process has been concerned with industrial nations; therefore, many of the interesting questions in the area can be answered only with data from economically developed socialist and liberal democratic states. Finally, one major assumption underlying this study (one which will be discussed later)—that chief executives have control over some important policy sectors—is more tenuous when applied to nations of the Third World. As Aaron Wildavsky and Naomi Caiden (1974; also see Tsurutani, 1973) have argued, budgeting and planning in "poor and uncertain nations" allow for minimal influence on the part of the top decision-makers; the constraints embedded in the budgetary process greatly circumscribe the impact that elites can have on the priorities that emerge.

Thus, due to theoretical and empirical considerations, this study has been limited to succession in a group of advanced industrial systems. Specifically, I will look at the United States, Sweden, Britain, Germany, Japan, Canada, and Austria, on the Western democratic side, and the Soviet Union, Poland, Bulgaria, Czechoslovakia, Hungary, Romania, and the German Democratic Republic, on the socialist side. These particular systems were selected with an eye to including what seem to be important variables, which would plausibly affect the linkage between elite succession and public policy.

---

be going to the economic sector. However, these reforms were rarely carried out to any substantial degree in the countries examined; scholars generally agree on that, though they find it difficult to put precise figures on the changes that did occur (see Schroeder, 1976; Keren, 1973). Moreover, even if these changes were substantial enough to cause concern, they would not seem to distort the findings of this study, because one would have to argue that such effects were systematically related to succession, a dubious argument.

THE INDEPENDENT VARIABLE

As noted above, the analysis will be concerned with what is popularly considered to be succession; that is, any change in the preeminent leader in the system. The central issue here will be one of "actor dispensability"—how much difference does a new leader make (Greenstein, 1969)? However, I will be equally concerned with addressing issues related to the succession process. To what extent do factors concerned with succession, aside from personnel change, affect policy priorities? Are changes in incumbents necessary or sufficient for policies to change, or is it the succession process—the issues it invokes, the conflict it stirs up, and the like—what affects the policy environment?

One way of getting around this problem of "multi-collinearity" between people and process is to examine successful and unsuccessful successions; that is, to look at instances where the process did not produce a new leader, as well as those cases where an actual turnover in incumbency occurred. If policy change occurs only when elites turn over, then it can be asserted that the rotation brought on by the selections of leaders—and not the threat of such rotation or the changes in mass expectations—is what seems to alter public policy. However, if both instances produce similar changes in policy, then one would have to conclude that the process of attempting to choose a new leader plays a critical part in generating policy innovation. While the primary focus in the analysis will be on changeovers in personnel, then, this study will include some control cases as well where succession did not produce a turnover in the leadership.

On the democratic side, this expanded definition of succession meant that the analysis included *all* the elections that occurred from 1950 to 1976, irrespective of their outcomes. For instance, Dwight Eisenhower's victory in 1952 will be compared with his reelection in 1956; this in turn will be contrasted with John Kennedy's narrow win in 1960.

In the British case, to cite another example, comparisons will be drawn between Harold Wilson's triumphs in 1964 and 1966, as well as the transition to Edward Heath in 1970 and back again to Wilson in 1974.[6]

While these two contrasting types or outcomes of successions are easy to distinguish in liberal democratic nations, the same cannot be said for socialist polities. There is no equivalent of a "reelection" in a socialist state. Therefore, I chose to focus on a change process which—similar to reelection—affects the leader's power in socialist states, but does not unseat him: that is, major changes in the composition of the Politburo. The logic here is that when Politburos turn over in socialist states, this tends to signify a change in the preeminent leader's mandate—generally indicative of increased support among the elite stratum but sometimes indicative instead of a decline in the power of the General Secretary. In this vein, Khrushchev's defeat of the Anti-Party group in 1957 was not terribly dissimilar from Harold Wilson's reelection in 1966 (Linden, 1967). In both cases, the key factor was a rise in mandate, signified by Politburo changes in the Soviet case and by an increase in Parliamentary seats for Labour in the British example. Thus, insofar as Politburo shifts indicate a new mandate (usually larger), they are similar to reelections in the West, and both instances would seem to affect how leaders, East and West, rule and the priorities that they advocate.[7] While

[6] In a Parliamentary system, where leaders can call for elections, a reelection can be a major tool for consolidating power (see Holt and Turner, 1969). In Presidential systems, there are also examples where large reelection victories are sought in order to enhance the leader's power in policy-making. One has only to point to Lyndon Johnson's and Richard Nixon's elaborate plans for reelection. This reflected not only the usual dose of political uncertainty, but also their desire for a strong mandate in order to engage in major policy initiatives.

[7] I did not look at major Cabinet shuffles in the liberal democratic states because their policy impact is not obvious, either in the literature or in theory, and because such changes usually occur around election time, so their impact is hard to gauge.

it is fully admitted, though, that the analogy is not perfect,
I will still examine the impact of Politburo shake-ups, keeping in mind that they signify (depending on the particular
case) either an expansion or a contraction of the First Secretary's support. If nothing else, they do indicate some kind
of shift in the distribution of power in the system, and
mean similar things across the Soviet bloc.

Aside from their utility as control cases, moreover, major
changes in the Politburo (defined as changes in one-fourth
or more of the membership) and reelections are interesting
in themselves to analyze. Even if they have no impact, that
would be important to find out, since political scientists at
times have attributed important policy ramifications to both
kinds of events. Reelections are thought to increase the
prospects for change; this is a common interpretation, for
example, of both Dwight Eisenhower's and Harold Wilson's
second terms of office. Similarly, the rout of the Anti-Party
group in the Soviet Union in 1957 was taken to be a significant victory for Khrushchev and the major stimulus
behind several subsequent policy innovations. Thus, it
makes a good deal of sense to look at shifts in political
power, whether or not they led to shifts in leaders as well.

THE DEPENDENT VARIABLE

In the quantitative portion of this study, the dependent
variable—changes in policy outputs—has been operationalized as shifts in budgetary priorities over time for all the
units in the group and, for the communist party states,
capital investments as well. I have chosen to focus on this
type of policy for a number of reasons. First, budgets are
comparatively easy to compare across nations and across
time; they are interval-level data, and they are similar cross-
nationally in terms of how they are constructed and their
revenue constraints. As Aaron Wildavsky (1975:3) put it:

> The fundamental sameness of budgetary strategies around
> the world flows from the functional equivalence of the

budgetary processes. Everywhere there are those who want more than they can get, and others whose business it is to show them they can't have it (also see Pryor, 1968; Koval, 1973; Doern, 1971; Klein, 1976; Campbell, 1977).

Furthermore, budgets can be seen as fairly representative policy documents. So many public policies find monetary expression in the budget in socialist and liberal democratic states; indeed, budgeting everywhere is concerned "with the translation of financial resources into human purposes" (Wildavsky, 1975:3). Thus, given that the concern in this analysis is with looking at as broad a range of policies as possible, it would seem that budgets would be the ideal documents for study; they are highly inclusive types of public policy. If one cannot look at all policies, budgets are certainly a good place to begin.[8]

However, perhaps the most important reason for looking at budgets has to do with their *political* importance. As Kenneth Boulding (1966:10) has argued, "The budget seems to be the prime expression of political decisions. . . . The essence of the political process in any system is to reach a decision on the budget and to make the decision effective." Certainly, this is the common view of budgets in Western democratic states. Indeed, scholars in the Second World echo these same arguments with respect to the West. For example, one Soviet economist has described budgetary decision-making in the United States as "a highly political process . . . (in that) many important political battles in the United States involve the division of the economic pie" (Usoskin, 1973:38).

Moreover, they make the same argument for the Soviet

[8] In doing cross-national and cross-system research, it is very difficult to establish functional equivalence among public policies. While, ideally, it would be optimal to look at a broad range of policies, this is impossible, given the tremendous methodological problems involved. Thus, what I have done is to "settle for" budgets and the two case studies, a compromise which is not that disturbing, given the importance of these policy areas and their obvious relevance for leadership succession.

Union, in that the budget is "a direct reflection of the Leninist policies of the Communist Party and the Soviet state" (Garbuzov, 1971:22; also see Tulebaev, 1969, 1963). Just as in the West, then, the interdependence between the political and economic roles of the budget is something which has been noted by Soviet officials as being an accurate description of how budgets function in their system as well:

> The financial system of the USSR actively pursues the tasks of material production and enhancing the economic power of the country, its cultural development and improvement of the social welfare of the Soviet people. A critical role in the achievement of these goals is played by the state budget of the USSR and the budgets of the union republics. . . . Most importantly, it should be noted that the budget is not simply a financial plan, but a document concerned with the state, its policies, and all the responsibilities of the state and the party (Usoskin, 1973:42; also see Lewis, 1976; Pichotin, 1971).

Thus, the political relevance of budgetary policy East and West is readily apparent, and this would seem to justify the use of such policies in this study.

This justification is further enhanced by the power that chief executives have, at least potentially, over budgets. Certainly, if one is interested in the policy impact of executive turnover, one needs to look at policy areas where elites exert some control; otherwise, the hypotheses could not be tested adequately. In the case of budgets, it would seem that their political importance makes them almost by definition an area of great elite concern. Budgets do seem to be potentially susceptible to the direction of, and hence changes in, political leadership. What Kermit Gordon, a former budget director, has argued about the American budget—that "it is the President's plan and the implied priorities are his priorities" (Gordon, 1969:58)—has been noted for other chief executives as well. In his cross-national comparisons of the budgetary process, for instance,

Aaron Wildavsky (1975) has concluded that budgetary strategies and processes resemble one another in a variety of countries, and one major similarity is the centrality of the chief executive in this process. A second similarity Wildavsky (1975:3) found is the nature of political interaction; whether in France, Britain or the American states, "behind every government budget lies conflict." Thus, in view of the political salience of budgetary policy and the role of the leader as the major participant, it would seem that the rotation of political elites would directly affect budgetary priorities. If the budget is the leader's "plan," then changes in leaders should change the plan.

But can a similar argument be made for socialist nations? Are budgets as sensitive to leadership guidance in such polities as they are in the West? While Soviet scholars are not as straightforward on this issue as their American counterparts (which is not surprising, given their reticence to discuss any policy role for the First Secretary), two types of evidence can be cited to support the central role of socialist chief executives in budgetary decision-making. First, one can reiterate the point made above that Soviet budgets are highly political policies, perhaps even more so than in the United States, given the greater scope of the Soviet budget. Would any socialist leader, therefore, stand on the sidelines while such important policy is made?[9] Second, it seems rather clear that, just as in the West, socialist successions are guided by priority battles and most of the "priorities" have to do with budgetary allocations. Sidney Ploss (1971:271) provides one case in point for the Soviet Union

---

[9] It has been argued by some that the Soviet budget (or any budget in a planned economy) is constrained a great deal by the Five Year Plan. However, in practice, the Plan seems to act as a very general directive that guides budgetary expenditures and that interacts with actual expenditures. For a discussion of the veritable lack of connection between the plan and the budget, see George Feiwal (1972). This has been supported, for example, by Leonid Brezhnev, who reported in 1973 that industrial investment rose by 7.3 percent as opposed to 5.8 percent as called for by the plan. See *Pravda*, December 16, 1973, p. 1.

when he argues that in both the Khrushchev and Brezhnev successions the central issues included "choices between guns and butter in budgetary allocations." In fact, even those seemingly "non-budgetary" issues which crop up during succession often have a substantial impact on the budget. De-Stalinization, for instance, led not only to decompression but also to dramatic shifts in budgetary allocations in Eastern Europe and the Soviet Union, and succession in Northeastern Europe and the Soviet Union has been linked to shifts in public consumption outlays (Pryor, 1968; Bunce, 1980a; Mieczkowski, 1978). The point, then, is that Soviet and Eastern European decision-makers behave as good Marxists; they are fully aware of how much politics and economics are intertwined in budgetary expenditures and capital investments.

Thus, most of what government does, East or West, is translated into financial as well as political action, expenditures as well as substantive programs. These expenditures, moreover, reflect to some degree executive priorities and power in the policy process. Therefore, if one is interested in succession and its impact on policy, one logical and indeed excellent area of investigation is shifts in budgetary priorities.

However, there is one caveat that should be made. While the political character of the budget, East and West, is undeniable, this does not mean that I am stacking the deck in favor of finding a strong correlation between leadership succession and budgetary innovation. As noted briefly in Chapter One, budgetary policy-making is in many ways a constrained decision process; the potential for elite impact may not be matched by a great deal of real impact. Thus, to the reasons listed above for using budgets as my primary quantitative indicator of public policy, I can add a final one: they provide a fair, but *tough*, test of the impact on public policy of executive turnover. If elites can alter budgetary allocations by virtue of their rotation in office, then succession would indeed be an important political variable precisely because it affects such an important and highly controversial policy area.

The Quantitative Methods

In order to assess the impact of succession on budgetary expenditures and investments, I have utilized an interrupted time-series research design. This design is particularly well-suited to my research needs because it features an intermittent independent variable (such as elite succession) and a continuous dependent variable (in this case, budgetary expenditures). Moreover, as James Caporaso (1973:17-18) points out, this design

> is appropriate to data distributed over time . . . and where there is theoretical reason to believe that some event should cause a change in the behavior of the series. The key question involved in this design is whether the occurrence of the events in question had an effect or whether the behavior of the series after the events represents an undisturbed continuation of the series from its previous state. . . . Two questions are involved. Did a non-random change occur in the vicinity of the experiment? Is this change attributable to the occurrence of the experimental event?

Before we discuss the methodology in detail, it is necessary to linger for a moment on the notion of "impact." In the theoretical literature on succession and policy change, there are two basic models of change. The first, which is the more common notion—and one that was discussed in Chapter One—is that, if innovation is to appear, it must come early in the new administration (Wilson, 1966; Gross, 1972). The logic behind this assertion is explained by Jeffrey Pressman and Aaron Wildavsky (1973:130):

> The advantages of being new are exactly that—being new. They dissipate quickly over time. The organization

ages rapidly. Little by little the regulations that apply to everyone else also apply to it. Accommodations are made with other organizations in its environment. Territory is divided, divisions of labor are established, favors are traded, agreements are reached. All this means that the new organization now has settled into patterns of its own which defend it against disruption.

However, an alternative pattern of policy innovation is also plausible, based on the argument that innovation does not require "newness" in leadership so much as experience (Gouldner, 1953; Kaufman, 1971:99-100). Whereas new personnel lack the organizational contacts, expertise, and authority to introduce and to implement policy change, those with tenure have greater capability to innovate. This in turn implies that the impact of succession may not be immediate and short-lived but, rather, delayed and expanding over time.

Because both patterns of change do seem to be plausible (and testable), I decided to use two methods to assess the impact of succession: one which focuses on the behavior of expenditures immediately after succession—the honeymoon period (based on one timepoint in the new administration)—and a measure which compares a series of points after succession with the behavior of the series before succession. In both cases, impact is measured by testing the extent to which priorities in the new administration differ from previous outlays in the short run and across the entire administration. In the first case, I used a technique developed by James Caporaso and A. Pelowski (1971): that is, I regressed expenditure *shares* of the budget (thereby controlling for inflation and the tendency of budgets to increase geometrically)[10] against time for the period prior to

---

[10] I actually handled the data several ways: gross expenditures, expenditures in constant prices, expenditures per capita, and, finally, as shares of the budget. The latter calculation was selected for this study, because it both approximates how policymakers look at the budget and

succession (i.e., the entire previous administration) and calculated a predicted expenditure for the first complete budgetary year of the new administration. This prediction was then subtracted from the actual expenditure, and the difference represents the impact of succession. This figure in turn was converted into a t test, by placing the difference over the standard error of the regression (predicting) equation. The result indicates statistical significance, or the probability of such a difference, given previous patterns of change.[11] Thus, the degree to which the behavior of expenditures prior to succession can predict the behavior of expenditures in the first year that the new administration has control over the budget is the measure of the immediate impact of leadership turnover.[12] The extent to which the prediction is "off," then, and the degree to which this deviation is greater than past annual deviations, is the "impact" of succession. I will term this impact innovation because it signifies that budgetary priorities are rather different from those which existed before the succession.[13]

---

controls for inflation. How the priorities or shares of the budget are arranged each year seem to be political decisions, irrespective of changes in the size of the whole budget.

[11] In the tables in subsequent chapters, I report the share difference and whether it is significant. However, it should be emphasized, though, that significance will *not* be construed as any direct estimate of the impact of succession; rather, the concern will be with the frequency of significant results and the overall patterns in the data. While it is not terribly justifiable to use significance levels when there is no sample and in time-series analysis, they do have the appeal of controlling for past variance and thereby taking the context of shifts into account—which is not directly revealed by share differences. Hence, I have included both in the analysis, but relied heavily on the latter and on scatter plots to interpret the results.

[12] It should be made clear that, in order to get around the problem of too few time-points and thus the possibility of undue influence of outlying values, I looked at expenditures both in all administrations previous to the one examined, as well as those just in the prior administration. Both notions of prior behavior yielded the same results.

[13] There may be some objection to terming such deviations innovation, but it is my view that the establishment of new *priorities* is innovation.

The second model of change, which posits that innovation will come later in the new administration, can be tested through a comparison of priorities across entire administrations (Caporaso and Pelowski, 1971). This approach calls for subdividing the data into separate administrations and comparing their mean differences. The extent to which contiguous administrations are different in terms of budgetary priorities suggests that different leaders have, in the long run, different priorities and that elite succession therefore has a general effect on budgetary policies.

Thus, the impact of succession will be measured from the perspective of immediate and long-term policy change. In both cases, the extent to which new administrations are different in their priorities from their predecessors will be the indicator of impact.[14] The only difference between the two approaches, then, is the timing of the innovation or its lag. Both measures together will pick up any deviation in expenditures, whenever it occurs. This is one of the assets of using two measures instead of one; the other is that it helps us to pin down more carefully which change processes are involved.

THE INTERPRETATION OF THE QUANTITATIVE RESULTS

This leads to the issue of the interpretation of the results. The design seems to be well suited to the assessment of change, because it compares previous behavior with allocations after the onset of the independent variable. Moreover, because the design incorporates multiple observations of the independent and dependent variables, the overall behavior of each "impact" can be presumed in the aggregate to be typical and representative. There is little likelihood, then, that the findings will be wrong or biased.

However, even the most foolproof research design can-

[14] It should be mentioned that this is a rough test of impact, since one "impact" could be a conscious decision to continue previous priorities.

not guarantee the investigator a correct interpretation of
the results. This design is no exception to that generalization. Most important, I cannot prove that leadership
succession changes public policies; I can only show that
policies change more after succession than before. As Edward Tufte (1974:5) notes, causal interpretations are always
frought with great dangers:

> Statistical techniques do not solve any of the common
> sense difficulties about making causal inferences. Such
> techniques may help organize or arrange the data so that
> the numbers speak more clearly to the question of caus-
> ality—but that is all statistical techniques can do. All the
> logical, theoretical, and empirical difficulties attendant
> to establishing a causal relationship persist no matter
> what type of statistical analysis is applied. There is, as
> Thurber moralized, "no safety in numbers or anything
> else."

Does this mean that the entire analysis must be reduced
to mundane statements about correlations between succession and policy change? Emphatically not! If the theoretical
literature supports a causal connection (and it does), and
if the results of the analysis are consistent and in the direction anticipated, then one has every right to contend
that a causal linkage exists between succession and policy
change. This is all the more convincing given the size and
diversity of the observations and the comparatively long
time-series involved in the analysis. The quantitative results
and empirical theory, therefore, will be joined throughout
this analysis to tie together, to the extent that one can,
succession and budgetary policy-making in a causal relationship.

THE CASE STUDIES

The commitment to establishing causality leads to the second mode of evidence that will be used in this study, the

case studies. As noted above, I chose to include case studies in this book because of the contextual information that they can provide. Two cases were selected for examination: welfare policy in the United States in the 1960's and agricultural policy in the Soviet Union since the death of Stalin.

These two countries were selected for more intensive study because they are major powers and representative of two contrasting types of political systems, socialist and liberal democratic; thus they are of particular interest to political scientists. Moreover, as will be discovered later in the quantitative analysis, the impact of succession on public policy in these two nations is rather typical of their system types and consistent across time. Thus, a more in-depth study of policy change in these two nations would be as generalizable as a case study can be.

The rationale behind selecting agriculture and welfare policy in the Soviet and American cases, respectively, is also straightforward.[15] As with the logic behind looking at budgetary policy, in the case studies I wanted to examine policies that fall within the jurisdiction of chief executives. Moreover, I wanted to provide a tough test of the impact of succession; just as with budgetary policy-making, so agricultural and welfare policies are very hard to change for similar reasons. They are engulfed by tremendous conflict over money, techniques, and programs, and they incite strong feelings on the part of elites and masses in both political systems. Performance levels in these areas, moreover, have been notoriously poor, and there seem to be few if any easy answers for increasing agricultural productivity and cleaning up the "welfare mess." Third, it can be argued that, as with budgets, agriculture in the Soviet Union and welfare in the United States are issues that seem to permeate political dialogue during succession. They are, there-

[15] For a discussion of the political salience of agricultural policy in the Soviet Union, see Hahn (1972); Volkov (1975). As for the importance of welfare on the American elite agenda, see Steiner (1974).

fore, highly salient areas of crisis, yet resistant to change, and thus ideal for the purposes of this study.

However, there is a fourth and very important reason for looking at these two policy areas, and that is that, unlike budgetary data, they involve programmatic as well as monetary decisions. One common critique of budgetary analysis is that it understates change by ignoring the rise and fall of various programs within a given budgetary category (Natchez and Bupp, 1973). While, for my purposes, this problem is not particularly bothersome, since it simply means that the quantitative analysis will provide a particularly tough test of the impact of succession, it would be useful for the generalizability of the findings to look at more programmatic aspects of public policies. This is especially the case when one realizes that both agriculture and welfare policies involve programs and techniques, as well as lines in the budget; therefore, the results of the two types of analysis—the quantitative and the case study—can be compared rather directly. Agriculture and welfare policies, therefore, seem to provide precisely the kind of evidence one needs to buttress the quantitative analysis. How these two issues respond to changes in political power at the apex of each system, then, can tell us more precisely *how* succession affects public policy in socialist and bourgeois democratic systems.

Thus, I would argue that agricultural policy in the Soviet Union and welfare policy in the United States seem to be, for my needs at least, functionally equivalent public policies. They are areas that are politically salient, highly controversial, and involve programmatic as well as monetary indicators of public policy priorities in their respective systems. These qualities in turn mean that they can complement and augment the other source of evidence in this investigation—the quantitative assessment of the impact of succession on budgetary allocations. Thus, the development of agriculture in the Soviet Union and welfare policy in the United States in the postwar era will help to fill in more explicitly—to flesh out—the linkages between leadership succession and policy change specified by the statistical analysis. I will be able to get some sense from these two policy areas of precisely *how* new leaders do or do not make a difference.

CONCLUSION

In a recent overview of comparative public policy research, Howard Leichter (1977:594; also see Leichter, 1979) has argued that

> what is needed is an approach to comparative policy analysis which will bridge the gap between the broad range generalizations typical of the multination aggregate studies, and the more narrowly focused, but richly detailed analysis of specific cases.

This is precisely what I hope to do in this study, by dividing labor between two different but complementary approaches or modes of evidence—the case study and the quantitative analysis—in order to test the impact of succession on public policy. By bridging this gap, I hope to emerge, not just with evidence of change or a series of correlations, but with a *causal* sense of the relationship between leadership succession and policy outputs in socialist and capitalist states. When these two modes of evidence are combined with good theory, they can explain how, how much, and why leadership succession affects public policy.

THREE

Changing Leaders and Changing Policies: The Western States

There is nothing quite like the ease with which officials of a
newly elected administration take over the departments and
agencies of government. Only later do the difficulties emerge. In
the beginning a sense of immense power is conveyed. For a short
time anything seems possible.
—*Daniel Moynihan* (1973)

The first complete budget of any new administration is its most
important. It is . . . the first full statement of priorities, policies
and proposals for meeting national needs.
—*Jimmy Carter* (1978)

INTRODUCTION

In Chapter One it was hypothesized that elections should
affect policy priorities in the immediate aftermath of the
succession. This assertion was based on the argument that
decision-making during the honeymoon period provides
an optimal environment for policy innovation, combining
a strong desire on the part of the new chief executive to
be innovative with an unusual capacity for carrying out
these new ideas. The campaign experience, the availability
of information, a sense of optimism and of adequate time,
the existence of a supportive and ambitious inner circle
surrounding the new leader, wide support among the public, Congress, and the bureaucracy, and the impact of newness—which means a lack of commitment to the past and
a desire to make a mark—would all appear to work in
concert to encourage the development of new policy priorities in the honeymoon.

However, even during this time innovation is not easy—

[59]

it is only comparatively easy. Conflict, complexity, and political culture all work to limit the extent to which new leaders in bourgeois democratic systems advocate and implement new policies. This fact suggested in turn (in Chapter One) several subsidiary hypotheses. First, impact will be constrained even during the honeymoon so that change, while more than in the past, will be at the margins. Second, the honeymoon period will usher in new priorities which will, essentially, freeze until the next succession. Thus, innovations should cluster at the beginning of administrations, but rather quickly fall into what become the new routines. Innovation is, therefore, cyclical, peaking in the honeymoon and stabilizing until the next transfer of power.

The final set of hypotheses is centered around the conditions under which innovation would be more or less likely, following the transition in executive leadership. Here, I hypothesized that newly elected parties and/or chief executives will be more change-oriented than those which have simply been returned to power, that large mandates will be more conducive to innovation than small ones,[1] and that leftist parties will be more change-oriented than rightist ones. Thus, to the extent that certain electoral conditions expand either the power of the leader (i.e., a large and/or increasing mandate) or the chief executive's desire to make changes (i.e., the victory of a new party), one would expect a rise in the impact of succession. Conversely, a decline in power or incentives to innovate would seem to reduce the policy effects of leadership turnover.

[1] This hypothesis is somewhat controversial. If one sees innovation as arising from incentives, and innovation to be a last-ditch effort, then a large mandate would seem to allow leaders to rest on their laurels. However, if power is emphasized, then a large mandate would be, as I have argued, conducive to change. This contradiction is apparent, for example, when one compares the American state versus the comparative literature on party competition. The first position is exemplified by Key (1949:307) and Cnudde and McCrone (1969). The second notion of the effects of competition can be found, for example, in Kirchheimer (1966) and Downs (1957).

A Quantitative Assessment

In this chapter, I test these hypotheses by examining—through electoral and budgetary data—the short- and long-term effects of succession on budgetary priorities in seven nations (the United States, Great Britain, Japan, West Germany, Sweden, Austria, and Canada) and twenty-three American states. The primary focus is on shifts in the budgetary totals, as well as in the outlays (expressed in shares of the total budget) for a number of specific categories, such as health, education, and welfare, and, to a lesser extent, transportation, housing, and public safety.[2] The independent variable, elite succession, is operationalized to include *all* elections which took place between 1950 and 1974, whether or not they led to changes in the top leadership.[3] As discussed in Chapter Two, the analysis will measure the impact of succession in two ways: (1) by assessing the extent to which past expenditures priorities (that is, of the previous administration) are different from those in the first year the newly elected chief executive has control over the budget; and (2) by comparing the mean budgetary priorities of each administration and seeing the extent to which they differ from one another. Taken together, these two methods (along with scatter plots) indicate how much impact succession has, what form that impact takes, and how permanent the "disruption" in priorities is.[4]

[2] The difficulties of procuring cross-national data over a twenty-seven-year time period meant that the bulk of the analysis had to be on aggregated categories. However, a number of preliminary tests on less aggregated categories showed results similar to those reported below.

[3] As noted in Chapter Two, I looked at elections which did not yield a change in leadership in order to have a control case where an election occurred, but the incumbent remained in office.

[4] This method is discussed in greater detail in Chapter Two. However, I should reiterate that the first method compares past expenditures and their variation with those allocations registered in the first year that the new administration has control over the budget, and divides the difference between real and predicted levels by the standard error of the regression (or the predicting) equation. The second method compares the behavior

In Table 3-1 I have presented the results of the first test, which assesses the immediate impact of democratic elections. Given the extent to which past priorities do *not* predict very well the priorities of the new administration, it can be concluded that thus far the central hypothesis of this study does seem to be confirmed. Elections do seem to affect public expenditure priorities in a significant manner[5]—in all seven liberal democratic states and with respect to most elections—but not in a way that one could construe as dramatic. The findings, then, are striking and consistent. In *every* country, the changing of the political guard was translated into some, and sometimes a great deal of, policy change. Sweden, the United States, Great Britain, Canada, and Austria all feature a comparatively large amount of expenditure change, while Japan and the Federal Republic show somewhat less of an impact. However, even in the latter two cases, succession does seem to correlate with budgetary innovation.

But do these innovations last or are they simply symbolic gestures that fade away with the aging of the administration? In Table 3-2 I have presented a comparison of the difference in priorities across all the administrations the data cover within each country in the group. This table clearly indicates that elections have an *enduring* effect on budgetary priorities, as well as the short-term impact re-

---

of allocations over the entire administration by computing difference of means tests, based on changes in budgetary priorities (not absolute levels) in each administration. This gives us a sense of the probability of the changes, though the *t* scores themselves are of less interest. For this reason, I presented in the tables the actual shares change with the significance of that change starred. For a discussion of both methods, see Caporaso (1973).

[5] This conclusion (as with those reported throughout this chapter) is based on several facets of the findings: the number of significant *t* tests, the size of the share differences (which are directly comparable, and which can give some indication of differences between expenditure priorities before and after an election), and, finally, the scatter plots of the data. No one measure was emphasized, because each one taps different things and would be misleading if used alone.

TABLE 3-1

The Immediate Impact of Succession on Budgetary Allocations

Country	Administration[a]	Total Expenditures[b]	Health[c]	Education[c]	Welfare[c]
Austria	Raab* (1953)	+ 8221*	+ .3%	+ 2.1%	− 3.2%*
	Raab (1956)	+ 6126	+ .8%*	− 2.3%	− 2.9%*
	Raab (1950)	+ 3623	+ .3%	+ 3.0%*	+ 1.0%
	Gorbach* (1962)	+ 4111	+ .2%	+ 2.4%*	+ 3.2%*
	Klaus* (1966)	+ 4000*	− .3%	− 5.2%	− 6.5%*
	Kreisky* (1970)	+ 19644*	+ .3%*	− 4.0%	− 2.3%*
	Kreisky (1971)	+ 21230	− .5%*	+ 1.6%	+ 2.1%*
	Kreisky (1975)	+ 22067*	+ .4%*	+ 3.5%*	+ 3.5%*
Canada	St. Laurent* (1957)	− 158	+ 2.0%*	+ 1.1%	+ 4.4%*
	Diefenbaker* (1958)	+ 192	+ 1.5%*	+ 1.1%	+ 1.2%
	Diefenbaker (1962)	+ 320	+ 1.0%*	+ .5%	+ 1.1%
	Pearson* (1963)	− 600	− 1.5%	+ .3%	+ 3.1%
	Pearson (1965)	− 601	+ 1.0%*	+ 1.0%*	+ 6.2%*
	Trudeau* (1968)	+ 2365*	+ 1.3%*	+ 2.1%*	+ 5.3%*
	Trudeau (1972)	+ 2295*	− .3%	+ 1.4%*	+ 3.1%*
	Trudeau (1974)	+ 2120*	+ .9%*	− .1%	+ 4.1%*
Germany	Adenauer (1957)	+ 300	− 2.0%	+ 1.0%	+ 2.1%
	Adenauer (1961)	+ 400	+ 1.0%	+ 4.0%*	+ 5.2%*
	Erhard* (1962)	+ 200	+ 1.0%	+ 1.0%	− 1.3%
	Kiesinger* (1965)	+ 301	+ 2.0%	+ 3.0%*	+ 3.3%*
	Brandt* (1969)	+ 509*	+ 3.0%*	+ 4.0%*	+ 4.9%*
	Brandt (1972)	+ 692*	+ 4.0%*	+ 4.1%*	+ 3.1%*

TABLE 3-1 (cont.)

The Immediate Impact of Succession on Budgetary Allocations

Country	Administration[a]	Total Expenditures[b]	Health[c]	Education[c]	Welfare[c]
Great Britain	Macmillan (1959)	+ 2002*	− 3.1%*	+ 1.3%	− 1.3%
	Wilson* (1964)	+ 2009*	− 3.2%*	+ 2.2%*	− 1.5%
	Wilson (1966)	+ 700*	+ 4.0%*	+ 2.2%*	+ 2.6%*
	Heath* (1970)	− 202	− 3.4%*	− 3.9%*	− 1.5%
	Wilson (1974)	+ 3005*	+ 4.3%*	+ 3.7%*	+ 3.5%*
Japan	Kishi (1958)	+ 2391*	+ 3.2%*	+ 3.6%*	− 3.3%*
	Ikeda* (1960)	+ 5001*	+ 1.1%	+ 5.4%*	+ 1.1%
	Sato* (1963)	− 200	+ 1.4%	+ 2.3%*	+ 4.4%*
	Sato (1967)	+ 2341*	− 1.6%	− 1.4%	+ 2.1%
	Sato (1969)	− 202	− 1.6%	− 1.5%	+ 1.3%
	Tanaka* (1972)	+ 211	+ 5.4%*	+ 3.0%*	+ 1.6%
	Miki* (1974)	+ 2599*	+ 4.5%*	− 1.6%	+ 3.5%
Sweden	Erlander (1956)	+ 388*	+ 1.3%*	+ 2.4%*	+ 3.3%*
	Erlander (1958)	+ 462*	+ 2.2%*	+ 3.3%*	− 1.2%
	Erlander (1960)	+ 508*	+ 3.6%*	+ 1.3%	+ 4.4%*
	Erlander (1964)	+ 609*	− 3.4%*	− 1.2%	+ 3.3%*
	Erlander (1968)	+ 731*	+ 4.3%*	+ 4.2%*	+ 3.6%*
	Palme* (1970)	+ 520	− 1.3%	− 3.5%*	+ 3.6%*
	Palme (1973)	+ 668*	− 4.6%*	− 2.4%*	+ 3.5%*
United States	Eisenhower* (1952)	− 284*	− .2%	− .7%	+ 5.2%*
	Eisenhower (1956)	+ 1159*	+ .1%*	+ .4%*	− 1.2%
	Kennedy* (1960)	+ 1272*	+ .1%	+ .1%	+ 3.5%*
	Johnson* (1963)	+ 1489*	+ .3%*	+ 4.3%*	− 2.2%
	Johnson (1964)	+ 929	+ .3%*	+ 2.2%*	− 5.6%*
	Nixon* (1968)	+ 4068	+ 1.0%*	+ 2.5%*	+ 4.4%*
	Nixon (1972)	+ 3265*	+ 1.1%*	+ 1.1%	+ 3.2%*

[a] The administrations reported are the new administrations, and the year in parentheses is the year they were elected. Normally, however, the year following this is the first year the new administration controlled the budget and, hence, all of the calculations were based on that year rather than on the electoral year. The asterisk is used to designate a new administration, as opposed to one which has been returned to office. The importance of this distinction will become apparent later.

[b] The numbers reported in this category represent the difference between the allocations expected (rounded off to dollars, Deutsche Marks, etc.) for the first budgetary year of the new administration, if previous levels were to continue, minus the actual expenditure level. Those numbers with an asterisk are significant at at least the .05 level. Significance was determined by taking the result of the difference between real and expected levels and dividing this by the standard error of the regression equation. This gave a t score, which indicates how likely the difference is, taking the variance of past outlays into account.

[c] These figures were calculated as in column one, except that they represent shares of the budget, rather than actual expenditure levels.

Sources: See the Appendix.

ported in Table 3-1. Moreover, when the scatter plots of these priority shifts are examined, the pattern of change outlined above—that is, clusters of change grouped in the honeymoon period, followed by a stabilization of these new priorities until the next election—seems to be confirmed. To take American education outlays as one example, it is clear that new leaders do new things, but rather quickly get stuck in their ways. Kennedy, Johnson, and Nixon all made a difference, and that difference remained fairly steady until a new incumbent came into the Oval Office. Thus, newly elected chief executives do pursue different policy objectives, particularly in their initial period in office, and the changes they introduce tend to last until the next succession.[6]

TABLE 3-2
Average Priorities by Administration

Country	Administration[a]	Health[b]	Education	Welfare[c]
Austria	Raab* (1953)	.1%	6.5%	22.1%
	Raab (1956)	.2%*	8.2%*	20.1%*
	Raab (1960)	.2%	8.5%	19.3%*
	Gorbach* (1962)	.3%	8.4%	23.1%*
	Klaus* (1966)	.4%	8.9%*	25.7%*
	Kreisky* (1970)	.5%*	10.3%*	24.8%*
	Kreisky (1971)	.6%*	11.1%*	24.2%
	Kreisky (1975)	.5%*	12.2%*	24.5%
Canada	St. Laurent* (1957)	1.1%	.9%	14.1%
	Diefenbaker* (1958)	2.9%*	1.9%*	17.2%*
	Diefenbaker (1962)	4.7%*	1.2%	21.1%*
	Pearson* (1963)	5.2%*	3.6%*	23.2%*
	Pearson (1965)	5.1%	2.9%*	22.8%
	Trudeau* (1968)	5.9%*	4.3%*	22.0%*
	Trudeau (1972)	5.8%	4.2%	21.0%*
	Trudeau (1974)	6.1%*	4.1%	21.1%
Germany	Adenauer (1957)	3.3%	1.4%	22.3%
	Adenauer (1961)	3.2%	1.6%	24.5%

[6] It should be noted that outlays within administrations in all of these countries are incremental, averaging an R^2 of .92. The greater number of such years, as opposed to honeymoon periods (in which R^2's drop considerably) explains why expenditures over time are generally incremental.

TABLE 3-2 (cont.)
Average Priorities by Administration

Country	Administration[a]	Health[b]	Education	Welfare[c]
	Erhard* (1962)	3.4%	2.1%*	20.2%*
	Kiesinger* (1965)	3.2%*	3.4%*	18.3%*
	Brandt* (1969)	3.9%*	6.8%*	22.1%*
	Brandt (1972)	4.8%*	7.8%*	21.4%*
Great Britain	Macmillan (1959)	8.7%	10.8%	15.5%
	Wilson* (1964)	8.9%*	11.5%*	16.3%*
	Wilson (1966)	8.8%	12.1%*	16.2%
	Heath* (1970)	9.2%*	12.5%*	17.1%*
	Wilson* (1974)	9.6%*	13.1%*	17.5%
Japan	Kishi (1958)	2.3%	12.3%	7.6%
	Ikeda* (1960)	1.8%*	11.9%	6.9%*
	Sato* (1963)	2.2%*	12.2%	8.9%*
	Sato (1967)	1.9%*	12.1%	9.2%
	Sato (1969)	1.7%	12.3%	9.5%
	Tanaka* (1972)	1.6%	13.1%*	11.3%*
	Miki* (1974)	1.8%*	13.0%	13.4%*
Sweden	Erlander (1956)	3.4%*	9.5%	22.1%*
	Erlander (1958)	3.6%*	10.9%*	22.2%
	Erlander (1960)	3.4%*	10.7%	23.1%
	Erlander (1964)	3.8%	12.3%*	24.5%*
	Erlander (1968)	4.1%*	13.2%*	25.4%
	Palme* (1970)	4.6%*	15.0%*	26.6%*
	Palme (1973)	4.7%	15.4%	28.2%*
United States	Eisenhower* (1952)	2.8%*	8.1%*	15.5%*
	Eisenhower (1956)	2.8%	9.4%*	17.6%*
	Kennedy* (1960)	3.3%*	12.1%*	15.5%*
	Johnson* (1963)	4.2%*	14.7%*	15.6%
	Johnson (1964)	6.4%*	16.3%*	14.9%*
	Nixon* (1968)	7.1%*	18.0%*	15.6%*
	Nixon (1972)	7.4%	19.2%*	16.0%

[a] These are the new administrations, and those with an asterisk represent a turnover in the chief executive. The year in parentheses is the election year, and in most cases the year after this is the first budgetary year of the new administration (in the American case, the lag is two years).

[b] These are the average shares of the budget for those years the administration exerts control over expenditures. The numbers with an asterisk are significant at the .05 level, as calculated from a difference of means test.

[c] Other categories, such as transportation, housing and agriculture showed similar patterns as well.

Sources: See the Appendix.

Before I test some of the subsidiary hypotheses and explain the differential impact of elections within these tables, it would be useful to examine some other categories. In Table 3-3 I have presented additional data which assess the short-term influence of leadership changeover on budgetary categories that are less aggregated and less politically important than social-welfare expenditures. As is clear from this table (and through comparisons of average expenditure shares by administration), the findings reported above appear to be representative of other categories in the budget, such as public safety, transportation outlays, and like. Again, one finds that elections have an impact on policy priorities both over the short and over the long run. Moreover, this is true for all the Western nations and for most administrations. Thus, the conclusion drawn above does not seem to be a function of the particular category that has been examined; instead, the guiding hypothesis seems to describe the relationship between elections and budgeting in general.[7]

SOME FURTHER EVIDENCE: BUDGETARY CHANGE IN THE AMERICAN STATES

There is, of course, another way that one can look at the relationship between budgeting and succession, and that is to examine expenditure patterns at the sub-national level of government—specifically, the tie between priorities and gubernatorial succession in the American states. There are several reasons why it would be informative to look at budgeting below the national level of government to test the hypotheses. First, such an analysis would help to get around the familiar "many variables small N problem" that undermines genuine comparative research (Lijphart, 1971:177; also see Rose, 1973). Because succession at the national

---

[7] Again, I did perform similar tests on other, more fragmentary, budgetary data and in other nations with similar results.

TABLE 3-3
The Immediate Impact of Succession: Some Extra Categories[a]

Country	Succession	Public Safety	Housing	Industry	Transportation	Conservation
Germany	Kiesinger (1965)	−1.3%	+ .53%*	+2.2%	+2.2%	
	Brandt (1969)	−1.4%	+ .79%*	+2.4%	+4.9%*	
	Brandt (1972)	−2.0%*	+ .89%*	+1.3%	+2.8%*	
Great Britain	Wilson (1964)		+1.3%	+3.5%*	+3.6%*	
	Wilson (1966)		+2.2%*	+3.8%*	+2.8%*	
	Heath (1970)		−8.1%*	−1.2%	+2.7%*	
Japan	Sato (1969)			+2.4%*		+1.3%
	Tanaka (1972)			+3.2%*		+1.2%
	Miki (1974)			+3.0%*		−1.8%*
Sweden	Erlander (1958)		+3.3%*		+3.3%*	
	Erlander (1960)		+2.4%*		+2.1%*	
	Erlander (1964)		+2.2%*		+3.2%*	
	Erlander (1968)		+2.6%*		+2.3%*	
	Palme (1970)		+2.3%*		−1.0%	
	Palme (1973)		−1.1%		+1.4%	

[a] The sources for this table are the same as for the preceding tables. The administrations named are the new ones. The figures starred are significant at at least the .05 level, reflecting the same *t* test procedure as in Table 1.
Sources: See the Appendix.

level is so infrequent and the number of industrialized liberal democracies limited as well, one is forced to work within a rather limited universe. By looking at state level successions, however, we can expand the cases (and the conditions under which succession occurs) considerably.

Second, by assessing the impact of gubernatorial turnover in the American states, I will be able to assess the effects of succession in a policy environment that is different from national-level politics. Governors seem to be in some ways more powerful than Presidents and yet in other ways more constrained. On the one hand, some scholars treat Governors as dominant figures who can do pretty much as they please. For example, it has been argued that the power of the Governor has supposedly grown a great deal in recent years. Especially in comparison with the state legislature, the Governor has a disproportionate amount of resources upon which to draw. For instance, he tends to be more politically experienced, to command a larger staff, to play a more permanent and visible role in policy-making, and to be much better paid than the less professional legislators in the state houses. Thus, it can be argued that the Governor in most states more easily dominates the legislature than the President dominates Congress (Lockard, 1966). In this sense, one can say that Governors, even more than Presidents, are the chief legislators in their polity.

> The governor sets the agenda for public decision-making; he [sic] largely determines what the business of the legislature will be in any session. Few major state undertakings ever get off the ground without gubernatorial initiation. And in setting the agenda of legislative business, he [sic!] frames the issues, determines their context, and decides their timing (Dye, 1973:177; also see Sharkansky, 1970).

Moreover, this power is directly related to the budget. Indeed, as Thomas Anton (1967:34) has noted, "The Governor's control over the state budget is perhaps his [sic] most formidable power."

However, others argue that, if Presidents and Prime Ministers are highly constrained policy-makers, this is even *more* true for Governors. The biggest difference between a President and a Governor is that while the former has some control over revenues and staff resources to produce a budget, the Governor in actuality has neither. As Anton (1967:36) has explained, "Governors may be regarded as 'money-providers' or as 'budget-balancers'; only infrequently can they be viewed as decision-makers in the determination of state expenditures." In fact, in studies of budgetary outlays at the state level, incrementalism seems to be even more characteristic than at the national level, and any deviation from this tends to have more to do with changes in revenues (i.e., the economic development of the state) than with changes in the political environment (Dye, 1969; Winters, 1976). Thus, the power of American Governors is thought to be very limited, despite their commanding role in state politics. While the Governor proposes and the legislature disposes, he proposes under often severe policy constraints. Thus, from this perspective, in testing the impact of succession on budgetary priorities in the American states, I would seem to be providing the acid test for the influence of succession on public policy.

In Tables 3-4 and 3-5 a summary of the analysis is presented. Once again—and this is somewhat surprising—the guiding hypothesis has been upheld. While the changes in priorities do not seem to be as sharp as those found for the national level, it is still reasonable to conclude that there is a relationship between budgetary change and changes in political leadership in the American states. I have drawn this conclusion for several reasons. The first is basically a statistical consideration, and that is the difficulty of obtaining statistical significance with a limited number of cases (see Kish, 1970). Second, it should be noted, as discussed above, that the Governor does work within a highly con-

TABLE 3-4
The Immediate Impact of Succession: The American States

Priority Shifts[a]	Public Safety[c]	Welfare	Education	Highways	Health[d]
Priority shifts: 0-2%	50	32	25	21	50
Priority shifts: 2.1%-3.0%	30	25	28	31	29
Priority shifts: 3.1%-4.0%	10	24	20	24	12
Priority shifts: 4.1%-5.0%	2	8	10	15	1
Priority shifts: 5.1%-6.0%	0	2	7	0	0
Priority shifts: 6.1%-7.0%	0	1	2	0	0
Priority shifts: 7.1%-8.0%	0	0	0	0	0
Number significant (out of a possible 92)[b]	24	45	47	24	43

[a] This represents the percentage difference between the predicted share minus the real share, the prediction being derived from the trend in shares of the previous administration.

[b] Significance is reported in order to give some idea about how likely this deviation was, given priorities in the previous administration (see Table 3-1 for a description of the technique). The figure, 92, is derived from four elections times twenty-three states (which are all the states that had four-year governorships from 1950 to 1970).

[c] This is the number of share differences that conform to each of these categories in the analysis. Thus, for example, in the first budgetary year of fifty administrations, the difference between expected and real shares in public safety was equal to or less than 2 percent.

[d] In similar tests run for total outlays, 33 of 92 were significant at least at the .05 level.

Sources: See the Appendix.

strained environment. Given the tremendous pressures against change in the states, innovation is difficult. Therefore, insofar as it can, succession does produce what I would consider to be a substantial amount of policy innovation in the American states.

The fact that these innovations seem to occur more often later in the new administration than in the first blush of the new regime (a pattern which is revealed clearly in the scatter plots), moreover, further strengthens the case for arguing that succession influences public policy in the states. Severe constraints would seem to force a strategy of

TABLE 3-5
Priority Differences Among Gubernatorial Administrations

Priority Differences[a]	Public Safety[c]	Welfare	Education	Highways	Health
0-2.0%	30	16	14	21	25
2.1-3.0%	23	30	19	27	22
3.1-4.0%	12	15	22	20	14
4.1-5.0%	4	6	9	1	8
5.1-6.0%	0	2	5	0	0
6.1-7.0%	0	0	0	0	0
Number significant (out of a possible 69)[b]	29	46	41	33	30

[a] This represents average share difference between adjacent administrations.

[b] There are 69 tests, based on 3 tests per state and 23 states.

[c] This number is the total number of cases where the priority differences between administrations for public safety was, for example, equal to or less than 2 percent.

Sources: See the Appendix.

gradual change, wherein elites would build up, in an incremental way, support and dollars for pet priorities. It would take until the middle of their administration, then, for innovations to finally begin to appear, a strategy which approximates—and seems to explain—the pattern of results reported in Tables 3-4 and 3-5. Thus, what I am suggesting is that succession in the states has an impact which is often lagged, but which conforms to what can be described as innovation through experience.

Thus, as far as the Western democracies are concerned, changes in leadership do correlate with changes in budgetary priorities—in New York or Mississippi, Austria or the United States. The consistent pattern in the data, linking succession with innovation and its absence with stability, coupled with the theory developed in Chapter One contrasting honeymoon decision-making with "politics as usual"—incrementalism—suggests a causal linkage between elections and budgetary change. A change in leadership, then, does seem to be one political variable that does generally influence the budgetary process.[8] New Governors, new Presidents and new Prime Ministers all seem to make a difference.

Explaining the Results: The Impact of Mandate

Having drawn that general conclusion, however, it would be useful to backtrack a bit and to examine the variance in the results. While elections on the whole do seem to encourage budgetary innovation, there seems to be a fairly wide range of impact apparent in the data. Sometimes succession has a dramatic effect—for example, in Sweden and in the United States—and sometimes policy change is less striking—as in the German Federal Republic. How can this variance be explained?

One way to understand the differential impact of succession is to code the various elections according to some key variables that were hypothesized in Chapter One to affect the linkage between turnover and policy innovation. I have done just that in Tables 3-6 and 3-7, where each nation's and each state's political characteristics—such as executive mandate, party and personnel turnover, and leftism of the governing party—are recorded.[9]

The first factor is mandate—the size of each leader's vote

---

[8] In the eternal search for political variables that affect public policy in the liberal democratic states, one obvious factor—the electoral process—has been left out. For examples of the many studies that have compared the impact of political versus economic variables, see Richard Winters (1976) and Rudolph Klein (1976).

[9] The reader may be rather put off by the fact that there are no statistical summaries of the results presented in Tables 3-6 and 3-7. However, there is no way to put the results together—short of adding up significance tests, which is misleading—and thus I must leave it to the reader to look at previous tables and compare the results on the basis of the political variables coded in Tables 3-6 and 3-7. I should also note that these political variables were also coded by elections (but not reported here), and that these findings will be included in the discussion that follows.

TABLE 3-6
The Impact of Successions: A National Summary

Country	Average Competition[a] Votes	Seats	Average Leader Mandate[b] Votes	Seats	Average Spread Between Top Two Parties[d] Votes	Seats	Party Turnover[e]	Elite Turnover Rate[f]	Percentage Time More Leftist Party in Power[g]	Ranking of Impact[h]
Austria	55[c]	51[c]	58.5[c]	72.1[c]	3.7	4.3	Yes	4	50%	Medium
Canada	67	67	43.3	53.0	9.1	23.3	Yes	4	54%	Medium
Federal Republic	82	89	49.6	52.6	9.4	10.4	Yes	5	25%	Low
Great Britain	85	87	45.3	52.5	2.5	8.4	Yes	8	33%	High
Japan	50	55	46.6	52.5	24.4	31.0	No	8	0%	Medium
Sweden	36	41	46.3	48.0	27.5	28.1	No	2	100%	High
United States	85	—	54.6	—	12.3	—	Yes	6	33%	High

a This is the vote/seats of the second place party doubled.

b This is the vote/seats of the winning party averaged over time.

c This underplays the high competition in Austria, because of the influence of the grand coalition until 1966. Since that time, the comparable average competition figures would be 86 and 89, and the average mandate would be 48 and 53.

d This is the average percentage spread in votes and seats between the top two parties.

e This signifies whether the system is turnover (at least one party change) or dominant.

f This is the number of chief executives 1952-1975.

g This is the percentage of time the most leftist party has been in power for the data points analyzed.

h These rankings are based on a composite of the size of share shifts following succession and the significance levels associated with these shifts. For example, high impact indicates that over 60 percent of the share shifts for a given country were statistically significant and that the great majority of these shifts were over 2 percent. They are, obviously, rough, and the reader can refer back to Tables 3-1 and 3-2 to get a sense of the differences in impact. They are provided, then, to ease the reader's job of deciphering the results.

Sources: See the Appendix.

TABLE 3-7
A Summary of the American States

State	Average Competition for Governor[a]	Average Competition for Governor and Legislature[b]	Average Governor Mandate	Party Turnover in Governorship[c]	Turnover Rate[d]	Percentage Time More Leftist Party in Power[e]	Number	Ranking of Impact[f]
Alabama	35	13	Large	No	4	100%	20	Medium
California	85	80	Medium	Yes	3	40%	16	Medium
Connecticut	94	77	Medium	Yes	2	80%	7	Low
Delaware	97	81	Small	Yes	4	40%	19	Medium
Georgia	22	12	Large	Yes	4	80%	21	Medium
Idaho	100	88	Medium	No	2	0%	9	Low
Illinois	96	88	Small	Yes	7	40%	14	Medium
Indiana	92	75	Medium	Yes	3	40%	17	Medium
Kentucky	90	68	Medium	Yes	3	20%	20	Medium
Mississippi	32	12	Large	No	3	100%	19	Medium
Missouri	86	68	Medium	No	3	0%	18	Medium
Montana	95	73	Medium	Yes	3	20%	12	Low
Nevada	86	74	Medium	Yes	2	40%	13	Low
New Jersey	94	82	Medium	Yes	3	80%	10	Low
New York	98	89	Medium	Yes	2	20%	14	Low
North Carolina	84	40	Large	No	3	100%	14	Medium
Oklahoma	82	48	Large	Yes	3	60%	15	Medium
Pennsylvania	95	94	Small	Yes	4	60%	12	Low
South Carolina	18	10	Large	No	3	100%	14	Medium

Utah	94	81	Large	Yes	3	40%	14	Medium
Virginia	80	36	Large	Yes	4	80%	15	Medium
West Virginia	94	68	Medium	Yes	4	60%	10	Low
Wyoming	96	80	Medium	Yes	4	20%	11	Low

[a] This is the percentage vote of the second place party doubled.

[b] This summarizes governor mandate: 0-5 percent over next candidate is small; 6-15 percent is medium; and over 16 percent is large.

[c] This is to separate one party from turnover states (where party rule has changed at least once).

[d] This is the number of governors 1950-1970.

[e] This represents the percentage of time the Democrats were in power.

[f] This ranking is a composite of the size of share differences in the short and long term and the significance, statistically, of those differences. For example, "medium" reflects approximately 40-60 percent of the shifts are significant, and about half of the differences in shares between administrations are more than 2 percent. These rankings, of course, are not meant to be definitive, but rather roughly indicative of the results reported in Tables 3-4 and 3-5, and hence helpful in understanding the discussion that follows.

Sources: See the Appendix.

and/or seat margin in the legislature[10] As noted in Chapter One, one would expect that a large and/or growing base of support would expand a leader's power and hence would enhance as well the prospects for budgetary innovation. However, the data reveal that in fact priority shifts are more likely under conditions of both small and large mandates (refer to the pattern of results in the earlier tables and Tables 3-6 and 3-7). In both the Western democracies and the American states, the relationship between executive victory and legislative support, on the one hand, and priority shifts, on the other, is curvilinear; moderate competition seems to be where innovation is *least* likely. This is true both when individual elections and when states as a whole are treated as the units of analysis. Thus, it is at the pole of power and at the pole of competition that budgetary change is most probable.

It would appear, then, that the impact of mandate, or party competition, tends to follow the pattern predicted years ago by V. O. Key and Robert Dahl, not the pattern predicted by Anthony Downs or Otto Kirchheimer; that is, competition between parties seems to work to encourage *innovation*, not to stifle it.[11] However, one can also see another path to innovation in the data—high mandate—which confirms the common argument that policy change

[10] In party systems where more than two parties actively compete, this measure gets at competition better than simply doubling the minority party vote. In the latter case, states would look less competitive than they are because the second-place vote would not be close to fifty percent. However, for comparison's sake I included this original measure as well in Tables 3-6 and 3-7.

[11] Refer to note 1 and also see, for a supporting argument, Dahl (1966). Thus the issue of power to change policy—which would seem limited under conditions of high competition—does not seem to be relevant. Apparently leaders have enough power, even with skimpy mandates, to change things around. This may be because, when seat margins are narrow, Prime Ministers and Presidents can enforce greater party discipline in the legislature—each legislator feels his or her cooperation is needed, if policy is to be made at all.

requires power. The point, then, is that innovation in budgeting reflects one of two conditions: strong desire to change
policies, which may be enhanced by competition, or great
power, which is reflected in a large mandate. When either
are present to a substantial degree, the impact of succession
on budgetary priorities is enhanced. This generalization
holds, moreover, no matter how competition is operationalized, and whether one looks at nations or states, individual
elections or elections aggregated by polity.

THE IMPACT OF "NEWNESS"

A second plausible way to explain the results is to differentiate among successions that usher in new leaders and/
or new parties and those which involve a mere continuation
from the previous administration. It would seem obvious
that new leaders and new parties would advocate priorities
that deviate from those of their predecessors, not just because of ideology, but also because they interpret their
election as an indication that the electorate is dissatisfied
with the policies of the previous administration.

This argument is in fact upheld by the data. In the
American states, new parties and new Governors are more
likely to shift priorities than when elections continue the
rulers of the past. In the case of the nation-states, however,
the impact of "newness" is not so apparent. The reason for
this comparatively weaker result would appear to be the
presence of dual effects—that is, the tendency of reelection
to be accompanied by increasing mandates in the Western
democracies. Thus, Presidents and Prime Ministers are not
only reelected; they also tend at the same time to have an
increase in mandate, which seems to be in itself conducive
to innovation. By contrast, no such linkage between reelection and expanded power occurs in the American
states; in fact reelection often correlates with a *downturn* in
mandate. Thus, it can be concluded that mandate, or party
competition, is important to innovation, as is newness, but

that reelection with a decrease in mandate tends to dim the prospects for innovation. If accompanied by an expanded mandate, however, returning the incumbent to office can affect policy about as much as the inauguration of a new leader.

The validity of this interpretation can be seen clearly in the case of Germany (Gunther, 1970). As Konrad Adenauer's mandate declined in the late 1950's, the impact of elections on public policy declined as well, reflecting the decrease in his power *and* the policy biases entrenched by his repeated reelections to office. However, his replacement by Ludwig Erhard and Kurt Kiesinger ushered in more change, because, while the competition between the Christian Democrats and the Socialists was still growing (which tends to discourage policy change), there was a turnover in the post of Chancellor which enhanced the impact of succession. However, change in policy really began to occur when *both* the mandate increased (rather than decreased, as in previous years) and the executive office turned over at the same time: that is, with the victory of Willy Brandt in 1969 (Edinger, 1970). In 1972, with a reelection but an enlargement of his mandate, Brandt once again changed priorities.

Thus, what seems to matter is newness *or* an increasing mandate. This explains, for example, Tage Erlander's repeated innovations in Sweden throughout the 1950's and 1960's, despite his long tenure; Harold Wilson's impact in 1964 versus 1966; Dwight Eisenhower in 1956 and Lyndon Johnson in 1964; and the impact of Julius Raab versus Bruno Kreisky in Austria. Increasing one's mandate or being a first-termer tend to foster innovations in public policy. However, what really seems to be the most critical is being new.

Another way to conceptualize "newness" is to look at turnover rate. Indeed, there does seem to be a strong correlation between elite turnover rate and the policy effects of succession at the national and state level. In the American states, for instance, a high turnover rate leads to more innovation in budgetary priorities than lower rates of elite rotation. Similarly, one can contrast England, a country with a high turnover, with Austria, a nation with few executive changes. The former shows far more policy change in response to succession than the latter. Thus, there does seem to be a tendency—as the organizational literature has hypothesized—for high turnover to correlate with innovation (Price, 1976). Whether this peaks with very short tenure, as some scholars have suggested (Wilensky, 1967), is difficult to say, since there is only one such state in the group, Japan, that shows *very* rapid turnover in chief executives.[12] While the Japanese case is supportive of the notion that a revolving door of Prime Ministers can lead to a great deal of policy stability over time and after each election, one would need more cases to really accept this hypothesis. However, at the least, I can conclude from this data base that a fair turnover rate (say, tenure averaging four years) does seem to be more conducive to greater policy change after succession than longer tenure in office. A protracted bias in the policy network brought on by the dominance of one leader does seem to routinize policy priorities.[13]

Being new also seems to be important with respect to party rule. If one compares, for example, dominant with high turnover party systems, one finds the former to show fewer changes after succession than systems where two parties alternate in power. For example, in the American states, party turnover is more conducive to innovation after an

[12] The short tenure of Western officials has been noted by a number of scholars and linked with an inability to affect the ongoing policy process. Anthony Downs (1974) calls this "the law of inescapable discontinuity."

[13] Sweden, of course, is an important exception. There, leftist dominance and an expanding mandate seem to explain budgetary innovation following succession. While it was not included in this study, the Swedish findings were similar to those in Norway, where the Social Democrats have also (up to 1965) been dominant.

election than party continuity. This is also the case at the national level. In that context, new parties have a higher probability of ushering in policy change than old parties. Again, though, mandate (or competition) seems critical; this is why, for example, Lyndon Johnson's election in 1964 is so dramatic in its policy effects, and why the Swedish pattern of party dominance shows more policy change than the Japanese case. Thus, there do seem to be two paths to innovation: the interruption of a prevailing mobilization of bias in the policy network when one party dominates at the polls, and a shift upwards in mandate with or without a transfer of power from one party to another.

THE EFFECTS OF PARTY IDEOLOGY

The contrast between the Swedish and Japanese cases suggests the importance of a third factor: the ideological complexion of the governing party. Here the argument is that leftist parties (within the context of their own systems) tend to be more willing to change priorities than do rightist ones, primarily because change is a more legitimate enterprise to the left than it is to the right. In the American case, for example, James Sundquist (1968:201) makes such a distinction between the Democrats and the Republicans:

> A change in national administrations is a time of reappraisal and redirection. Historically, when the power shift is from Democrats to Republicans, the redirection takes the form of sorting out of democratic ideas and programs—the discarding of some, the acceptance of others and through that means, their admission into the national consciousness. . . . The Democrats innovate . . . and the Republicans consolidate.

This would lead us to expect that dominant party systems of the left should show more innovation after succession than do those of the right, and that leftist parties should sponsor more innovation than rightist ones within the same polity.

The data reported throughout this chapter indicate that ideology is indeed an important consideration. If one divides the American states into clusters, reflecting the percentage of time the Democrats rule (for instance, high = 80-100 percent of the time, medium = 40-79 percent of the time, and low = below 40 percent), one finds that leftism does correlate somewhat with the impact of succession. The small but apparent difference, of course, is not terribly surprising when one considers the extent to which parties in the American context tend to be indistinct ideologically.

Similarly, if one places Sweden, Austria, and Canada in the most leftist group at the national level (that is, where the left party has been in power at least 60 percent of the time), the U.S. and Britain in the next leftist group (from 40-60 percent) and Japan and Germany in the third and least leftist group (less than 30 percent of the time), there is some confirmation for the hypothesis that countries ruled by their more leftist parties will show more policy impact in response to succession than countries dominated by the right. This is most evident, for example, when the extremes are contrasted; that is, Sweden with Japan and Germany. However, both Great Britain and the U.S.—which are highly competitive systems dominated through the 1950's by the right—demonstrate a strong impact of succession, nearly equal to that of Sweden. This would seem to indicate once again that change occurs in response to two conditions: competition combined with turnover (as already noted) and the preponderant dominance of a left party. Where the impact of succession is less likely is when there is dominance by the right, moderate competition or competition without party turnover. The examples here would be Canada (especially in the 1950's), Germany, prior to 1965, Japan since the early 1950's, and Austria prior to 1966. In all of these cases, either dominance of the right occurred with low to moderate party competition, or there was high competition with no party changeover.

Thus, to return to an earlier distinction, what seems to

be happening is a mixture of the will and the way: leftist parties have the will, especially when they have a lot of power or when they are under fire from a rightist party that has ruled in the past and could do so again. Rightist parties are also innovators, *if* they feel the threat of leftist competition. Several seemingly contradictory hypotheses, therefore, have been upheld here which verify one common conception of competition—that of V. O. Key (1949)—and the impact of party ideology. Competition is conducive to innovation, and affects the left and the right. Similarly, leftism, especially when it occurs within the context of dominant systems, also leads to policy change following the election.

To what extend do these generalizations about leftism work when one looks at elections rather than at countries as the unit of analysis? In the American states, the differential impact of a Democratic versus a Republican victory is small, but in the expected direction. However, competition again seems to be the key; the American states are generally very competitive (compared with nation states, for instance), and this means (as is implied in the analysis above) that rightist parties tend to innovate as much as leftist ones in order to maintain their competitive edge. Thus, what I am saying is that, given high party competition in the states, Democrats and Republicans seem to be similarly willing to reorder priorities.

In the case of the national elections, there is a similar contrast, though, not surprisingly, far more striking. In those elections which ushered in the more leftist party, budgetary change is large; where rightist parties won, however, it is much smaller. For instance, one can contrast budgetary change in Germany under Adenauer versus Brandt, Canada under Trudeau versus Diefenbaker, England under Wilson versus Heath, or more generally, Sweden versus Japan. It is, therefore, clear that leftism does correlate with propensity to change budgetary priorities.

But change is one thing and the direction of change is

another. It is important to emphasize that, whether leftism is defined within or across systems (i.e., Democrats versus Republicans at the national and state level, as opposed to the Swedish Labour Party versus the Conservatives of Japan), dominance by the left—over time and at each election—tends to lead to a disproportionate rise in social outlays. This is particularly the case when the left dominates over time and/or when it receives a strong mandate. Parties of the right, as one would expect, respond to competition as well, by priming social outlays when they are under electoral pressures from the left. Thus, as in macro-economic policies (Hibbs, 1977; Frey, 1978; Cameron, 1978; Tufte, 1978), so in budgetary strategies ideology matters but is tempered by competition. Parties, therefore, have not "ceased to function as mechanisms of policy innovation" (King, 1969:136). Similarly, dominant leftist parties, like the Swedish Labour Party, live up to their reputation as innovators:

> Sweden's recent record of policy innovation, much of it closely related to post-industrial socio-economic trends, and much of it regarded as extremely advanced by international standards, seems to owe more to the established elite attitudes than to popular discontent expressed through new channels. . . . Even where "ad hoc" pressures have existed, they have served more as a trigger to initiate elite activities . . . than as an alternative agency of political change (Castles, 1976:208-209).

In contrast to dominant right parties, it seems that leftist parties do not need the threat of electoral competition to be innovative: it flows directly from their ideology, which in turn encourages greater emphasis on social-welfare priorities.

Thus, several important factors—party and personnel rotation, party competition, high mandates, and leftist dominance—could be identified that seem to enhance the extent to which elections alter budgetary policies, and the kinds of priorities that are favored. These factors, more-over, seem to be *critical*: they distinguish well between high and low impact, and they work across nations as well as across individual elections. I, therefore, can argue with some confidence that elections will have a greater impact on policy when they usher into power a new party, a new leader, and/or the more leftist party within the system. Fi-nally, party competition seems to be important, though not mandatory: nations with close elections and party turnover tend to be more change-oriented after elections than those with moderate competition. Clear dominance, however, works much the same as high competition in encouraging policy change after elections. Thus, high mandate and nar-row victories seem to be the most conducive to policy in-novations.

While I cannot point to any one political factor and say it is mandatory, then, I can list a number of conditions under which the impact of elections on public policy seems to be enhanced. There are indeed many roads to policy change after an election—some affect the desire for change (i.e., competition, party and personnel turnover) and some affect capability (i.e., leftist party dominance or an increase in mandate)—but the similar result is a strong impact of elections on budgetary priorities. The variance in the re-sults, therefore, can be explained to a substantial degree with a battery of rather familiar political variables that af-fect elite desire and capacity to change public policy.[14]

Before getting too carried away with this notion of var-iance, though, we should note that, whatever the effect of mediating variables, there is still one general conclusion: elections have significant effects on budgetary policy, wher-ever they occur, in Alabama or in Austria, in South Carolina

---

[14] In the course of the analysis, other explanatory variables were ex-amined—specifically, the effects of coalition and consociation and the impact of Presidential versus Prime Ministerial systems. However, it was found that none of these factors went very far in explaining the results.

or Sweden. Moreover, the impact generally tends to occur in the honeymoon and to level off once new priorities become the new routines. In this sense, there does seem to be an electoral cycle that calibrates the budgetary process in bourgeois democratic polities.

Conclusion

In the past ten years, political scientists have built a strong case for "actor dispensability," the idea that public policies are made by organizations and past priorities, but not by decision-makers (Greenstein, 1969). At the same time, the role of elections in decision-making has been criticized for failing to be "issue referrenda" (Polsby and Wildavsky, 1971:209). Thus, the pervasive picture is of a decision process in which policies seem to develop almost by themselves, unencumbered by the electoral process, the mass publics, or even the political leadership stratum.

This analysis, however, refutes these arguments by putting elections and elites back into the policy process in bourgeois democratic states. Elections rotate policies as well as leaders in nations as diverse as Japan and the United States, and states as different as New York and Mississippi. Moreover, policy change occurs precisely where some theories would have predicted—in states with high party competition, where leaders and parties change, when the election mandate expands, and where leftist parties win. But some change occurs with nearly every succession, whatever the level of party competition or executive rotation rate. In fact, where elections are concerned, incremental decision-making (and all the constraints it implies) is the *exception* and not the rule. It does seem to matter who rules in democratic political systems.

The question then becomes, how can all this be reconciled with what is the most dominant model of decision-making in political science today—the notion of incrementalism?

The answer is that I seem to have uncovered an electoral cycle, wherein newly elected leaders make changes in public policy only to have those changes become routinized until the next election. This pattern—incrementalism interspersed with short bursts of innovation—is rarely noted in studies of budgeting, yet is a "typical" cycle in many case studies of policy and organizational innovation. As one student (Walker, 1973:67) of the area has summarized: "Policy changes do not normally occur continuously or at regularly spaced intervals in most policy areas, but rather are clustered during periods of high activity followed by periods of consolidation and even stagnation." Thus, the quantitative analysis seems to confirm what many analysts of innovation have already suspected, that changes do indeed occur in response to shifts in certain factors—such as the increased desire and capability of leaders to innovate in the honeymoon—and occur in a predictable and cyclical fashion. Just as incrementalism is a rather common mode of decision-making, so is innovation. While the latter summarizes politics *within* administrations, as this analysis has demonstrated, innovation is what characterizes the politics of the honeymoon period.

In addition, the findings also help to resolve what has been a common contradiction in many studies of elections. As has been noted, for those who approach liberal democratic succession as a dependent variable, elections have been generally viewed as processes that maintain the status quo (to a fault); they are said merely to select "personnel, not policy" (Dye and Zeigler, 1972:141). However, for those few scholars who treat elections as independent variables, wholly different conclusions tend to be drawn. They emphasize the potentially *unstable* qualities of elections. Typically, this view emphasizes that

the problem of succession is central to all political systems; it is an inevitable consequence of Time and Man's mortality. . . . On the process of succession depends the

stability, welfare, and progress, sometimes even the continuity of the polity (Brecher, 1966:1; also see Stanley,
1965).

If one juxtaposes these two perspectives, one comes up with
the ironic conclusion that liberal democratic elections are at
the same time "too" stable, and yet perhaps not stable enough!

However, if a more consistent standard is adopted—that
elections hold open the possibility of institutionalized
change—then one can see how the findings fit in with this
seemingly contradictory notion of the impact of elections.
The electoral cycle does allow for change, but hardly opens
the floodgates. Elections and the interim between them
provide, therefore, a balance between the need for change
and policy reevaluation, on the one hand—which elections
and the honeymoon provide—and the need for stability
and predictable expectations, on the other—which occurs
within administrations through incremental decision-making. In this sense, the electoral process is functional and
works as an agent of change. These two qualities are not,
therefore, mutually exclusive; they may in fact be mutually
supportive. Innovation *and* incrementalism in budgetary
policy seems to be regulated by the electoral process in a
routinized manner.

This leaves us, however, with one final issue. Incrementalism versus innovation is one issue, and the impact of
leaders versus their environments is another. It should be
clear from the analysis thus far that changes in public policy
result from the interaction of two processes, campaigns and
decision-making, honeymoon style. It has to do, then, with
a complex interaction of pressures and incentives, with the
flexibility of policy-making and the malleability of the policy
environment. But where do leaders fit into this model? Are
they just simply responding to new structures and hence
as limited in their influence as they are in their mid-terms,
where incrementalism holds sway? Part of the answer to
this question lies in this chapter, and it is "no." Elections

without turnovers have less policy effects than successions which usher in new chief executives. However, even here we must be tentative. There are exceptions in the analysis; change is usually not dramatic even under optimal conditions, and even new leaders operate within—albeit a new—structural context. Given these qualifications, the next step is to look more intensively at how policies come about and at their origins in the mix between leadership and the policy milieu. It is to that task—a case study of American welfare policy-making—that I turn in the next chapter.

FOUR

Leadership Succession and Welfare Policy in the United States: A Case Study of the Impact of Elections on Public Policy

We shall soon with the help of God be in sight of the day when poverty will be banished in the Nation.
—*Herbert Hoover* (1928)

This nation . . . here and now declares an unconditional war on poverty in America. . . . We shall not rest until that war is won.
—*Lyndon Johnson* (1964)

Nowhere has the failure of government been more tragically apparent than in its system of public welfare. . . . It breaks up homes. . . . It often penalizes work. It robs recipients of dignity. . . . And it grows.
—*Richard Nixon* (1969)

INTRODUCTION

In the last chapter, I argued that elections seem to be critical mechanisms for budgetary innovation in Western nations and (to a lesser extent) in the American states. This conclusion was drawn because of the strength and consistency of the findings, and their correspondence to case studies of decision-making during the honeymoon period and models of policy innovation. The data revealed, therefore, a consistent and similar link between succession and budgetary change—across categories, countries, levels of government, and time. Moreover, the pattern of change was precisely as one would expect: that is, innovation in the honeymoon—reflecting the comparatively strong desire and capacity to innovate, on the part of the new governing team—followed by incrementalism for the duration of the

[91]

term—reflecting the diminution of the leader's power and incentives to reorder priorities. This cyclical notion of policy change, wherein new policies are introduced early in the term and freeze in at their new levels, is further calibrated, not just by elections, but particularly by certain types of elections. When elections enhance a leader's desire or incentive to innovate, or increase his capacity to dominate the policy process, succession has more impact. In this sense, the extremes of party competition, a change in the incumbent and/or ruling party, and the victory of the more leftist party all work to enhance policy change in the aftermath of succession. Thus, there does seem to be a great deal of theoretical and empirical support for the notion that new leaders have different priorities, mandates, and pressures than old leaders, and these distinctions make policy change more likely when leaders turn over or when elections occur than in the periods between transfers of power. The succession process, then, seems to provide leaders with the incentive and the capacity to reorder budgetary priorities.

This chapter will illustrate the causal linkage between succession and policy innovation by analyzing, based on secondary evidence, how Presidential elections in the 1960's shaped the course of American welfare policy. I intend this example to go beyond a case study that chronicles the rise and fall of welfare policies—that, after all, has been done a number of times. Rather, I will place the vicissitudes of welfare on the American elite agenda within the context of the linkage between succession and policy innovation and the alternation between "politics as usual"—or incrementalism—and the politics of decision-making during the honeymoon period. The overall goal is to incorporate all of this evidence to illustrate, expand, and further verify an empirical theory of elections as instruments of policy innovation. The basic argument will be that Presidential elections and the transition period that follows together provide unique, but predictable, opportunities for policy change to occur; that is, the transition period provides the newly elected chief executive with both the *incentive* to innovate—which comes primarily from the campaign experience and the "can do" mentality of new administrations—and the *capability* to do so—which is derived from the unusual support and compliance that mark the honeymoon period. Once the honeymoon is over, though, both the desire and the opportunity to reorder policy priorities wither away, and the policy process once again resumes an incremental pattern of development. That cycle—of change, then stasis—will be illustrated and further fleshed out in this chapter.

One might ask why American welfare policy was chosen as a case study of the relationship between democratic elections and policy innovation. The logic was that I wanted to look at an area that echoes back to the quantitative analysis of budgeting, yet deals with programs as well as dollars. Welfare is such an area. In addition, I wanted to examine an area that falls clearly into the domain of the chief executive; if this condition were not filled, one could not really test for the impact of executive turnover. Certainly, welfare policy meets this test very well because it is a redistributive policy; indeed, "White House interest and activity must be considered the sine qua non for change in relief policy" (Milius, 1976:1). Finally, and perhaps most important, it seemed imperative to look at a policy that is highly salient to both elites and the public at large. There is little question that, since 1960, welfare policy has been high on the agenda of concerns of American policy-makers:

> Each of the three most recent Presidents of the United States—John Kennedy, Lyndon Johnson and Richard Nixon—gave the problem of the poor attention early in his administration. President Kennedy's first executive order dealt with improved distribution of surplus food; President Johnson's first meeting as President with the Chairman of the Council of Economic Advisors in-

structed the latter to move full speed ahead with work on an anti-poverty program; President Nixon's first major domestic proposal was to overhaul the widely criticized program of aid to families with dependent children (Steiner, 1971:vii).

Similarly, the mass public evinced great concern over the relief issue in the 1960's; in May, 1965, for example, thirty-three percent of those polled by Gallup considered poverty to be one of the three most pressing problems in America.[1] However, while welfare reform and poverty became salient issues during the 1960's, there was no indication that any consensus about "the welfare mess" has emerged. It could be said, while the welfare "problem" evoked great pressure for policy change, most efforts at reform were paralyzed by the controversies engulfing the issue.

Thus, welfare policy seems to be an ideal case study for my purposes because it is highly salient to chief executives yet resistant to change. The development of welfare reform in the United States in the 1960's, therefore, would seem to be a useful example of how executive succession affects public policy.

WARFARE AGAINST WELFARE: AN OVERVIEW OF AMERICAN WELFARE POLICY

Perhaps the most striking characteristic of American welfare policy in the twentieth century has been its sporadic development. Rather than simply evolving incrementally, federal welfare policy has grown in fits and starts, sharp changes interspersed with longer periods of slow and more consistent change (Steiner, 1971; Moynihan, 1968; Skolnick and Doles, 1971). As evidence, one can point to the clustered pattern of changes in welfare: the Social Security

[1] See the *Gallup Poll Index*, 1 (June 1965). By 1968, though, the fickleness of the public became evident as this figure dropped to 3 percent and Vietnam came to dominate the public agenda.

Act of 1935 (which ushered in the first federal efforts in this area); the long lag until the Kerr-Mills Act of 1959; John Kennedy's renewal of the food stamp program in 1961 (which had been abolished after World War II); the Manpower Development and Training Act of 1962; Lyndon Johnson's Economic Opportunity Act of 1964; and, finally, Richard Nixon's abortive welfare reform—the Family Assistance Plan—first introduced in 1969. More recently, one can point to the Supplementary Security Income Program which came into being in 1974. This list reflects the fact that throughout the 1940's and 1950's there was little concern with welfare; however, in the 1930's and 1960's, major changes in the system occurred.

How can this pattern be explained? There are, it seems, two possible interpretations. The first and more common one is that "the crises of today are the programs of tomorrow" (DeGrazia, 1969:66). As evidence for this argument, one can look to the 1930's, when the Depression brought on greater need for public assistance, yet lowered the capacity of state and local governments to respond. The resulting crisis, of course, began the federal role in relief policy in the United States. Similarly, one could point to the purported welfare crisis of the 1960's.[2] In those years, welfare policy was attacked for being insufficient and unequal in its coverage and benefit levels, ineffective in reducing poverty, inefficient in its administrative application, and, finally, altogether too expensive, with costs spiralling seemingly out of control. For example, critics pointed to the fact that, beginning in the late 1950's, welfare expenditure began to grow at a rapid pace; from 1960-1972, social welfare expenditures increased four times, from 29 percent of the federal budget in 1960 to 32 percent in 1965, to 37

---

[2] It should be emphasized, however, that what is called a crisis in the United States is considered normal procedure in Western Europe and Canada. American welfare costs are not unusual, even if one takes into account how limited the coverage is (see, for instance, Rein and Heclo, 1973).

percent in 1972 (Skolnick and Doles, 1971). Within the welfare category in the budget, moreover, some programs grew at even faster rates, particularly Aid to Families with Dependent Children (AFDC), food stamps, and Medicaid. While in 1965 these programs comprised 21 percent of all such outlays, by 1972 they represented 41 percent of all welfare allocations at the federal level (Skidmore, 1975). These figures would probably not have been so disturbing except that most policy-makers and the public saw precious few results for all the money spent. Income distribution seemed to remain as unequal as always,[3] the percentage of families below poverty level was still very high, and benefit levels varied tremendously from one jurisdiction to another. All of these problems, however, as disappointing as they were in an objective sense, were made all the more unpalatable by the gap between the seeming intractability of poverty and the optimistic rhetoric of the 1960's. Much seemed to be ventured and yet little was gained, and this made the welfare problem even more acute in the eyes of many Americans. Thus, it can be argued rather easily that welfare innovations increased in the 1960's as in the 1930's because a crisis was perceived, and it was felt that the government could and should do something about it.

However attractive this argument may be in terms of linking crisis with innovation—a linkage that is pervasive in studies of public policy and organizational behavior—it does not tell us *why* elites chose to play up this "crisis" more than others, or why they introduced the new policies they did when they did. All the "crisis" argument says is that there was a need for change; what it does not tell us is why this need led to the adoption of certain policies and the

---

[3] See Plotnick and Skidmore (1975:viii; Burke and Burke, 1974:7-10). However, more recent evidence indicates that some inroads have been made, particularly if one takes into account in kind transfers (the fastest growing programs, such as food stamps) as well as income (see Doolittle, et al., 1977).

rejection of others. Nor can one explain the *temporal* pattern of welfare reform on the basis of this argument. What was it about the 1960's that encouraged so much experimentation at particular times and not others? Why did essentially similar problems in the 1950's bring on only incremental adjustments in the status quo?

Thus, to understand the ebb and flow of welfare innovation, one needs to focus on the impending crisis in welfare (the creation of a "need"), and the ways in which decision-makers responded to these needs. Whereas the crisis in welfare opened up the possibilities for new approaches and ideas, it was the electoral process and decision-making in the White House and Congress that determined both the extent to which the crisis was recognized and the nature of the programs designed to combat it. While Dwight Eisenhower opted out of welfare innovation for the most part, Presidents Kennedy, Johnson, and Nixon behaved as policy entrepreneurs, using welfare reform both to expand their political power and to spearhead their often anemic domestic programs. Considerations of power and policy priorities in the White House, when combined with a salient issue—poverty in America—worked together in the 1960's to produce welfare reform. But at the base of this linkage was the electoral process which transformed the issue, political power, the policy perspectives of the Presidency, and even incumbency to make reform in the welfare arena a real possibility.

THE ORIGINS OF THE WAR ON POVERTY

As noted above, the first major innovation in relief policy in the postwar era was the Economic Opportunity Act of 1964. However, as James Sundquist and others have so amply documented, to understand the roots of the Economic Opportunity Act, one needs to go back into the 1950's, when Congress and the Presidency both began to reconsider the issue of poverty, a topic that had last received attention in the 1930's (Sundquist, 1969, 1968; Anderson, 1970).

While professing to be a fiscal conservative, Dwight Eisenhower did increase the role of the federal government in several policy areas and thus opened up the possibility of federal intervention in welfare policy as well. In his second term, the first civil rights bill of the twentieth century was passed, along with the Kerr-Mills Act (which helped the elderly with hospital costs) and the National Defense Education Act of 1958. Paralleling this trend of an increased federal role in social policy was the 1954 Supreme Court decision on segregation, the Little Rock crisis of 1957, and the passage (but successful Presidential veto) of two laws concerned with area redevelopment and job training. In addition to legislation, there were also in these years some Congressional investigations of poverty: the Joint Economic Committee and John Sparkman chronicled rural poverty in America, and Senators Paul Douglas and Eugene McCarthy held hearings in Congress on poverty, unemployment, and malnutrition in the United States. Finally, one can point to another influential indicator of interest in this period: Professor John Kenneth Galbraith and Averell Harriman (then Governor of New York) added to the concern in the latter part of the 1950's by criticizing in an outspoken manner the inequality of income distribution in the United States.[4] However, these incidences were just that—isolated stirrings of discontent with the status quo. The more pervasive sentiment in the 1950's was to "sustain the concept of public assistance as a declining business that could be safely left to wither away" (Steiner, 1974:50).

This conviction, however, came into question in the 1960 Presidential election. During his campaign for office, John Kennedy was deeply moved by the poverty of West Vir-

[4] Congress was the antechamber for many of the later policies that were labelled "executive" innovations (see Sundquist, 1968; Chamberlain, 1969; Moe and Tell, 1971).

ginia, and Hubert Humphrey, his major rival for the Democratic nomination, embellished the issue further by playing up his modest background as contrasted with that of the millionaire Kennedy (Sundquist, 1969; Skidmore, 1975). While the West Virginia primary was the major turning point in the nomination process, and this embellished the importance of this particular campaign for Kennedy, its entire impact extended beyond the final vote tally. Throughout the campaign, and especially in West Virginia, Kennedy was exposed to poverty for the first time, and this filled in the many gaps that he had in his political experience, his policy priorities, and his sense of national needs. Upon election, Kennedy, an activist, yet a political novice, realized he had no domestic program; therefore, he turned to several sources of ideas—the programs of the past (such as the abortive ventures in social policy in the 1950's) and the campaign experience. Both worked to make him an aggressor in social policy, a stance that fit in with his political style, the biases of his surrounding advisers, and the tenor of his campaign for office. Thus, the campaign worked to encourage innovation by providing Kennedy and the faithful around him with ideas, experience, and the desire to "do something once elected."

Once in office, Kennedy immediately took up the poverty issue by reviving the food-stamp program and expanding the surplus commodity program, two actions that Congress had in fact suggested to Eisenhower in years past. In addition, Kennedy—again relying on many of the ideas that had circulated around Congress in the 1950's—sponsored the Area Redevelopment Act (1961) and Manpower Development and Training Act (1962). While these policies were not new, they did imply a tentative recognition of poverty as an important issue, and one that could be solved by introducing some new services and greater opportunities for employment among the poor in depressed regions of the country. In the early part of his administration, then, Kennedy was innovative, yet seemed to approach the poverty issue in a gingerly fashion. While he was innovative in the sense that he recognized poverty to be a problem of dependent families as well as old people and that he offered more services for the poor—such as job training and food stamps—he was not willing to go one step farther and present to Congress an extensive long-term, multi-dimensional program on poverty that would upgrade substantially the federal government's role in public assistance. Welfare reform in this period was, therefore, a classic example of the piecemeal strategy that seems to characterize most reform efforts in America, a strategy which at times has eventually led to dramatic shifts in public policy.

Kennedy's reluctance to lead a concerted assault on poverty, however, slowly changed over the course of his administration. By 1963 pressure had been building for a bold attack on poverty in America. Two disturbing and well-circulated indictments of poverty had appeared—Michael Harrington's *The Other America* came out in 1962 and Dwight McDonald's "The Invisible Poor" was published in *The New Yorker* the following year. At the same time, some problems in the existing welfare system had become more visible: expenditures had jumped (this process had actually begun in 1959), AFDC (or ADC, as it was called then) payments and the number of recipients had begun to rise, inequalities in benefits among the states became more apparent, and finally, the structure of poverty—as a problem primarily of the young and minorities, and not just the aged—became more well-known than in the past. Moreover—and this is critical to any innovation—information about poverty became readily accessible to decision-makers. Just as Robert Kennedy's Commission on Juvenile Delinquency provided a great deal of data on poverty and crime among the young, so the work of the Ford Foundation had a similar impact with respect to poverty, enhancing what Daniel Moynihan (1965) has called, "the professionalization of reform" efforts in the 1960's. Under its grey (read "poor") areas program, for example, Ford had tested out a number of theories about poverty, and had demonstrated to some extent the utility of a multifaceted approach that emphasized community involvement, urban renewal, and "preparing people for jobs" rather than vice-versa (Sundquist, 1969; Yarmolinsky, 1969). Instead of explaining poverty simply as a deficit of funds, the Ford Foundation attributed poverty, not just to income insufficiency, but also to deficiencies in housing, education, and political and social participation. This particular view of poverty was to permeate welfare reform throughout the early and middle 1960's, and became known as "the services approach" (Steiner, 1971).

Finally, and perhaps most critically, towards the end of his administration, John Kennedy increasingly saw public assistance as an issue around which he could organize and expand his flimsy electoral coalition. Early in his term, eyeing his slender margin of support in Congress, Kennedy arranged his legislative program to build some consensus. Later, however, with the 1964 election on the horizon, Kennedy began to see poverty as an issue which could appeal to the broad masses of the voters. After all, it was in keeping with the spirit of the New Frontier, and was a valence issue as well: who after all could come out *for* poverty? This meant that the poverty issue could attract large numbers of new supporters with few risks of alienating previous allies. Kennedy could play it safe, and at the same time appear bold and imaginative. Only much later did welfare reform, with its high cost and limited success, develop pockets of opposition.

Thus, in late 1962 and throughout 1963, John Kennedy encouraged his staff, particularly the Council of Economic Advisors, to develop ideas about combatting poverty. Their response to Kennedy's encouragement was typical "bureaucratic politics"; that is, "Each department [jockeyed] for position, attempting to gain control of the antipoverty effort (or at least win more funds) by selling programs which only it could administer" (Blumenthal, 1969). What resulted was a rich hodgepodge of proposed programs, including Medicare and Medicaid, job training, vocational rehabilitation, and community action (or regional corporation programs, as they were then called). Although Kennedy's advisors were split on the advisability of poverty as an election issue, Kennedy decided in November of 1963 to place policy regarding poverty at the center of his legislative proposals for 1964. One can be certain that he would not have done this in a non-election year; he felt that such a domestic innovation would help him to win the 1964 election. In this case, contrary to the usual cliché concerning politicians' avoidance of major issues during an election year, policy innovation in the welfare area was seen by Kennedy and many of his advisors as a way to *expand*, not contract, his electoral appeal. This was a cautious, pragmatic, and yet at the same time innovative approach to welfare policy and a response to both serious issue concerns and "the electoral connection" (Mayhew, 1974). Just as many politicians before him, Kennedy tried to expand his power by creating a new issue and appearing to act in a forthright manner to resolve it—to give the electorate a handle on his administration and to see him as innovative and energetic. While this issue would later become highly controversial, in 1963 it was not and therefore seemed to be an ideal way to arouse popular passions and to expand electoral support. Thus, Kennedy became a policy entrepreneur in the welfare arena in part because of the electoral cycle—it had stimulated his first efforts in the area and had emboldened him later to construct a full-fledged program in order to expand his mandate and give him a reelection issue. Thus, campaigns, elections (and reelections), changes in leaders, and the Presidential honeymoon can work together to produce new public policies.

Kennedy never had a chance to test whether these new directions in poverty policy would in fact enhance his electoral appeal—the assassination intervened. However, Kennedy's death did not end the concern with poverty policy in the Executive Branch; if anything, desire and capability to change welfare policy were magnified in the years immediately following Camelot. Kennedy ensured that welfare policy would be high on his successor's agenda, by making it a hot issue in the executive and legislative branches and developing a policy community committed to reform in this area and highly resistant to being dispersed. Thus, before one too quickly dismisses JFK's ventures into the welfare thicket, it should be remembered that he made it a politically important issue. For those who followed him, welfare reform became an imperative of sorts. In this sense, Kennedy "invented" the welfare issue. His successors, however, were the ones who implemented new policies and hence could be termed "innovators."[5] And the electoral process played a major role in these developments.

THE JOHNSON YEARS: REHABILITATION NOT RELIEF

As Kennedy did before him, Lyndon Johnson took on the welfare issue immediately after his accession to office. When told of his predecessor's plans for a legislative package dealing with poverty, Johnson quickly assented to the idea and encouraged Kennedy's advisors, the CEA task force, to continue the work. However, the more Johnson thought about the idea, the more he wanted it to be *his* policy (Skidmore, 1969; Donovan, 1970). He then asked Sargent Shriver to set up a new task force, which was empowered to go full speed ahead on welfare reform. This was the beginning of the War on Poverty, an innovation which combined many of the ideas of the Kennedyites with the mandate and legislative power of the Johnson administration.

What differentiated Johnson's approach from Kennedy's

[5] For example, Sundquist (1969) notes that until 1964 the term "poverty" had never appeared as a heading in the index of either the *Congressional Record* or the *Public Papers of the President*.

was his full commitment to a broad-gauged program, his interest in gathering as much information as possible before the program was actually written into legislation, and his haste in converting all those ideas into law. Johnson widened considerably the net of consultants involved in poverty policy, bringing in numerous academics and professionals into the Executive branch. While JFK originated the heavy use of task forces in executive decision-making, it was Johnson who really plugged them into the policy process (Thomas and Wolman, 1969; Glazer, 1969). What is most striking about Johnson's approach to poverty policy was its potential for producing fundamental changes in policy. The task forces in the Johnson White House provided optimal conditions for the generation of new ideas because they pitted outsiders against insiders, focused on specific policy concerns, had only limited duration, and finally, insulated "idea people" from actual policy implementors. A premium, then, was put on producing new policies rather than on justifying old ones, and new ideas rather than feasible ones. Moreover, the variety of the participants' backgrounds meant that a variety of options were in fact discussed. Thus, by virtue of their power, their diversity, and their temporary status, the Johnson task forces could be legitimately a "policy community" (Walker, 1974), committed to change, and vested by President Johnson with developing a full War on Poverty.

However, the "policy community" would not have been conducive to innovation if it had not received the full support of the new President. In the transition from one administration to another, there is a great deal of uncertainty and much competition to pay respects to the new successor (Stanley, 1965; Henry, 1960). In this climate, the effect of a new President's showing strong interest in particular issues would work to encourage subordinates to come up with a range of proposals in relating to those issues. This tendency would be made easier if a critical mass already existed committed to such notions; this, of course, was precisely the case with the poverty issue in 1963 and 1964. Thus, many members of the Executive branch were using the poverty problem to win Johnson's favor, keep their jobs, press personal concerns, and perhaps move up a notch or two in the White House. Ambition once again seems to have been the mother of policy innovation.

But the importance of ambition in fostering policy change was not limited simply to subordinates and to members of the poverty task force; it affected Lyndon Johnson's behavior as well. Having been humiliated as Vice President and uncertain of his mandate, Johnson wanted to establish his credentials as President. This sense of insecurity was combined with a grandiloquent personality and an enduring concern with government action on behalf of the needy. As Doris Kearns (1976:211, 218-219) explained it, Lyndon Johnson was a "twentieth century booster" and a highly ambitious politician:

> A multitude of changing conditions and attitudes conspired to convince a President who was bent on achievements that would leave his mark on the country's history that the Great Society was not a utopian vision, but the inevitable direction for progressive action. . . . Johnson demanded support for the Great Society . . . to improve all the conditions of society as a matter of faith. . . . It would accomplish more for the nation than had programs of any other administration, compelling history to acknowledge the greatness of its progenator.[6]

Johnson's commitment to antipoverty policy, then, grew out of his need for power and his long-time concern for

---

[6] As Kearns notes, Johnson never wanted power for power's sake; he saw power as the handmaiden of good works (1976:214). Johnson was thus a policy entrepreneur, which seems to be a prerequisite for innovation. James Burns (1968:418-419) has argued that one reason why Johnson could do so much was because he came to the Presidency in its strongest hour—that is, he was helped immensely by the "institutionalized Presidency."

innovation in social policy. As with Kennedy, moreover, the desire for power worked with (not against) the desire for policy innovation. Neither Johnson in 1964 nor Kennedy in 1963 saw any real trade-off between the acquisition of power and the introduction of new policy initiatives. Thus, the process of acquiring political power can provide both ideas and incentives conducive to innovations in public policies.

All of the factors that have been outlined so far—Johnson's political role, his background, the impact of the transition period, the availability of information on poverty, the sense (left from the Kennedy days and snowballing ever since) of welfare in crisis, and finally, the role of the task forces—worked both to ensure innovation in public policy and to shape the very nature of the Economic Opportunity Act (EOA). One of the most striking aspects of this legislation (passed in 1964 and substantially amended in 1965) was the extent to which it was an "in-house document": "The most significant feature of the Economic Opportunity Act . . . was that it was legislated almost entirely within the executive office branch and indeed virtually without prodding from Congress or other outside clienteles" (Bibby and Davidson, 1967:220, quoted in Brecher, 1973:36). A second unusual characteristic was the speed with which the bill was written; it was sent to Congress on March 16, 1964, less than four months after Johnson acceded to power. Johnson clearly wanted to take advantage of Congressional guilt about Kennedy, popular support for the new incumbent, the democratic majority, and his own popularity in Congress—in short, the power that flowed from his honeymoon period. Johnson wanted his mandate and an election issue, and this meant visible poverty legislation in quick order. He also wanted a valence issue, just as Kennedy had, that would move the public and have the added benefit of fighting such salient problems as crime, unemployment and juvenile delinquency. Thus Johnson was running for office and seeking a firm mandate in his first year as President;

this, plus the convenient supply of ideas, his position of power, and his concern with poverty, converged to make the Economic Opportunity Act a dramatic innovation in welfare assistance. Ambition, ideological preferences, and political power, therefore, converged in 1964 and linked succession with policy innovation.

A final ingredient, however, was the notion of a crisis. As James Q. Wilson has observed, "Many organizations will adopt no major innovation unless there is a crisis" (Wilson, 1966:198). While leaders may have the power, ambition, and interest to act, these are amplified when a need to take action is perceived. In such a circumstance, the risks of not acting become high, and hence "pressure to make a change" combines with the desire and incentive to make a change. Thus, if one were to summarize why the EOA came into being, one would have to include the ambition of its framers, their interest in the issue, their power over the policy process, the availability of a number of options and ideas and, finally, the perceptions of a policy crisis, or a "forcing action." But at the base of all these variables is the electoral process, which defined the crisis and power of the decision-makers and their propensity to take action.

While all of these factors did shape the "innovativeness" of the Economic Opportunity Act, it was the hearts and minds of its major framers that gave the act its unique personality. The dominant approach was, to quote from Lyndon Johnson's State of the Union Message in 1964, that "the War on Poverty is not a struggle simply to support people, to make them dependent on the generosity of others. It is a struggle to give people a chance" (quoted in Lander, 1967:4). By "a chance," Johnson meant a whole range of things, including job training and placement, day-care centers, community participation in policy decisions on poverty, adult education, low-income housing, small-business loans, medical care for the poor—in short, a "structural" approach to poverty, as opposed to what Daniel Moynihan (1968) has called the "cold cash" method of alleviating poverty. This crazy quilt of services reflected two things: a commitment to attacking the causes, not the fact, of poverty, and, second, the way in which policy disputes were resolved in the Johnson White House. Basically, the Economic Opportunity Act reflected Johnson's admiration for consensus politics; instead of choosing among alternatives, he tended to include them all (Kearns, 1976:136-137, 186). Thus, for example, Daniel Moynihan and Willard Wirtz won their job proposals; Abraham Ribicoff won an emphasis on services; Johnson won on education; Adam Yarmolinsky, Robert Kennedy, and the Ford Foundation's ideas were incorporated into the Community Action Program (CAP); and Sargent Shriver won on the creation of the Office of Economic Opportunity (OEO). Thus, ironically, the very process of putting the Economic Opportunity Act together encouraged both consensus and innovation, and the consensus in fact encouraged the innovation to come into being.

Perhaps even more rare than the combination of consensus with innovation is the ease with which the Economic Opportunity Act passed through both houses of Congress (226-184 in the House, and 61-34 in the Senate, both votes reflecting strong party lines). One reason for this was the simplicity of the proposal. The Economic Opportunity Act was a straightforward set of policies, which included the creation of the Job Corps, Neighborhood Youth Corporations, and the work-study program (Title 1); the Community Action Program, adult basic education, and Head Start (Title 2); the rural loan program and migrant labor services (Title 3); small-business loans (Title 4); job training (Title 5); the Office of Economic Opportunity, Vista (the domestic Peace Corps), and the Economic Opportunity Council (Title 6); and, finally, an act to separate these services from the calculation of income for social security beneficiaries.

However, it is also important to emphasize that the Economic Opportunity Act was passed quickly because Congress was ready to act fast in 1964. There was a "can-do" President in the White House (to use one of Johnson's favorite words), a man who was a graduate of both Houses (indeed, one could say summa cum laude), and there was a large democratic majority, which acted in concert. In addition, Congress felt guilty about its role in undermining the social legislation of John Kennedy. Even if Congress had not been willing, though, Lyndon Johnson would have twisted its arm. The Economic Opportunity Act received a tremendous amount of publicity from the White House; for example, Johnson went on a tour of Appalachia while the bill was in the House, and Congress was barraged with information, statistics, and liberal doses of "the Johnson treatment."[7] Thus, the Economic Opportunity Act became law because the ideas and incentives were there to propose new policies, the Chief Executive put himself squarely behind those policies, and the "Zeitgeist" in Congress and the nation favored new ventures in social problem-solving. Therefore, one can argue, as was the case with John Kennedy and with the quantitative analysis in Chapter Three, that policy innovation comes in the honeymoon period because the electoral process has provided both the desire and the capability for new leaders to change policy priorities. The campaign and the honeymoon, or the desire to innovate when combined with unusual capabilities to do so, seem to be the key to understanding the pattern of welfare reform in America. In the case of Lyndon Johnson and the Economic Opportunity Act, one can point to his succession to office, the process of his selection, his mandate, and the nature of the incumbent himself—his ambition, his values,

---

[7] What is surprising, however, is the poor quality of information decision-makers had about poverty in America in the early and even middle sixties. For example, in discussions in the White House during this period, they defined poverty in terms of families (of whatever size) with an income under $3,000. Moreover, they greatly underestimated the number of welfare recipients who were not really trainable, and failed to recognize the massive exodus of Southern poor from the South to the North during the 1960's.

and his activism—as the reasons behind the development of the first major change in American welfare policy since 1936.

However, in the years following 1964 there developed a lull in welfare innovations, a pattern similar to the routines present in the Kennedy administration, and in the quantitative analysis presented in Chapter Three. Specifically, in the later years of the Johnson era there developed a large gap between what was ventured and what was gained; in fact, "the war on poverty dwindled into a skirmish" (Burke and Burke, 1974:10). There have been any number of explanations for this "slippage" (Sundquist, 1968; Liebman, 1974), the most convincing of which is the simple fact that in 1965 Lyndon Johnson became involved in another and far more costly war in Southeast Asia. As he complained to Doris Kearns (1976:251-254):

> I knew from the start that I was bound to be crucified either way I moved. If I left the woman I really loved— the Great Society—in order to get involved with that bitch of a war on the other side of the world, then I would lose everything at home. All my programs. All my hopes to feed the hungry and shelter the homeless. But if I left that war and let the communists take over South Vietnam, then I would be seen as a coward. . . . I knew that Harry Truman and Dean Acheson had lost their effectiveness from the day that the communists took over China . . . so you see, I was bound to be crucified either way I moved.

The War on Poverty paid for that escalation. Rather than a comprehensive attack, the Economic Opportunity Act programs contributed to perhaps one-fifth of the welfare budget in the late 1960's and never reached the funding levels envisioned in 1964. As Sar Levitan has argued, the Economic Opportunity Act really ended up as a supplement to older programs, such as AFDC and Social Security. Because of Vietnam and Johnson's resistance to income support for the poor—in short, because of Lyndon Johnson's own policy priorities—the Economic Opportunity Act never really had the dollars to live up to its grandiose rhetoric (Levitan, 1969; Liebman, 1974).

Another problem with the War on Poverty—a problem that flowed directly from the haste and consensus that had underlined the making of the poverty policy in 1964 and 1965—was that its programmatic base was ambiguous and haphazardly tied together so that few could disentangle the content, goals, or even the implementation process implied in the EOA. This was most apparent in the implementation of the Community Action Program (CAP) and the formation of the Office of Economic Opportunity, both of which were highly controversial and plagued by a series of "maximum feasible misunderstandings" (Moynihan, 1969; Miller and Rein, 1969; Donovan, 1970a). Most applications were ad hoc, and neither the CAP nor OEO ever clearly defined their roles. This in turn was hardly helped by the fact that decentralization was heavily emphasized in the program, which meant in practice a proliferation of interpretations of the proper role of CAP and a proliferation of control and coordination problems for OEO.

Some have gone even further in their critique and argued that the problems the EOA encountered have less to do with the program itself than with the very nature of decision-making and policy implementation in the United States. Peter Marris and Martin Rein (1969:235), for instance, in their analysis of CAP, have drawn such a conclusion:

> The more widely the freedom to initiate change is spread, the more difficult it becomes to control the outcome. In this lies the complementary weakness of reform in America. A vision of opening opportunities for millions of maltreated youngsters might end with a dozen children in a makeshift nursery school.

The *process* of building consensus, then, sealed the fate of the Economic Opportunity Act. There seems to be an either/or quality to reform in America: one can either propose innovative policy and watch its impact wither away, or pursue existing priorities and be more assured of smooth implementation and meaningless impact. It seems that the price of consensus is the dilution of new programs once the policy is implemented, as each group wrangles over its share and its interpretation. The dilemma of welfare reform, then, takes on a Catch-22 quality that was described twenty years ago by Wallace Sayre and Herbert Kaufman (1960:718-719) in their analysis of New York City politics:

> Changes of any magnitude thus encounter a long, rocky, twisting path from conception to realization. They are likely to be blocked almost at the start unless their authors revise and modify them to appease strong opponents. . . . After all the bargaining and concessions, a plan may well have lost much of its substance, much of its novelty. If plans are radical, they seldom survive; if they survive, they seldom work major changes in the governing system.

However, such blanket assertions about the failure of the Economic Opportunity Act as a function of the impossibility of innovation in America do not really address the specific facts that limited the impact and implementation of that particular policy. Innovation in America cannot be dismissed so easily as something which is structurally impossible; rather, specific events and forces seem to make change difficult, though not impossible. With each policy, one can isolate the reasons why change did not occur, and the Economic Opportunity Act is no exception. Certainly, one reason why the War on Poverty ran out of ammunition was because of its poor funding and its peculiar fascination with job training and the "roots" of poverty. *How* poverty was understood in the 1960's ensured to a great extent the failures to combat it:

> The Kennedy-Johnson public assistance legacy . . . was a services approach that had failed, a work and training

approach that could not get off the ground, an asserted interest in day care but no viable day care program, a reorganization of the welfare apparatus in Health, Education and Welfare, some procedural changes in the lame duck period and a steadily increasing number of AFDC recipients (Steiner, 1971:105).

By trying to get at the "root causes" of poverty and by assuming that poverty was caused by inadequate preparation for entering the work force, the policy-makers of the 1960's failed to expand job opportunities (assuming somehow that jobs would open up for the newly trained), to ensure a living wage so that the poor could afford to work, and to transfer money to those who, because of children or poor education, could not really work. The great bulk of AFDC recipients and the working poor, then, were left out. What was left in was too small to make much of a dent in the poverty ranks. Thus, *how* policy-makers defined poverty determined the programs they developed and the impact of those programs. In the case of the War on Poverty, the failure flowed, first, from the assumptions behind the program, and then from the funding problems, the structure (or its lack thereof) of power in America, the fuzzy goals of the Economic Opportunity Act itself, and the gap between the magnitude of the legislation and the problems it sought to solve.

By 1967 sentiment among government officials and the mass public had started to turn against the War on Poverty. All the statistics pointed to an increase in the welfare rolls (from 1962 to 1967 the number of Americans on welfare had increased from 3.5 to 5 million) (Burke and Burke, 1974:10), in welfare spending, and in crime and delinquency; as a result, there was a decline in public sympathy for recipients of welfare, the civil rights movement, and Lyndon Johnson. The "Zeitgeist" had changed from sympathy to antipathy, and Congressional action reflected this downturn of support. The dominant interpretation of the "welfare mess" was that welfare recipients were lazy and corrupt; therefore, Congress in 1967 moved to reform AFDC so as to require that single parents work, or train for work, unless they had a child under age five. The new law also provided some (though hardly enough) funds for day care and provided more work incentives by allowing recipients to keep more of their earnings from employment before they lost their welfare benefits. At the same time, Congress passed an AFDC freeze, which was supposed to cut off federal matching funds after June 1968 (this was later retracted). Finally, striking out again at inefficiency, Congress began to whittle away at the Economic Opportunity Act programs, and Lyndon Johnson gave up the fight. By 1969, the amount devoted to such programs in the budget dwindled to a mere eight percent of all federal anti-poverty dollars (which testifies, among other things, to the growth of AFDC and food stamps). Thus, the "services approach" of the early 1960's gave way in the twilight of the Johnson era to what has been called a "work or economic incentives strategy" (Steiner, 1974; Marmor and Rein, 1973). At the same time, the pendulum by 1967-1968 had swung back to ad-hoc, incremental decision-making, rather than any concerted policy effort that aimed for an overhaul of the welfare system. The pattern of innovation in welfare policy, therefore, assumed the familiar decline in innovation following the honeymoon period. As with the quantitative analysis, so in welfare policies, the flurry of innovations characterizing the first year of the new administration slipped back to incremental change in the later years of the administration.

This reappearance of incremental decision-making by 1966 and 1967 led many observers to pronounce welfare reform dead in America. Pointing to the expanding dollars spent, adherents of the right complained about inefficiency, fraud, and lack of work incentives, while those of a more leftist persuasion criticized the inequalities in benefits, the humiliation involved in going on welfare, the woefully inadequate funding and services provided for the poor by the federal, state, and local governments, and discrimination against the working poor, two-parent families, single people, and childless couples (Doolittle et al., 1977)[8] While throughout the 1960's aid to the aged, blind, and disabled and veterans' pensions all improved with incremental but cumulatively innovative adjustments, the same could hardly be said for AFDC recipients, who after all comprised the bulk of those on welfare.

However, some scholars began to take a different view of the progress on the poverty front in the late 1960's. Pointing to the same data that documented the spiraling costs of the AFDC and food stamp programs (due to expansion of recipients, not to the size of the benefits), some observers argued that *this* was the reform, that welfare was reaching more people than ever. As Gilbert Steiner (1974:48) put it: "Admitting more of the needy poor to the welfare rolls is the quintessence of welfare reform." Rather than berate the statistic that, while in 1940 only two percent of American children were on welfare and by 1969 the comparable figure was ten percent, the optimists saw this as a positive indicator of the reach of the welfare system. This, then, was the ironic outcome of the Economic Opportunity Act; it expanded the welfare ranks by providing more goods, more information, and more awareness, and this signified, not its failure, but its success:

> So the self-support amendments of the Great Society period helped open the door to welfare growth, without being destined to do so. The door opened wider as welfare rights groups spread the message of welfare as a right; as mayors and governors decided to accept the

[8] The inequality and inadequacy of public aid among the states can be seen in the fact that only 25 percent of the states provide funds on a level commensurate with need (as defined by each state) for AFDC. For the rest of the states, payments vary from 22 percent of need in Mississippi, 48 percent in Missouri, 59 percent in Ohio, 65 percent in Georgia, and 70 percent in Alabama. For further discussion, see Platky (1977).

new liberalism rather than change the consequences of
the new militancy; [and] as the legal services movement
successfully challenged state efforts to limit eligibility
. . . (Steiner, 1974:69).

Unfortunately, there is one flaw in this argument, a flaw
that should seem familiar to those who criticize incrementalism. While more and more people were being covered,
the adequacy of that coverage was limited by the structure
of the system and the size of the benefits. No incremental
adjustment was going to reduce disparities between New
York and Mississippi, or provide aid to the working poor
or childless couple. If the "base" is wrong or inadequate,
no additions to the base will be sufficient: the bias in the
system will continue, no matter how much tinkering goes
on or how many adjustments are made. The problem of
cost efficiency, discrimination, and inequality, then, cannot
be ameliorated by expanding the reach of the existing system; gaps will widen, costs will keep rising, and some needy
group will never be reached.

It was with these arguments in mind that the second
major attempt to change American welfare policy in the
postwar era—the Family Assistance Plan—was developed
in 1968-1969. And, again, it was no accident that this program appeared immediately after the election of Richard
Nixon, i.e., during the start of a new administration. The
politics of succession and the fact "that old data came to
the attention of new men [sic]" (Bowler, 1974:3)—a repeat
performance of those other honeymoons of 1960-1961 and
1964-1965—once again ushered in new policies and a new
way of thinking about the welfare issue. The ambition and
the policy interests of the new President, the newness, expertise, and ambition of his advisors, and the politics of the
honeymoon period combined to produce what some suggested would be "the most innovative change in public assistance since the 1935 Social Security Act" (Burke and
Burke, 1974:3, 19; Steiner, 1971:90).

The Family Assistance Plan

As seems to be inevitably the case with innovations in welfare policy (as in most policies, for that matter), the origins of the Family Assistance Plan go back into the previous administration. From 1967-1968 several members of the Johnson administration—namely, Sargent Shriver, Worth Bateman, and several other officials at Health, Education, and Welfare and the OEO—began work on several negative income tax plans. Their feeling was that the federal government should take over more of the welfare burden (to ease fiscal pressure on the states and cities, and to equalize benefits) and pay recipients in cash, not kind, according to "inability to pay" income taxes—hence the term "negative income tax" (NIT). As Sargent Shriver described the program, the NIT "would reach all the nooks and crannies of the poor" (Steiner, 1971:121). However, their interest in this proposal failed to impress either Wilbur Cohen or Lyndon Johnson; it was too radical, too expensive, too "monetary," and too long-term in its impact (the planners projected an implementation phased over five years). Thus, from 1965 to 1967 OEO kept proposing its "National Poverty Plan" and getting rebuffed as Lyndon Johnson, Wilbur Cohen, and Wilbur Mills resisted any major overhaul of the welfare system during this period. After all, at that time Johnson was neither running for reelection nor retiring; he was ambivalent and this immobilized the policy process.

But the movement toward NIT was afoot in a number of quarters. William Ryan, a Democratic Congressman from New York, introduced a guaranteed income bill in Congress in May of 1968, a bill that was in fact written in OEO (see, especially, Bowler, 1974; Marmor and Rein, 1973). In 1967, Daniel Moynihan wrote a paper criticizing the welfare system for encouraging dependency and the breakdown of family life. This paper was circulated widely among government officials and provided opponents of the existing order with a handy list of problems inherent in the existing "welfare mess." One should also note in this regard the formation in 1968 of a commission within the executive branch charged with developing LBJ's final legislative package for Congress. While members toyed with several radical measures, they ended up (at the behest of Johnson) patching up the current welfare system by suggesting, among other things, a means test for AFDC and increases in social security benefits. However, in the process of formulating the program, the commission did indicate a number of problems in public assistance policy and hinted at the persistence of a welfare crisis.

Thus, as in the early 1960's, so by 1968 the conditions for a major overhaul of the welfare system seemed optimal. Several prerequisites for policy innovation had reappeared in full force: a competent and thorough critique of the current system had developed (made even more potent since it developed from both within and outside government); a "policy community" committed to change and accessible to leading policy-makers had evolved with linkages to both the executive (through OEO and secondarily, HEW) and legislative branches of government; more and better information was available concerning the performance of the current system and the plausibility of several alternatives to it; several trial runs with negative income tax had occurred, which made members of Congress, OEO, and HEW more comfortable with the idea of a new approach; and, finally, the NIT did have bipartisan credentials in that Milton Friedman and John Kenneth Galbraith both endorsed it (poverty policy makes some strange bedfellows). However, there were several missing ingredients— there was no policy entrepreneur in the White House to activate these forces, and there were no incentives to encourage major decision-makers to introduce thoroughgoing welfare reform. The logic of incrementalism as a device to reduce conflict and complexity prevailed; the linkage between innovation, ambition, and conflict had not yet materialized, since Johnson was not running for reelection. However, the accession to power of Richard Nixon was to change all this by tying policy innovation to political power in the new White House and crowning a new President committed to the idea of welfare reform.

How did Richard Nixon, a Republican President with a narrow electoral victory, facing a Democratic-controlled Congress, become the first President to introduce a negative income tax proposal—the Family Assistance Plan (FAP)?[9] The first thing to be noted is that, just as in the case of his predecessors, Nixon had been very affected by his campaign experiences and by what he perceived to be the big issues bothering Americans. While the 1968 campaign did not dwell particularly on welfare and in fact was a rather negative campaign, with Hubert Humphrey limply defending Johnson and Nixon hatcheting democratic administrations and the progress of the war in Vietnam, Nixon did seem to develop a strong concern with welfare— the inequality of the system, the expense of it, its salience to the electorate, its tie with other big issues such as race and crime, and, perhaps most importantly, the seeming "uncontrollability" of AFDC. Thus, right after his election (again, the parallel with Johnson and Kennedy is striking), Nixon created a task force on welfare headed by Richard Nathan, a Republican from Brookings Institution, and staffed by numerous holdovers from the Johnson administration. Starting with the premise that inequality among the states in welfare payments was the most intolerable aspect of the current system (a revelation that was certainly aided by the Southern strategy), the task force moved to the idea that the federal government had to provide a nationwide floor of support. Robert Finch, Nixon's Health,

[9] See Burke and Burke (1974:52-73; Moynihan, 1973; Marmor and Rein, 1973). Of course, I am not suggesting that the 1968 campaign actually developed the issue of welfare; this came later in the transition task forces.

Education, and Welfare Secretary-designate, found the idea very attractive and began promoting it to the President, with whom he had particularly close relations.

However, the real turning point came three days after the inauguration, when Nixon formed the Council of Urban Affairs and appointed Daniel Moynihan and Robert Finch to a subsection concerned with welfare. Over the next few months, the battle lines were drawn: Moynihan and Finch supporting variations on the Nathan plan, and Arthur Burns pushing a less ambitious plan that included strong work incentives and excluded much of the working poor. In the Cabinet and various sub-Cabinet meetings from February to April, the various plans were debated and the idea of a negative income tax came under bitter attack. While Arthur Burns and Maurice Stans attacked NIT, Moynihan answered their criticisms with the defense that NIT was fairer than the current system, would pare down the bureaucracy, and would provide a work incentive through a sliding scale of income and public aid—all of which were in line with traditional Republican concerns. However, Moynihan's trump card was that he played to Nixon himself—his ego, his desire to become a great President, and his need for a quick domestic policy innovation. In a barrage of memos and personal exchanges, Moynihan managed to convince Nixon that, like Benjamin Disraeli, he could become a conservative reformer who could achieve both power and policy objectives by introducing liberal policy reform—in this case, FAP. By April tremendous pressure was on Nixon to come up with a domestic program; by that point the media had played back a number of times Nixon's 1967 statement that "I've always thought that this country could run itself domestically without a President" (quoted in Bowler, 1974:40-41). Nixon, therefore, needed a domestic policy and Moynihan responded with FAP.

It was not, however, just the existence of a domestic policy vacuum, the pressures and possibilities to be creative during the honeymoon, the impact of Moynihan, Finch, and some Johnson holdovers in HEW, or Nixon's campaign experiences that sold him on the idea of FAP; it was also the nature of the policy itself. A federal floor on welfare payments would endear Nixon to the Southern states, because their low payments would be subsidized by the federal government up to the minimum level; this would ease any future worries about bringing their benefits up to need levels and would, essentially, freeze their welfare burden at a low level. In the case of the North, while FAP would bring in few dollars, it would also freeze their benefits, and perhaps even reduce them if their levels were above the federal minimum. This would mean, essentially, that the floor could be interpreted as a ceiling, which in the future would ease the burden of welfare spending on the North as well. Thus, given the widespread displeasure with the current welfare system, FAP could work to expand Nixon's mandate.

Second, Nixon wanted to hit many issues with one policy and could use FAP to address urban, racial, and economic problems as well as the issue of "law and order." FAP was above all an efficient political issue. Third, Nixon saw welfare as *the* domestic crisis. Projections indicated furth r growth in welfare rolls and Nixon reasoned: why should he, a Republican, preside over a continually expanding welfare sector that was bequeathed to him by the Democrats? Relatedly, it was worrisome that this explosion of the welfare rolls implied that a large mass of disaffected, poor young people was developing who, in the political context of the late 1960's, would surely exacerbate the political unrest in the country. Finally, FAP was that rarest of species, a low-risk policy innovation. By introducing it, Nixon could use his conservative cloak to protect his own flanks and win the support of liberals in the process, thereby expanding his mandate and gaining a new and critically important policy in the bargain. He could in addition take advantage of the honeymoon period, when, as he argued himself, policy innovation was much easier. A policy such as FAP would give an innovative stamp to his administration and remove the pressure from the critics, particularly from those who claimed he was essentially a foreign policy President.

But even if FAP did not pass, Nixon would gain something for the effort. He would be credited at least for trying and he could play up the recalcitrance of Congress and its inability to confront squarely new public policies. While Nixon would not have the new policy, he would have exposed the sloth and opportunism of Congress and the numerous problems in the welfare system bequeathed by his Democratic predecessors. He could, therefore, retire from the domestic arena with honors. Thus, FAP was that rare kind of policy innovation that entailed few risks and many opportunities for both changing the system and expanding the President's power base. Once again, policy crisis, political ambition, heightened political power, and the personal policy objectives of the President converged to produce an attempt at a major change in public policy; in 1969 in the area of welfare reform, incrementalism made much less sense than innovation.

For all of these reasons, Nixon was persuaded that FAP was precisely the kind of policy he should introduce in his first year in office. On August 8 he announced on television that he was proposing a federally financed income floor of $1,600 for a family of four. In addition he proposed that all states should pay a minimum amount (reflecting the cost of living in the state) to the aged, blind and disabled—essentially an income ceiling for them as well. However, the impact of the first part of the proposal was moderated by the fact that Nixon emphasized work incentives and requirements throughout the talk (Burns had indeed won some points) and stressed how efficient and moral such a system would be. He also conveniently left out the cost of the entire program and the fact that it would increase—in fact, double—the number of people on the public dole. FAP at this stage, then, was a wolf in sheep's clothing.

On August eleventh, FAP was sent to Congress. The basic provisions included the minimum income noted above with lesser federal contributions paid up to a total income of about $4,000; uniform, nationwide eligibility and standards to include in the program the unemployed, the working poor, and intact families as well as single parent families; partial replacement of AFDC (depending on whether or not states paid the minimum level); and, finally, restrictions on the food-stamp program to those not covered by FAP, such as unmarried or childless couples (this was later abolished). Thus, FAP was a boon to two-parent families, Southerners, and the working poor; for the rest, it was no real improvement. FAP continued to discriminate against childless couples and unmarrieds, and provided little in the way of assuring a minimum necessary income. Essentially, FAP was to bring perhaps twenty percent of the then welfare recipients closer to the level of the remaining eighty percent and would add about fourteen million to the welfare rolls (though perhaps only two or three million for full support). What it would not do would be to improve the benefits for the bulk of the population eligible for welfare; FAP's goals, therefore, were to equalize public assistance and increase the federal role in welfare policy, rather than to increase markedly the benefits that the poor received. Thus, Moynihan's characterization of FAP as an innovative policy and a "fundamental reform" needs some qualifications; his attack on the Great Society as being oversold with flamboyant rhetoric could be applied as well to his own packaging of the Family Assistance Plan (Moynihan, 1973:7-9 and 543-545).

From October 15 to November 13, 1969, the House Ways and Means Committee held hearings on FAP; eventually, in March of 1970, the bill was reported out and one month later was passed. However, in the Senate FAP ran into more opposition as the Senate Finance Committee complained about its inability to reconcile FAP with existing programs, such as AFDC, food stamps, and various manpower development and retraining programs. However, after the administration amended and clarified FAP, the Senate Finance Committee still refused to report it out, and efforts to force it out resulted in filibusters and in the eventual death of the legislation on the floor. In the Ninety-second Congress, FAP once again passed the House only to go to the Senate to compete unsuccessfully with several other related bills. By 1972, FAP was as dead as George McGovern's campaign for the Presidency, and his proposal to give $1,000 to every American family. The impetus for welfare reform had passed, leaving only a negative income tax for the old, blind, and disabled—the Supplementary Security Income—in its wake.

What had happened? Why did a broadly based NIT program dwindle into a more limited program restricted to the aged and crippled? There are, of course, a number of answers. Adherents to the Moynihan school place the blame squarely on Congress (a position which Richard Nixon had mapped out months before). For example, Gilbert Steiner (1974:63; Moynihan, 1973:348-375) has made a typical interpretation in this vein:

> Too little for most liberals and too much for most conservatives, family assistance was out of phase politically; a proposal with which the Great Society would have been comfortable, offered instead by its enemies and offered after the bloom was off the Great Society.

Vincent and Vee Burke (1974:134) have gone one step further and argued that "from the beginning many democratic liberals found it uncomfortable to be associated with President Nixon on a social issue. They were loathe to concede to their old enemy the qualities of goodwill."[10] Thus,

---

[10] A more charitable, but similar, observation was made by Abraham

FAP failed, purportedly, because it was caught between Democrats, who wanted more and more credit, and Republicans, who felt uncomfortable about the cost and the blatant "cash" thrust of the proposal. Rather than succeeding by using a conservative cloak to put through liberal policies, Nixon ended up alienating *both* liberals and conservatives, and his coalition of conservative state Governors and reformers concerned with equity fell apart. Welfare reform was crucified by partisan politics; the cost of extracting support was simply too high.

A second interpretation, offered by M. Kenneth Bowler, points the blame more squarely on the Oval Office. Thus, Bowler attributed the failure of FAP to "the inability of the administration to clarify the relationship of FAP to the existing welfare system" (Bowler, 1974:28). From the beginning, it was unclear how FAP would fit in the AFDC, and the Nixon administration did not help to clarify this matter by first announcing that FAP would replace AFDC and then later arguing that the two programs would somehow coexist. Similarly, the administration was vague about how the cash transfers would be reconciled with in-kind programs. While such ambiguity reflected the desire of the administration to move fast and to placate those benefitting from the existing system by leaving current programs intact, the result was quite the opposite. The equivocal nature of the legislation ended up stalling Congressional action and alienating such key groups as the National Welfare Rights Organization.

Another major debit which was built into the proposal itself was that by opting for equality through levelling and at the same time holding down costs, FAP could have only

---

Ribicoff: "Its (FAP's) defenders in the administration attempted to set it as a liberal guaranteed income package to liberals and as a workfare plan with tough work requirements to conservatives. FAP tried to be both liberal and conservative, but few understood that the welfare and workfare aspects were intricately entwined" (quoted in Burke and Burke, 1974:ix-x).

a limited impact on the benefits levels received by those already on AFDC. It was in fact a modest program that would tend to increase benefits in ten states to perhaps one-half the poverty level (for the non-working poor) and freeze AFDC benefits elsewhere to current amounts. In this sense, FAP would discourage states from providing anything beyond the federally defined minimum need; there were no incentives, therefore, for states to up the ante beyond the low government ceiling. Thus, FAP was in a sense federal aid to the South and the working poor; for everyone else, it maintained the old faults—inequality of benefits among states, humiliation through stringent means tests and mandatory work requirements, continuation of the "minimum" minimum wage which maintained the existence of the working poor and, finally, exclusion of the young, unmarried, and childless couples from any federal aid. For these reasons, the objections to FAP in Congress that it was no major improvement over the status quo had a truthful ring. The problem with FAP was not just partisan politics; it was that the policy was not, except in the precedent it would set, all that coherent or revolutionary, and perhaps was even counterproductive.

A third common explanation for the failure of FAP harkens back to the problems that undermined the implementation of the Economic Opportunity Act: namely, the conflict in pluralist societies between satisfying the demands of various groups, while at the same time writing coherent legislation. In welfare reform, one group's meat seems to be another's poison, and this dilemma helped to stalemate FAP:

> The conflicts between fundamental reform and cost constraints, between the will to change and the requirements of keeping bipartisan supporters, were not candidly admitted. Four program goals came into sharp conflict— adequate relief in distress; effective (perhaps punitive) work incentives; substantial state and local financial re-

lief; and reduced federal costs over the long run. The efforts to harmonize these objectives proved unworkable, and the problems raised were not clearly delineated. They were patched over, and the patchiness was revealed when special interest groups reviewed with the Congress one or another program feature. . . . In the end, the bid for political support from ideologically antagonistic sides exacted its price and legislative stalemate ensued (Marmor and Rein, 1973:18-19).

Thus, to the extent that FAP could not offer any Pareto optimal solution to the welfare "crisis" and in fact threatened many administrators, bureaucrats, and recipients, it could not receive much Congressional support.

Finally, one can explain the demise of FAP by employing a more idiosyncratic factor: the manner in which Nixon sold his program to Congress and to the American public. After his speech in August, Nixon sent the legislation to Congress. In contrast to Johnson in 1964, though, Nixon seemed to let the proposal drop. He neither used the Office of the Presidency to drum up support, nor did he or his staff do much Congressional lobbying on behalf of FAP. This seeming death wish for the bill fits in both with Nixon's well-known antipathy for domestic politics and Congressional liaison work, and with his essentially negative approach to decision-making (Barber, 1973:60-62; Wills, 1970). After proposing FAP, he seemed to avoid it, feeling assured that a hostile Congress and a hostile welfare bureaucracy would destroy the proposal anyway. Thus, while Nixon could go along with the idea of FAP, he could not carry it through; he did not and would not test his power on the domestic field of battle. As is the case with so many policies—for instance, Lyndon Johnson and Wilbur Cohen on NIT—little change occurred, not because the system prevented it, but in part because policy-makers themselves vetoed it on the grounds of "political unfeasibility." In the case of FAP, such a strategy was doubly appealing, because

Nixon could have the image of an innovator without the burden of really carrying the innovation through.

Thus, there seems to be a number of plausible explanations of why FAP flopped; the nature of Congress, the policy itself, and Richard Nixon together seem to explain why Nixon failed to put through his negative income tax proposal. While FAP highlighted many of the problems in American welfare policy—and this was its essential contribution—its failure to be passed meant that it did nothing to correct these deficiencies. The "welfare mess" remains with us to this day; FAP was the last major attempt at thoroughgoing reform of the system. Even Jimmy Carter, his campaign promises to the contrary, opted out of welfare reform. "Reform follows reality" (Steiner, 1974) thus seems to be an unanticipated and yet enduring consequence of the Great Society and other innovations gone incremental.

Conclusions

The decade of the 1960's witnessed the rise and fall of welfare reform in America. It began with some faint rumblings in the Kennedy administration, reached a crescendo with the War on Poverty and the Family Assistance Plan, and then fell back to a "pianissimo" with the decisive defeat of Nixon's FAP in the Ninety-second Congress. This ebb and flow of welfare reform is hardly the picture of incremental—slow and consistent—change; rather, the pattern resembles more a clustering of innovations interspersed with longer spells of small change (see Zaltman et al., 1973; Walker, 1974). Nor does the incremental notion of the process of decision-making (as opposed to the pattern of outputs) describe very well the nature of welfare policymaking in the 1960's; while it captures the essence of the policy process in the middle and end of administrations, it is not very accurate in describing the politics of the honeymoon period. Thus, "doing what you did before"—the essence of incrementalism—does not explain very well what happened with welfare reform over the past two decades. It captures part of the picture, but not the whole thing.

However, in indicating the inappropriateness of the incremental model for much of welfare policy development, I do not mean to imply, as others have, that welfare reform is a rare or unpredictable exception to the general rule.[11] Rather, I see the issue in a broader and more stable sense. Incrementalism seems to *coexist* with innovation, and the two modes of policy-making seem to be interconnected and alternate with one another. Incrementalism, therefore, describes only part of the policy process; the other part is innovation, and both are eminently rational responses to their respective policy environments. This case study of welfare reform, therefore, confirms what was uncovered in the quantitative analysis—the regularized alternations between small and large changes in public policy, with the large changes resulting primarily from the installation of new chief executives.

Thus, I would concur readily with the argument common in organizational behavior studies that

> . . . consolidation/innovation is not a zero sum game. . . . Just as every organization must on occasion respond to the forces of change in a consolidative manner, so also does every organization have opportunities to anticipate the need for change and to meet these through innovation (Gawthrop, 1969:214).

Incrementalism may be a necessary approach to decision-making most of the time, but the same can be said for

---

[11] In fact, most critiques of incrementalism emphasize deviant cases and do not posit an alternative model that works in a regularized manner. See, for instance, Natchez and Bupp (1973); Schulman (1975). It is important to note that this pattern occurs in a number of other policy areas as well. It seems to work, for example, with health care and federal aid to education in the United States (see Bailey and Mosher, 1968:2-71; Cronin, 1969; Klarman, 1974; Marmor, 1973; Heclo, 1974). For a parallel historical case to the one I have been developing, see Eckstein (1958).

innovation as well. To amend David Braybrooke and Charles Lindblom's (1963:73) formulation, then, while "non-incremental alternatives usually do not lie within the range of choice possible in the society or body politic," they do enough of the time to justify a second model of decision-making in liberal democratic states.

The issue then remains: what shape should that model take? I would begin by concurring with Gilbert Steiner (1971:321-322) that the issue is far more complicated than attributing innovation to the "Zeitgeist" or to some other "idiosyncratic" factor:

> [We cannot embrace] . . . The facile non-explanation of political change implied by the line that the guaranteed income (or equal employment opportunity or pollution policy) is "an idea whose time has come." The time only "comes" when the combination of forces necessary to effect change is properly put together.

On the basis of this case study, of the quantitative analysis in the last chapter, and of theories of policy change and honeymoon decision-making, one can put together more precisely that "combination of forces" that creates policy innovation, as opposed to incremental change. Those forces include *long-term policy developments* (current policy priorities, the priorities of one's predecessors, the existence of a crisis, popular concern with the issue, a history of Congressional and bureaucratic interest in and knowledge about the issue, and the creation of an influential policy community committed to change and hostile to the status quo) and *short-term influences*—namely, the impact of the election and the honeymoon period on agenda-setting and Presidential decision-making. Thus, while the climate for change in welfare policy seemed optimal in the 1960's, a catalyst was needed to transform need into public policy, and that catalyst was as old as politics—the selection of new leaders who saw welfare reform as a way to expand their power and realize their policy objectives. Succession leads to innovation when the climate for change is right, and when high ambition and political power are joined together—in short, when desire and capability to innovate meet.[12]

This two-stage theory of policy innovation, of the development of a crisis and the creation of incentives and capabilities to make more changes, needs to be amplified. The first stage—the creation of a policy crisis—involves three different notions. The first, which was discussed in some detail above, has to do with performance; the policy must be seen as inadequate, so that policy-makers step up their efforts either to amend current approaches or to consider completely different ones (Cyert and March, 1965:113). In the case of welfare, this was apparent in the evolution from a services approach to minimum income. As Frederick Doolittle and his associates (1977) put it, "selling a new program is like selling a new car. In both cases it is useful to exaggerate the shortcomings of the previous models." However, for a crisis to have some impact, one also needs to feel that the policy area is *critical*. In the case of welfare, this criterion was met in that welfare was expensive and seen by elites as a real thorn in the side of many Americans. As Gaston Rimlinger has pointed out, the welfare issue has always evoked strong feelings in the United States:

> In the United States there has been a historical conflict between the need for socially assured income protection and the dominant individual values of American society. For a long time the balance of forces in this conflict delayed the enactment of a general Social Security system. It took an economic crisis that called into question the principles of the existing order to shift the balance enough for a victory of the forces seeking social income assurances (Rimlinger, 1973:232).

[12] While this is a new role for ambition theory, the dynamics are not terribly different from those posed in studies of ambition and elite responsiveness to mass demands (see Schlesinger, 1967).

Similarly, in the 1960's the salience of the poverty issue increased as welfare policy became intimately interconnected with the civil rights movement, crime, poverty, and civil unrest. In fact, one can easily correlate changes in public sympathy with civil rights, on the one hand, with changes in federal support for anti-poverty policy, on the other—just as public support for the former peaked in the late 1960's, so Congressional interest in policy on poverty peaked at the same time. By the end of the decade and into the 1970's, a federal stance of "regulating the poor" (Piven and Cloward, 1976) had developed, just as did public feeling that "the movement" had perhaps gone too far too fast.

For a crisis to impinge on policy-making in the Executive branch, though, high salience and poor performance are not sufficient; it is also necessary for decision-makers to feel confident that they can offer alternative policies that will work. It was the *optimism* of the 1960's that linked the welfare crisis with actual policy responses to that perception:

> The domestic promises Lyndon Johnson made between 1963 and 1967 were not only expressions of a grandiloquent personality, or reflections of the institutionalized fact that Congress must be asked for everything before it will give anything. They were valid statements of one strain in the national mood, the dominant strain at that moment among the educated, professional, managerial classes. The idea was both that institutionalized arrangements could be imagined (indeed, could be selected by reason) which could produce whatever social circumstances were desired, and that technology had infinite capacity to produce the good life at low cost (Liebman, 1974:15).

This confidence in turn stimulated policy-makers to reach out for ideas, to form policy-specific task forces, and to challenge existing approaches and priorities in anti-poverty policy. While a welfare crisis certainly existed in the late

1950's, government intervention, particularly at the federal level, was considered undesirable. By 1964, though, it was considered mandatory, and this transformed the crisis into a series of policy initiatives. Thus, elite perception of a crisis in a popular policy area, coupled with a propensity for federal government intervention, worked together to set the stage for policy innovation.

However, in the final analysis all the pressures in the world for policy change will have no impact unless decision-makers are convinced that a change in existing policies will be to their benefit—this is what I mean by the short-term, or catalytic component of policy innovation. The policy environment may be ripe for change, but elite action—to recognize the need and do something about it—is the sine qua non of policy innovation. In political science, it is all too often forgotten that elite decisions must intervene between "social forces" and public policy, and that any analysis of decision-making must take the opinions, values, goals, and needs of the principal actors into account. The study of policy innovation is no exception to this generalization.

However, most of the generalizations that can be gleaned from the literature on decision-making pile up constraint after constraint on elite desire or capacity to alter existing policy priorities. Scholars chant over and over that innovation is too risky, that the "collective wisdom favors the status quo," that human beings are routinized, and that the time, information, and resource constraints force elites to use past behavior as the base for action (Watson, 1969; Kaufman, 1971; Sorenson, 1963). The problem with such litanies is that they miss the conditions under which incrementalism is risky, when change seems far better than stasis, when doing what was done before is irrational, and when innovation would improve public policy, enhance a leader's power, and help him to win over subordinates.

Thus, innovation can make sense, particularly if one focuses on the electoral process and the honeymoon period. While elections are said to select leaders and form broadly based policy coalitions, they can also be said to be a forum for issues, ideas, and, most important, an intense learning experience for the candidate. Candidates do get a sense through campaigns of what people want, care about, and how they live; this in turn affects what task forces they form, the kinds of Cabinet choices they make, and the issues they emphasize in their first years in office. A second effect of elections is to signal to the contender the mood of the people for policy change—just as Kennedy sensed ambivalence in the 1960 election, so Johnson interpreted 1964 as a groundswell of support for the Great Society and so Nixon interpreted his minority victory as an indication to move slowly, to make policies palatable to both the left and the right. Finally, campaign experiences are used by candidates to fill in the many blanks they have in their policy programs. Campaign experiences are indicators in an uncertain world of what to do when in office.

But perhaps the most important aspect of campaigns is that they select new personnel, not just a President, but a whole coterie of officials, including over 2,000 appointees alone outside of the Executive Office staff. Because they are new or reelected with a higher mandate, Presidents in their honeymoon tend to look at policy differently than more experienced politicos. As one member of the Nixon administration expressed this quality in 1969:

> The time was right for dramatic change, especially with the change in administration. A new administration can always do things that an old one couldn't. Wilbur Cohen didn't have the guts to ask Johnson to make these changes. But a new administration can make changes— it doesn't matter if it's Democratic or Republican (quoted in Bowler, 1974:63).

Thus, to the extent that elections select new people (and hence start a new mobilization of bias in the system), publicize certain policies, provide some sense of public support for old and new directions in public policy, and encourage candidates to be active policy-makers, they act as mechanisms of policy innovation.

The impact of elections and campaigns is in turn affected by the politics of the honeymoon period. There is no question, for instance, that one critical component of the transition—the task force—is uniquely conducive to innovation. Task forces are formed outside of traditional policy networks; they are usually staffed by public officials and private experts who do not have to worry that much about political feasibility; and they are held responsible for coming up with new ideas in well-specified areas. Finally, they have direct access to the President and define their success "by the numbers of things they get started" (Thomas and Wolman, 1969:135; Corwin, 1972). Thus, task forces formed during the transition period bombard the new President with policy alternatives, and the President is responsive because during the campaign he probably has had little time to form a clear "policy" picture of himself in office. While campaigns generate some issues, they do not really develop a platform for action; instead, they pinpoint certain rather vague issue areas. Therefore, the new President uses past policies, campaign experiences, and task forces to get a hold on his new job. While he feels he has the power and support to do a great deal, he is not quite sure what he should do. He needs cues and he needs help. Here, the structure of decision-making in the honeymoon, when combined with the electoral experience, can lead to search and action on a variety of fronts. The new incumbent has strong desire to act, and a policy vacuum to fill.

The federal bureaucracy and Congress join with the task forces in filling in this vacuum by going along with the new incumbent and competing with one another to show the President that they have ideas as well. For many who were left out in the cold in the old administration, the honeymoon is an opportunity to reassert themselves. Similarly, those who dominated in the past will want to maintain their influence. In the scramble to pay fealty, then, and to get their ideas heard, members of Congress and bureaucrats compete with one another to present *their* policy notions to the new President.

The final component of the President's world—his Cabinet and staff—also work to encourage bold Presidential initiatives in the honeymoon period. The staff tends to be fiercely loyal and veterans of a long association with the President, and their long-sought and long-fought climb to the top gives them a sense of great power and the desire to do something big. Similarly, the newly appointed Cabinet members want to make a splash, to impress the President (whom many of them hardly know) and to demonstrate and take advantage of their power. All are fully cognizant of "the advantages of being new," and the extent to which establishing a position early on is mandatory for maintaining influence later.

Thus, what usually appear as blocks to policy change— the instability and conflictual nature of Presidential transitions, the separation of powers system, and the politicization of the Presidential staff and the federal bureaucracy— tend to *encourage* policy innovation, at least in the early period of the regime as elites vie for Presidential favor by suggesting new ideas. But the key to all this is the President. If he is ambitious, he will seek a policy that will expand his support, cement the allegiance of his coterie of faithful, put off criticism, and take advantage of the unique power of the President during a honeymoon period (Hess, 1974; Sundquist, 1968:395; Drew, 1975). At the same time he wants a policy that can be put together quickly, entails few risks (i.e., is "trialable," compatible with existing policies, does not infringe on existing policy coalitions, and is highly visible), and yet is sufficiently new that it stands out as the *President*'s innovation.[13] Both FAP and the War on Poverty fitted these specifications well, though FAP ended up stepping on more toes than its proponents had foreseen.

[13] This is why, for example, Presidents tend to pick up policies developed late in the administration of their predecessors—such programs are worked out, but not "old hat."

Thus, ambition and clear policy objectives on the part of the President; the availability of a crisis and reasonable policy alternatives; a desire to act fast and pressures on the President to innovate from the media, Congress and from within the Executive Office; and a heavy dose of Presidential power and public support—all work together to encourage policy innovation. Of course, these prerequisites do not always appear; they are far more likely in the honeymoon of a new President than at other times. This is what I mean by innovation as being at some points a rational and regularized response to the policy environment.[14]

Innovation, therefore, makes as much sense in the honeymoon period as incrementalism does at other times. With the aging of the administration, Presidential power wanes. Crises become a way of life, a routine, rather than the seeming catastrophes they used to be. Presidents come to see crises as daily awkward occurrences, not forcing actions. The President's propensity to act and freedom to make decisions, moreover, are curtailed as he is increasingly hemmed in by his staff, the bureaucracy, Congress, the Cabinet, and past behavior; public support shrinks, thus moderating Presidential ventures into new policy areas; and much time is spent amending and building support for the new ideas proposed in the first year of the administration (Hess, 1977). The innovations of the honeymoon period, therefore, seem inevitably to fall into routines, awaiting the next interim when policy reassessment and change become feasible once again. Most likely, that rare combination of desire and capability to act is not a fortuitous occurrence; rather, it will reappear either when the President returns to the campaign trail or during the next honeymoon period.

Policy-making in liberal democracies, then, seems to alternate between *incrementalism* and the constraints this

[14] It might well be asked how well the generalizations presented throughout this discussion apply to Western European chief executives. It would seem that they do (see Wilson, 1976; Brandt, 1977; Tsurutani and Mullen, 1977; Blondel, 1977; Brown, 1971; Crossman, 1976; Jones, 1971).

model implies, and *innovation*, a model incorporating considerably more freedom to act. This alternation does seem to be regularized, predictable, and rational: just as routines reflect elite adjustment to realities, so do innovations. Both, moreover, serve as policy correctives; routines sort out the viability of various new policies, while innovation reassesses old policies and opens the system to new ideas. Thus, decision-making in Western states is both incremental and change-oriented. To understand it, one must take both of these models into account. And to understand why these two approaches to policy-making alternate, one has to understand elections and their role as mechanisms of policy innovation in bourgeois democratic states.

But what does all of this say about the role of leaders in the policy process? One thing that seems clear is that all the factors noted above, which enhance the prospects for innovation during the honeymoon period, by definition expand as well the potential for influence by chief executives. They are the ones who in a sense activate the forces for change, precisely because they feel powerful and experimental during this period. They are new, they actively search for new programs, their milieu is geared to providing and being receptive to new ideas, the agenda is relatively open, there is a spirit of cooperation (if not toadyism), and they perceive activism as legitimate and desirable. The atmosphere is conducive to change, and the spirit is willing, and these two factors together explain the linkage between succession and policy innovation in Western states. They also imply a more leader-centered process of decision-making than when incrementalism serves as the dominant strategy. New leaders do choose what to do and want to do more when they are novices. And, as the organization literature tells us, ambiguity, a sense of crisis, control, and consensus, all of which characterize honeymoon politics, enhance the influence of individuals and the prospects for innovation. This is why, among other things, reelections yield less policy change than turnovers; the latter enhance precisely those characteristics of crisis, control and the like during the transition period.

But even if the model of honeymoon decision-making is subject to the influence of the new chief executive, the environment after all dictates options, pressures, and incentives. It sets the parameters within which leaders operate—more flexible, to be sure, and more change-oriented than at other times—and those parameters allow for, if not specify, greater maneuverability on the part of principal policy-makers. Thus, to return to the "great people versus social forces" argument, I would have to come out somewhat on the side of a structural interpretation. It is true that leaders in the final analysis decide among options, feel more willing and able to scan the environment for new agenda items during the honeymoon period, and therefore have more impact during the earlier years of their administrations than at later times. Indeed, this is a crucial point in distinguishing between routine and honeymoon policy-making. However, this is clearly a case of less and more. If the past two chapters have demonstrated anything, it is the powerful effect of the environment, that constellation of incentives and pressures that help to shape what is considered and what is resolved, whether leadership is in flux or stable. In this sense, leaders merely reflect what are important changes in their environment, and therefore policies can always be understood as being to a certain degree responses to structural factors. And, to the extent that those vibrations transmit different messages defining the ease and desirability of policy change, those structural considerations always calibrate the policy cycle—when incrementalism holds sway and when innovation is the rule. While new leaders and leaders in general make some difference, particularly at certain times, the impact of elections tells us as much about environmental change as about personnel change. Leaders matter, but always within certain parameters.

FIVE

The Impact of Elite Succession: The Socialist States

Leading posts in the Soviet Union are not reserved for anybody
forever. The violation of discipline, the failure to draw
conclusions from criticism and self-criticism, and the ratification
of incorrect policies necessarily lead to demotion.
—*Leonid Brezhnev* (1974)

The election platform our party is now putting before the
people is completely realistic and also will be unconditionally
fulfilled. Can the governments of capitalist governments say any
such thing about their fulfillment of campaign commitments?
Certainly not. All sorts of pledges and demagogic promises are
forgotten by the bourgeois parties as soon as the election
campaign is over.
—*Mikhail Suslov* (1970)

INTRODUCTION

In the next two chapters I will examine the impact of leadership succession on public policy in the communist party
states—specifically, budgetary and investment allocations
in the bloc and agricultural policy in the Soviet Union. The
guiding hypothesis is that succession should have a strong
effect on priorities, reflecting the power that socialist leaders seem to have, their commitment to radical change, and
the close linkage between the succession process and the
generation of new issues in socialist nations (see Rush, 1974
and 1968; Golan, 1971; Jancar, 1971; Bromke, 1972; Brzezinski, 1969; Ludz, 1973; Beck et al., 1976; Korbonski,
1976; Hodgson, 1976). However, given the purported decline in elite power and ideological fervor, and the appearance of incremental decision-making in these systems
since the death of Stalin, one would expect that the policy

[140]

impact of succession will be tempered, over time generally, and within administrations (Lowenthal, 1974; Baumann, 1971; Korbonski, 1976; Rush, 1974:19-20; Rush, 1976; Rigby, 1970). Thus, the interplay between the overall character of decision-making in socialist states and the nature of the succession rite would lead one to anticipate a significant, but not dramatic, shift in priorities following the transfer of power. Moreover, this impact should, as in the West, settle into new policy routines once the succession is resolved. Socialist and capitalist systems, then, should be similar in terms of the short- and long-term policy effects of elite turnover. A new leader in Moscow should make about as much difference as a new leader in Washington, D.C.

SUCCESSION AND POLICY CHANGE:
A QUANTITATIVE ASSESSMENT

In this chapter I will test these hypotheses by examining how executive-level succession affects budgetary and investment priorities in, first, the Soviet bloc, and, second, the Soviet republics. As with the Western case, I will look at two types of impact—short- and long-term—and assess how much priorities change after a change in leadership.

In Tables 5-1and 5-2 I have presented the results of the test which assesses the difference between what priorities would have been if previous levels remained constant minus their actual levels in the first year the new chief executive exerts policy control. Both tables indicate that succession does correlate with policy change in a consistent manner across all categories, countries and time. Thus, the first hypothesis is confirmed: succession does seem to be a mechanism for innovation in budgeting and investment allocations. While the changes are not dramatic, they are clear; therefore, it is apparent from these tables that new leaders do advocate new priorities in socialist nations to about the degree they do in the West.

TABLE 5-1
The Immediate Impact of Succession on Budgetary Expenditure Shares: The Socialist Nations

Country	Time Points	Administration[a]	Total Expenditures[b]	Health	Education	Welfare[c]
Bulgaria	1950-1958	Zhivkov	294	2.06%	4.53%	2.98%**
	1953-1959	Politburo	802*	2.12%**	3.62%	5.67%**
	1957-1963	Politburo	309	3.05%	4.69%**	4.61%**
	1957-1967	Politburo	802*	3.06%**	3.05%.	2.21%
Czechoslovakia	1950-1954	Novotny	1259	1.68%	2.38%**	3.16%**
	1950-1954	Politburo	1642	2.01%	3.11%	.28%
	1957-1960	Politburo	1328*	2.65%**	1.14%	2.55%**
	1953-1970	Husak	1965*	2.33%**	3.28%**	4.10%**
East Germany	1950-1972	Honecker	3295*	2.21%**	3.12%**	4.69%**
	1950-1955	Politburo	3450*	1.29%**	1.19%	1.22%
	1960-1964	Politburo	2628	2.14%**	3.08%**	3.38%**
Hungary	1950-1957	Kadar	1964	2.38%**	1.10%	2.98%**
	1956-1964	Politburo	3954*	2.64%**	3.18%**	2.49%**
	1956-1971	Politburo	1219	3.98%**	4.04%**	3.39%**
Poland	1950-1957	Gomulka	1429*	3.39%**	3.34%**	4.12%**
	1960-1971	Gierek	1568*	2.12%**	3.19%**	4.08%**
	1960-1969	Politburo	599	2.46%	2.94%**	4.15%**
Romania	1950-1966	Ceausescu	4944*	1.23%**	2.69%**	2.48%**
	1950-1953	Politburo	210	.28%	.22%	1.22%
	1954-1957	Politburo	465	.29%	1.09%	1.64%
	1957-1963	Politburo	5211*	3.21%**	1.49%**	3.12%**
	1950-1972	Politburo	3688*	1.29%**	2.18%**	3.18%**

Soviet Union	1925-1929	Stalin	12090*	3.45%*	8.99%*	8.56%*
	1950-1954	Malenkov/Khru-shchev	398*	1.28%*	2.34%*	5.68%*
	1950-1958	Khrushchev/Polit-buro	345	2.35%*	3.12%*	4.28%*
	1957-1965	Brezhnev	649*	2.64%*	2.09%*	3.12%*

[a] The administrations reported in this column are the *new* administrations, and the years represent the previous administration, through the year the new leader (or new Politburo) first exerted control over the budget (i.e., Brezhnev, 1965; Honecker, 1972). When the term "Politburo" is used, it means major changes in the Politburo and not a change in the top leader. This is why the Soviet Union has only one strictly "Politburo" change; all other major turnovers in the Politburo membership were accompanied by a succession in the top leadership post as well. I sometimes had to leave certain leaders out of the analysis because their tenure was too short or the timepoints inadequate—Rakosi, Gero, Ochab, Dubcek, and the "first" leaders.

[b] The number in each column is the difference between the predicted share (on the basis of the previous administration) and the real share. In the case of total outlays, the number is the difference between real and predicted allocations, expressed in each national currency. Those with an asterisk are significant at the .05 level, as determined by a t test which places the difference over the standard error of the regression equation.

[c] Here, I am distinguishing between the period of dual leadership versus single leadership (Khrushchev's victory over the anti-Party in 1957). This of course was a Politburo change, but more importantly, it signified the victory of Khrushchev.

Sources: See the Appendix.

TABLE 5-2

Country	Administration[a]	Predicting Time Points[b]	Total Investment[c]	Industry	Heavy	Light	Agriculture
Bulgaria	Zhivkov	1950-1958	643*	3.02%*	2.94%	.89%	2.85%*
	Politburo	1953-1959	295	3.19%*	2.14%	2.14%*	2.11%*
	Politburo	1957-1963	340	1.14%	1.12%	.22%	1.40%
	Politburo	1957-1967	480	3.09%	3.38%*	1.15%	1.28%
Czechoslovakia	Novotny	1950-1954	1069	2.61%*	3.04%*	.89%*	3.54%*
	Husak	1950-1970	1223*	2.03%*	3.32%*	.05%	1.21%
	Politburo	1950-1955	969	2.89%*	2.48%	.48%	2.84%*
	Politburo	1950-1960	942	1.98%*	4.01%*	1.33%*	2.19%*
East Germany	Honecker	1950-1972	1387	2.94%*	2.98%*	1.29%*	2.22%
	Politburo	1950-1960	1888	1.03%	.82%	2.08%*	1.61%
	Politburo	1950-1964	2090*	2.33%*	3.13%*	2.33%*	3.15%*
Hungary	Kadar	1950-1957	1020	2.10%*	3.89%*	1.33%*	3.22%*
	Politburo	1950-1964	843	2.62%*	1.83%	1.01%*	1.04%
	Politburo	1956-1971	868	1.01%	1.74%	1.36%*	3.69%*
Poland	Gomulka	1950-1957	2246*	3.21%*	3.48%*	1.89%*	4.90%*
	Gierek	1950-1971	1849*	2.34%*	3.65%*	2.81%*	4.01%*
	Politburo	1960-1969	2210*	2.36%*	3.40%	2.14%*	2.43%*
Romania	Ceausescu	1950-1966	4056*	3.21%*	4.89%*		
	Politburo	1950-1953	1843	1.14%	3.65%*		
	Politburo	1950-1957	1820	2.83%*	1.22%		
	Politburo	1950-1963	3110*	2.11%	4.22%*		
	Politburo	1950-1972	3025*	3.10%*	1.01%		

Soviet Union						
Stalin	1924-1929	10653*	5.33%*			5.24%*
Khrushchev/Malenkov	1950-1954	949*	3.20%*	3.65%*	1.82%*	3.05%*
Khrushchev/Politburo	1950-1958	1021*	2.49%*	3.01%*	1.39%*	3.66%*
Brezhnev	1950-1965	2012*	3.09%*	3.05%**	2.01%*	2.94%*

[a] These are the new administrations.

[b] These time frames are the previous administration, with the last point being the first year of the new administration.

[c] The numbers in this column are the differences between the predicted and the real allocation. Those with an asterisk are significant at at least the .05 level, as reflected in a t test which places the difference over the standard error of the regression (predicting) equation. This gives some idea, given previous levels and their annual variance, what the probability of the expenditure level is. In the rest of the columns, the same prediction was made on *shares* of each category of capital investments.

Sources: See the Appendix.

However, as Tables 5-1 and 5-2 (and their scatter plots) also indicate, the argument that, given the growing regularization of the rite, the impact of succession on public policy should decline over time is in fact found wanting. In most countries, it seems to be holding steady and strong (for example, in Poland and Romania). If it is declining at all (for instance, in the Soviet case), the margin is not that great, and the trend levels off fairly quickly.

To take the second case as one example, it is clear that Stalin's rise to power had dramatic effects on public expenditures. However, while Khrushchev's accession to power did not have a similarly exaggerated effect, the impact of his victory was not by any means negligible; Khrushchev was clearly a leader who made a difference, though not as much as Stalin. If one looks at the third Soviet succession—Brezhnev in 1964—one does not see any continuation of the trend in declining impact. In fact, Brezhnev's victory in 1964 has every bit as much effect on budgetary and investment priorities as did the triumph of his mentor, Khrushchev. Thus, the purportedly "bold and imaginative" Khrushchev and the "pragmatist" Brezhnev had equally sharp effects on policy priorities (see Breslauer, 1976; Hough, 1976). I would, therefore, have to reject at least a portion of the second hypothesis. While there is some tendency for first successions to be unusually change-oriented, later ones do not pale that much by comparison. They certainly do not merely continue previous priorities, as has been suggested. Succession is still a mechanism of policy innovation in socialist states and, therefore, promises to be so in the future.

However, thus far in the analysis I have been looking at the immediate impact of succession. What about its longer term policy consequences? Are the innovations noted above merely a transitory response to succession that wither away once the crisis is resolved, or does each administration retain its distinctive policy stamp? In Table 5-3 I have provided an answer to this question. There, I have summarized the differences among administrations in their average shares of budgetary and investment allocations. The first thing to be noted in this table is that innovations do stick— succession does tend to make a difference over the long as well as the short haul. There is clearly a Brezhnev versus a Khrushchev set of priorities, a Gomulka versus a Gierek, and the like. On the basis of the findings so far, then, I would have to accept the argument that socialist successions are mechanisms of policy innovation, in both an immediate and a long-term sense. Moreover, an examination of the scatter plots reveals that the pattern of policy change that was found for the West—that is, innovations in the honeymoon, followed by a stabilization in these new priorities until the next succession—is also the case for socialist states.

TABLE 5-3
Differences Among Administrations: The Socialist States, 1950-1976[a]

	Bulgaria	Czecho-slovakia	German Democratic Republic	Hungary	Poland	Romania	Soviet Union
0-1%	2	3	2	2	2	2	4
1.01-2.0%	2	3	2	2	3	1	3
2.01-3.0%	1	2	2	3	4	3	6
3.01-4.0%	2	4	2	1	5	2	5
4.01-5.0%	1	2	0	0	1	0	3
>5.0%	0	2	0	0	1	0	3
Number significant[b]	4 (8)	10 (16)	4 (8)	5 (8)	14 (16)	5 (8)	19 (24)

[a] For the Soviet case, this includes the Stalin period as well (1929-1938). This table reports the average share differences between contiguous administrations. The lowest category, 0-1 percent, is inflated due to the small share devoted to health, light industry and construction. The categories included are shares of total outlays on health, education and welfare in the budget, and capital investments in industry (heavy and light, as well as the total share), agriculture, and construction.

[b] This is based on a difference of means test and is meant to indicate the probability of such share differences, given the variance in shares of each category. The number in parentheses is the total number of significant results possible, reflecting categories times administrations.

Sources: See the Appendix.

Thus, new leaders East and West do innovate, but get rather quickly stuck in their ways.[1]

However, if one compares the results reported in Tables 5-1 and 5-2 with the figures reported in Table 5-3, one does find some cases where policy change does appear to be rather transitory after leadership succession (for example, the German Democratic Republic) and others where the impact did not show up until several years into the administration (for example, Czechoslovakia and Hungary). Thus, the impact of Ulbricht's retirement was rather short-lived, while the rise of Husak and Novotny had more of a long-term impact. Despite these distinctions between the tables, however, I can on the basis of the general pattern of the results conclude that, if succession is to affect policy, it apparently must do so at the start of the new administration. Moreover, these early changes do seem to remain; these are not symbolic innovations, but rather changes in priorities that occur early on in the administration and tend to endure. Thus, I would conclude that, in the areas of both capital investment and social consumption expenditures, the impact of leadership turnover is strong, consistent, and durable. Succession clearly is, in the case of socialist states, a potent force for policy change.

SOME FURTHER EVIDENCE: THE SOVIET REPUBLICS

As an additional test of the two hypotheses, it would be useful to look—as I did for the bourgeois democratic states—at succession below the national level. Specifically, does leadership turnover have an impact on budgetary priorities in the Soviet republics? Do changes in the First Secretary at the republic level usher in the same visible effects on budgetary policy that were found at the apex of

[1] The honeymoon in socialist systems lasts, however, beyond the first year in office. Generally, though this varies by succession, the honeymoon lasts three years, reflecting the time it takes to build a mandate.

power? Second, does this impact follow the same pattern; that is, peaking in the honeymoon, and then stabilizing until the next succession? Finally, do the sub-national transfers of power adhere to the consistent impact, over time and across countries, found for the national level successions?

There are several good reasons for extending the analysis below the national level of government. First, as the previous tables indicate, there is some need to expand the number of successions that are analyzed. Even more than in the West, executive turnover at the national level is fairly uncommon in the Soviet bloc. By adding fourteen republics to the study, one gains forty turnovers (see Table 5-4), a

TABLE 5-4

Average Tenure of the Leaders of the Soviet Republics, 1955-1970

	First Secretary[a]	Secretary of Organization	Secretary of Agriculture	Secretary of Industry	Average Tenure/ Republics
Ukraine	5.33	2.00	3.20	2.66	3.29
Belorussia	5.33	3.20	3.20	2.66	3.59
Uzbekistan	4.00	4.00	2.00	3.20	3.30
Kazakhstan	2.28	2.28	5.33	4.00	3.47
Georgia	16.00	4.00	5.33	4.00	7.33
Azerbaidzhan	5.33	2.66	2.66	5.33	3.99
Lithuania	16.00	4.00	4.00	5.33	7.33
Moldavia	8.00	3.20	3.20	2.66	4.26
Latvia	5.33	2.66	4.00	4.00	3.99
Kirghizia	8.00	4.00	2.66	5.33	4.99
Tadzhikistan	5.33	3.20	3.20	2.66	3.59
Armenia	5.33	4.00	4.00	3.20	4.13
Turkmenia	4.00	4.00	4.00	3.20	3.80
Estonia	16.00	5.33	16.00	4.00	10.33
	7.59	3.46	4.48	3.73	4.23

[a] The numbers represent average years of service.

Source: Grey Hodnett and Val Ogareff, *Leaders of the Soviet Republics, 1955-1972* (Canberra, Australia: Australia National University, 1973).

sizeable increase and a real aid in testing a number of hypotheses.[2]

Second, in looking at succession in the Soviet republics, I am putting the hypotheses to a stringent test. As in the American states, in the Soviet republics decision-making is a highly constrained affair, precisely because they are subnational political units. Not only do republic leaders often have severe time and information constraints, but they also are constrained by the centralized structure of the Soviet system. Republic budgets are determined to a certain degree by the center.[3] There are, therefore, fiscal and political limitations to budgetary innovation at this level of government, limitations which, while not completely binding, would seem to constrain the impact of leadership turnover at that level of the system. If succession has an effect in that kind of environment, then one would have to conclude that it is indeed a powerful political variable.

But does this mean that leaders at the republic level cannot have any impact at all? Am I in a sense providing too rough a test? I would say no, because there are some indications that republic-level policy-makers do have some power. For example, Soviet students of budgetary decision-making have emphasized the relative independence of the budgetary process in the republics, particularly in recent years and especially in the area of social consumption expenditures. T. Tulebaev (1969:50-51), for instance, notes that

[2] This, of course, is not to argue that socialist countries are unique in the infrequency of their successions. Sweden, for example, has had only three Premiers since 1950. In his study of elite turnover over time in Mexico, the United States, West Germany, and the Soviet Union, John Nagle (1977) found that turnover rates in Cabinet/Politburo positions is higher in liberal democracies, but in legislatures/central committees, it is higher in socialist nations.

[3] However, the details are worked out by the subnational units (see Tulebaev, 1969; Yevdokimov, 1974). For a more detailed description of the Soviet budgetary process, see Bunce (1976).

> Every union republic has its own budget, as well as extensive rights in planning and developing economic and social-cultural activities. . . . The budgets of the union republics play a large role in education and welfare (also see Yevdokimov, 1974:28-30).[4]

This characterization has been supported in turn by Joel Moses (1974:250), who has found some indication of such independence in his study of sub-national parties in the Soviet Union:

> Regional parties in the Soviet Union are granted at least some autonomy to direct their concerns selectively to local problems . . . particular issue areas, such as cadre-organizational problems, social welfare, and substantive industrial and agricultural problems indicate some adaptation to environmental characteristics.

Finally, one can argue that the complexity of decision-making in the Soviet Union, particularly the budgetary cycle, would in itself guarantee some autonomy for regional elites. Thus, one can argue that, as with American Governors, republic officials in the Soviet Union can, though with difficulty, affect policy outputs in their sphere of government.

But the proof of this proposition would seem to be in the data themselves. If I do find impact, then leaders would seem to be more than mere pawns of the policy process. In Table 5-5 I have presented the results of the analysis that assesses the immediate impact of changes in the First Secretary on budgetary outlays. It is evident, given the size of the differences in shares, that the immediate impact of

---

[4] I should note in view of Tulebaev's arguments that I did not apply the analysis to budgetary investment, precisely because it is so difficult to tie elite behavior to such decisions. A great deal of investment at the republic level is outside the budget and controlled by the center. Therefore, assessing its changes after succession would be misleading.

TABLE 5-5

The Immediate Impact of the Succession of First Secretaries on Budgetary Outlays[a]

Republic	Total Expenditures	Social-Cultural Measures	Education	Health	Physical-Culture	Welfare	Administration
Armenia	202	2.14	3.61*	1.01*	1.01	3.49*	2.01
	298	3.05*	4.22*	3.22*	.09	3.20	1.48
Azerbaidzhan	465*	3.17*	1.21	2.18*	.05	1.64	2.78*
	204	2.08*	2.14	2.01	.16	1.22	.64
Kazakhstan	210	1.99*	1.23	4.03*	.72	3.37*	.32
	92	3.61*	3.61	4.74*	.43	3.82*	1.83*
	305*	3.02*	3.20*	4.78*	.18	3.49*	.27
Kirghizia	109	3.41*	2.29*	3.68*	.32	3.85*	2.94*
Latvia	85	1.08	1.41	1.30	.41	2.41*	2.06*
Moldavia	104*	4.51*	3.21*	2.89*	1.94*	3.29*	3.61*
Tadzhikistan	182	3.22*	4.11	3.35*	.36	2.10*	.82
Turkmenia	361*	3.13*	3.54*	4.65*	.84	1.22	.79
	29	2.49*	4.19*	3.41*	.52	3.79*	.44
	45	4.21*	1.36	2.82*	.55	3.77*	1.83*
Ukraine	109	2.67*	2.39*	1.29	1.36*	2.21*	.62
Uzbekistan	102	2.01*	2.19*	4.41*	.99	2.31*	1.40*

[a] The numbers in the columns are the difference between real and predicted expenditures, with the aggregate amounts in the total outlays category, and budgetary share differences for the rest. Those with asterisks are significant, reflecting t scores based on the difference between the projected expenditure and the real outlay divided by the standard error of the regression (i.e., predicting) equation. The percentages have been dropped, but each number is the share difference. Not all successions or all republics are included here because some did not allow for sufficient timepoints for the analysis to be done.

Sources: See the Appendix.

sub-national succession in the Soviet Union is strong, though less dramatic than at the national level. Thus, the statistical analysis upholds the hypothesis that changes in republic-level political leadership correlate with changes in budgetary priorities. Social issues do seem to be key succession issues at the republic level as well as at the apex of power, and these issues translate into priority changes after the succession process is resolved.

It is also apparent from the analysis that the second hypothesis—that the impact of succession should wither over time—is partially disconfirmed, just as it was at the national level. Whether one compares recent successions with those in the 1950's or the changing impact of successive rotations within each republic, the result is the same: the effects of leadership changeover on public expenditures is consistent (and moderately strong) over time. Succession influences the policy process in the Soviet republics now as in the past.

The question remains, however, as to whether the findings about the effects of succession are upheld when a longer time perspective is taken. Is the impact of succession transitory, or do the changes in budgetary priorities remain throughout the administration? Table 5-6 compares budgetary priorities of entire administrations with one another. Once again, the impact of First Secretary successions is consistent over time, though the impact is obviously not quite as pronounced as were similar turnovers at the national level of government. Different republic leaders do pursue different policies and, thus, changes in leadership consistently tend to bring on long-term changes as well as short-term changes in budgetary allocations.

However, it should be noted that this generalization is not as compelling for the sub-national data as it is for First Secretaries at the top of the system. Thus, the constraints I spoke of earlier with regard to republic level politics are indeed there, though hardly complete. There is room for innovation, but within some fairly limited parameters. At the national level, of course, these parameters are more

TABLE 5-6

A Comparison of Average Share Differences Between Administrations: The Soviet Republics[a]

	0-1%	1.01-2.0%	2.01-3.0%	3.01-4.0%	4.01-5.0%	>5.0%	Number Significant
Armenia	3	2	3	4	1	0	6 (12)
Azerbaidzhan	1	0	2	1	2	0	5 (6)
Belorussia	3	4	5	3	2	0	9 (16)
Kazakhstan	3	5	5	3	0	0	5 (16)
Kirghizia	2	3	2	0	0	0	4 (6)
Latvia	5	3	4	3	1	0	6 (16)
Tadzhikistan	1	2	3	0	0	0	6 (16)
Turkmenia	4	6	5	1	0	0	4 (16)
Ukraine	4	5	7	6	2	0	10 (24)

[a] The numbers in the columns are the total number of all categories that changed the specified amount from one administration to the next. The significance column is based on a difference of means test, and the figure in parentheses is the total of all possible statistically significant results. The categories are socio-cultural measures, education, health, physical culture, welfare and administration in the republic budgets.

Sources: See the Appendix.

elastic and thus succession has more room within which to make its influence felt. However, in both political spheres, succession appears to be a major mechanism of policy in-novation, given the context within which it must work.

Thus, I have found strong confirmation at both the top of the system and in regional politics for the hypothesis that leadership succession does in fact lead to changes in policy priorities in socialist states. As anticipated, succession is a powerful political factor in the Soviet bloc. I therefore accept the common view that "any change in leadership is bound to result in a change in the political system as well" (Korbonski, 1976:1). New leaders do make a difference, particularly in their honeymoons, and that difference is steady over time.

Explaining The Results

The question remains, however, as to why some successions seem to have more impact than others. Why, for example, do Soviet changeovers result in more changes than do Bul-garian ones? Or, why did the transition to Gomulka affect priorities more than the transition from Rakosi to Kadar? In other words, is there any pattern in the results that would suggest that certain factors work to enhance (or de-tract from) the influence of succession on public policy?

In Table 5-7 I have classified the various successions at the national level, according to what seem to be some salient political variables—that is, whether the succession changed leaders or merely altered the Politburo, the cause of the succession (death versus reduced policy performance, for example), and finally the tenure of the predecessor.[5] Turn-

---

[5] I did not construct a similar table for the republics because data on differences among the various successions at this level are for the most part unavailable; I simply do not know how the various successions would score on most of the factors noted above. However, I do know the length of tenure of republic leaders and thus will include them when I evaluate the results for the third subsidiary hypothesis.

ing to the first factor—the contrast between Politburo shake-ups versus actual First Secretary changeover—it is clear that new leaders do in fact make a big difference. While major purges in the Politburo do usher in policy change, an actual turnover in the top post has a much stronger effect.

However, the second distinction—differentiating causes of succession—is not very helpful. The common argument, that more change-oriented successions involving mass and/ or elite dissatisfaction with prevailing policy trends should involve more change than those successions brought on by death, is in fact not upheld by these data. Even if one refines the distinction further and compares really disruptive changeovers—such as Poland in 1956 and 1970, Czechoslovakia in 1968, and Hungary in 1956—with merely elite contested affairs—such as the Soviet Union in 1953, or Germany in 1971—there does not seem to be much of a contrast. Thus, for example, the Polish October does not look that different from Ceausescu's victory following the death of Gheorghiu-Dej in 1965 or Brezhnev's relatively smooth replacement of Khrushchev in 1964. While all three successions occurred under very different circumstances, their effects on public policy (which were strong) were remarkably similar. Thus, I would have to reject, insofar as budgetary and investment priorities are concerned, Myron Rush's (1974:20) hypothesis that "politically induced succession, since it involves dissatisfaction with ruler's performance, tends to be more disruptive than succession due to natural causes." Apparently, most successions, whatever their origins, do bring many past priorities into question and open the way for new directions in public policy. Given that all successions, whatever their immediate genesis, are a time of reassessment, and a time when successors have to prove their worth by peddling new ideas, this conclusion is not, I think, terribly surprising.

The third and final factor—that the predecessor's tenure should correlate with the policy impact of the rise of a

TABLE 5-7

A Comparison of Successions in the Soviet Bloc

Country	Leader	Period	Cause of Succession	Primes	Percentage of Significant t tests[a]
Bulgaria	Chervenkov	1950-1954	Death	Yes	—
	Zhivkov	1954-	Death	Yes	44%
Czechoslovakia	Novotny	1953-1968	Death	Yes	44%
	Dubcek	1968-1969	Mass unrest	No	—
	Husak	1969-	Soviet Intervention	No	77%
East Germany	Ulbricht	1953-1971	Soviet Selected	Yes	—
	Honecker	1971-	Retirement (forced)	No	77%
Hungary	Rakosi	1953-1956	Soviet Selected	No	—
	Gero	1956-1956	Mass unrest	No	—
	Kadar	1956-	Mass unrest & Soviet Intervention	No	55%
Poland	Bierut	1948-1956	Soviet Selected	Yes	—
	Ochab	1956-1956	Death—Elite Affair & Soviet Selected	No	—
	Gomulka	1956-1970	Mass unrest	No	100%
	Gierek	1970-1980	Mass unrest	No	100%
Romania	Gheorghiu-Dej	1945-1965	Soviet Selected	Yes	—
	Ceausescu	1965-	Death—Elite Affair	Yes	90%
Soviet Union	Stalin	1928-1953	Death—Elite Affair	Yes	100%
	Khrushchev	1953-1964	Death—Elite Affair	No	100%
	Brezhnev	1964-	Retirement—Elite Affair	No	90%

[a] This is a very rough measure of impact. I encourage the reader to go back to the previous tables and look at significance *and* share change.

Sources: See the Appendix.

successor—receives more clear-cut support. While the real world in the Soviet bloc does not cooperate terribly well in helping test this hypothesis—short tenure (with the exception of Rakosi and Bierut) is noticeable rare—one does find that long tenure seems to precede particularly large changes in policy following succession. Compare, for example, Poland in 1970 and the Khrushchev and Brezhnev accessions to power, on the one hand, with Hungary in 1956 or the transition to Zhivkov in Bulgaria. It would seem that the pressures on a leader to change his predecessor's priorities increase with the duration of tenure, and this pressure seems to translate into new budgetary and investment priorities. This generalization, moreover, also works at the sub-national level (see Tables 5-5 and 5-6). First Secretaries there who follow men of long tenure tend to change policy more than when the predecessor was in only a comparatively short while.

Thus, Peter Wiles's (1969:315) argument with respect to Stalin seems to be a generalizable one:

> It has often been remarked how many domestic problems Stalin left his successors; allowing them to pile up during the years of his tyranny because he was aging and inert, because he knew his system would last, because he was so great a tyrant that in a sense he had no problems. . . . He required neither justice nor rationality nor ideological soundness nor even formality. His successors required all of these and when they denounced him the dam broke.

This would lead one to predict, given the effects of long tenure, the pervasiveness of incrementalism and the enduring impact of succession over time, that the impact of succession in the future should not wither away. This is plausible both because a pattern of diminishing effects is not present in the data presented here, and because tenure at this point is very long across the Soviet bloc. In this sense, I would have to agree with Jerry Hough (1976) that the

succession following Brezhnev will have major policy ramifications—not just because of generational tensions (see
Connor, 1975; Hough, 1976) and the problems inherent
in a holding operation (see Hough, 1976), but also because
of the impact of a protracted mobilization of bias. However,
if we keep in mind the tendency for new priorities to become the new routines and for innovations to be important,
but circumscribed policy shifts, then one can in no way
predict dramatic changes in future successions. In the future, as in the past, succession should function as a way to
"tune" the system, rather than to undermine it. Succession
seems to be less of a crisis, even under "optimal" conditions
(i.e., following long tenure), and more a mechanism which
readjusts priorities and the benefits and losses accrued to
strategic groups in the system.

In seeking to explain the variance in the results, then,
we seem to find that the most important factors are the
presence of new people and the duration of the previous
regime. However, these two variables do not go that far in
explaining the results; there are some important exceptions. Moreover, these exceptions cannot be explained by
variables commonly cited in the literature as helpful in
differentiating the impact of succession on public policy in
the Soviet bloc. In contrast to the Western analysis, the
impact of succession in the East seems to be somewhat
idiosyncratic, if not consistent.

This in turn suggests that I have confirmed something
that scholars in communist area studies have been emphasizing a long time, the importance of context to understanding a lot (but hardly all) of what happens in such
systems. In their study of elite succession in Eastern Europe, for instance, Carl Beck and his associates (1976:61)
make precisely that argument:

> We emerge with the conclusion that, on the basis of the
> indicators used, political succession in Eastern Europe
> appears to be a stochastic process. We hold with a premise

that is slowly being accepted in the literature: that situational analysis, in which context is interpreted through the lens of social theory, is a more powerful way of describing and analyzing communist politics than is a monolithic framework. We are left with a view that these systems are more particularistic than universal.

I would have to agree with them, though with the reservation that there are some universal factors operating; they just do not explain all the variance. What precisely, then, is missing?

What one needs to do to go further in explaining the results is to examine the impact of *individual* leaders and their political environments, a procedure that is perhaps too common in communist area studies and not common enough in more general analyses of the origins of public policy. Just as there is a tendency in the policy literature to downplay the importance of situational variables—such as political context and style of the chief executive—and extol instead the explanatory power of more aggregate and structural variables—such as economic development, executive power, and the like—there is a tendency among area scholars to underemphasize structural variables and couch their explanations in references to the elite stratum. Such an emphasis, however, would seem to miss out on much of the dynamics of elite decision-making and policy innovation. As stressed in Chapter Three, while structural variables certainly affect the capability and incentives to innovate, they hardly "do the innovating." As Richard Hofferbert (1970:318) put it, "such considerations as elite role patterns, leadership and ideology are becoming residual categories in much comparative state inquiry. . . . But human beings have to act for there to be a policy." Particularly at the apex of a system, one can assert that leaders make policies, and "parties," "revenues," and the like do not. A leader has style, decision rules, preferences, and preponderant power; sometimes he or she even has a feeling of tremendous energy and ambition to make his or her goals and presence felt. While the process of policy-making can set certain parameters, it is the leader who decides *how* to work within those bounds. John Donovan's (1970:135) example of Lyndon Johnson is instructive here.

> An analysis of policy-making as reflected in annual budgets suggests that while the process moves incrementally, it is not impervious to policy leadership. President Johnson's difficulty was not that he could not move the process in the directions he wished to, but that he was moving in several directions at one time. The "process" did not fashion the War on Poverty and turn away from it. The "process" did not pledge the President to equality in June, 1965 nor did the "process" Americanize the war in Vietnam (also see Hage and Dewar, 1973).

Thus, what is being suggested is that, while succession is a process and as such its general impact can be assessed, it is in many important ways a personal process. Its policy impact, then, to some extent should also be personal. While the more recent literature on the American Presidency and the Soviet *vozhd'*, for example, has emphasized the increasing power of the former and the decreasing power of the latter since the 1940's, in the process the personalized nature of the two offices has been lost. Because of the power and the open role expectations of these posts, neither the impact of their rotation nor the variance of that impact should be all that surprising. While the general impact of succession in socialist states testifies to the validity of structural variables—such as the importance of elite tenure and the dynamics of the process, the variance, though limited, within that impact speaks to the importance of specific elites and specific contexts in explaining policy outcomes. This argument is only enhanced, moreover, by the finding that policy change is far more likely when elites actually turn over.

The fact that an actual change in incumbents is conducive to policy change also gets at what seems to be a contradiction running throughout this chapter (and one which ran through Chapter Three as well, when I looked at elections). When one juxtaposes the fact that decision-making in budgetary and capital investments in the Soviet Union and Eastern Europe tends to be incremental with the pattern of innovation found in this chapter, one comes to the confusing conclusion that policy in socialist states changes a great deal and not at all. The first response to this paradox is that incrementalism speaks to the *general* behavior of policy, East and West, whereas innovation speaks to more short-term patterns of change. Long time-series data can after all mask some important policy deviations. In this chapter, the method used to assess the impact of succession seems to pick these changes up. Thus, incrementalism is a general tendency, while succession deals with some specifics of policy development.

I should also emphasize in response to this seeming contradiction that the kinds of changes I have found are hardly, in an objective sense, dramatic or radical; they are, instead, best characterized as moderate deviations from the norm. As Hugh Heclo and Aaron Wildavsky (1974:220) have emphasized, though, even "small" changes can be important in a political sense:

> In expenditures, one man's [sic] margin is another man's [sic] profit. The tiny differences which may seem unworthy of argument yield the little extras that make life worth living. Policies, as we have seen, are bargained on these margins. A few percent on hundreds of millions . . . may make the difference between sufficiency and stringency, contentment and dissatisfaction, elbow room and the strait jacket.

While the authors are referring to incrementalism in Great Britain, the same can certainly be said of socialist states as well. Incrementalism and innovative policy change are not mutually exclusive phenomena; in fact, they seem to alternate in a regularized way with one another, East and West, in response to the succession cycle.

The lesson of this analysis, then, is that one should not stress one mode of policy-making over the other; incrementalism and innovation are *both* important patterns of decision-making because they address different types of decision-making, divisions of power, and policy and elite contexts. Because the general tendency is slow change does not make that the only tendency, nor does it make it the most important pattern to analyze:

> The search for patterns is, of course, a legitimate and significant social science pursuit, just as is the search for statistical significance. But the significant cases in both historical sociology and statistical analysis are often the deviant cases. They are the ones that help us identify both the strengths and weaknesses of the models and theories and they serve as a basis for comparison and to identify emergent phenomena (Beck, 1975:124).

Succession and innovation, disruption and routine, are both critical in socialist states, just as they were in bourgeois democracies. What I have uncovered in this study is incrementalism and innovation: incremental policy change as the rule, punctuated by periodic changes in priorities brought on primarily by leadership change. The process of policy-making tends to involve the generation of similar policy priorities each year until a new administration comes in and sets up its own priorities. These in turn become set until the next administration change. This cluster pattern can be seen (to harken back to the American case study), for example, in the behavior of Soviet welfare policies. Khrushchev increased welfare outlays sharply after he came into power; these levels then became a routine which was not broken until 1965, when Brezhnev again expanded the welfare share of the budget. This in turn has become routinized until the present day.[6]

Thus, policy innovation in the Soviet Union is not terribly different from that in organizations in general, or in Western governments, for that matter. As with the case of welfare reform in the United States, for example, or budgeting in general, the process is cyclical, with long periods of consolidation interrupted by short flurries of innovation. In the long run, the process looks linear; however, it is often not that at all. Thus, public policy can be, indeed seems to be, both incremental *and* responsive to elite succession. This is as true of the East as it was of the West.

THE DIRECTION OF CHANGE

Unfortunately, there is no equivalent in the socialist context for "left" versus "right" parties, and hence we have little reason to predict certain types of innovations over others. However, an argument could be constructed that priorities which are favorable to the mass publics will receive the bulk of the attention in the aftermath of succession. This argument is predicated on the fact that new leaders, in campaigning after assuming office and in facing a crisis situ-

---

[6] Actually, 1957 marked major increases in welfare outlays in every Soviet bloc state, which suggests that the Soviet Union had declared a war on welfare. It should also be noted that, in the 1950's as a whole, changes in welfare outlays tended to be similar throughout the Soviet bloc. For example, the correlations between Soviet and East German, Polish, and Romanian welfare allocations, expressed as shares of the budget for that period, were, respectively, .82, .94, and .98. By the 1960's, however, states increasingly went their own ways in welfare: the comparable correlations were only .40, -.70, and .54. I should in addition mention that Khrushchev should receive some credit for the welfare changes implemented in 1965. However, Brezhnev did choose not to forestall them (see Bunce and Echols, 1975). For discussions of innovations in Soviet welfare policies, see Bronson and Krueger (1971); Osborn (1970); Feiwel (1972); Barkaiskas (1973); Maier (1974). For a concise statistical summary, see *Narodnoe obrazovanie* (1971) and *Zabota partii* (1974).

ation, will try to quell potential mass discontent (which they have seen happen in East European successions) and at the same time build a positive base of support for the new regime (see Mieczkowski, 1978; Bunce, 1980a and 1980b). Such an emphasis, moreover, has ideological legitimacy in the period of developed socialism (see Kukushkin, 1975; Evans, 1977). Thus, when stability seems at stake, as it seems to be during succession, income, wages, social outlays, and consumer goods and housing production should all be inflated in contrast to their previous growth rates. However, when stability returns and leaders are fully in command, other priorities should begin receiving their fair share.

In fact, this is precisely what happens (see Tables 5-8, 5-9, 5-10 and 5-11). Public consumption is primed during succession, and left to incremental growth, once the lead-

TABLE 5-8
Capital Investment in Light Industry and
Housing and Public Expenditures on Welfare:
The Soviet Union, 1929-1977

	Average Light Ind. Share of Capital Investment	Average Housing Share of Capital Investment	Average Welfare Share of the Budget
Stalin: Succession period (1929-1931)	n.a.	.053	.085
Post-Succession period (1932-1940)	n.a.	.0233	.075
Khrushchev: Succession period (1954-1957)	.049	.025	.133[a]
Post-Succession period (1958-1964)	.040	.019	.131
Brezhnev: Succession period (1965-1968)	.045	.170	.141
Post-Succession period (1969-1977)	.041	.152	.144

[a] This figure underestimates the impact of the Khrushchev succession since little was done to expand welfare until 1957—when there was a dramatic upward shift.

Sources: Sovet ekonomicheskoi vzaipomoshchi statisticheskii. Ezhegodnik stran chlenov Soveta ekonomicheskoi vzaipomoshchi (Moscow: Statistika, 1976), pp. 130-59; *Narodnoe khoziaistvo SSSR za 60 let: Iubeleinyi statisticheskii ezhegodnik* (Moscow: Statistika, 1977), pp. 272-73, 653-56; R. W. Davies, *The Soviet Financial System* (Cambridge, England: Cambridge University Press, 1958), pp. 244-48.

TABLE 5-9

Average Annual Growth Rates in Consumption and Consumer Goods: Poland and the Soviet Union (Percent)

	Succession Periods (1956-59 and 1965-68)	Post-Succession Periods (1960-64 and 1969-78)
Soviet Union		
Light industry production	7.51	5.72
Light industry investment	7.62	3.51
Public consumption funds	10.40	6.32
Real income per capita	5.81	4.22

	Succession Periods (1956-59 and 1971-73)	Post-Succession Periods (1960-70 and 1974-77)
Poland		
Light industry production	9.11	6.92
Personal income	13.70	5.73
Total consumption outlays per capita	6.51	4.92

Sources: See the Appendix and Current Digest of the Soviet Press, Vol. 29, No. 5 (Jan. 11, 1978), p. 9; Vol. 26, No. 51 (Jan. 15, 1975), p. 12; Vol. 24, No. 3 (Jan. 24, 1973), p. 9.

ership crisis has been resolved.[7] Thus, as in the Western case (Tufte, 1978), political ambitions and the need for mass support work to encourage a political cycle in economic policy. The only difference is one of timing; campaigns in the East occur after, not before, succession. Second, such a cycle tells us, as it did in the Western case, that successions are not just mechanisms of policy innovation, but also harbingers of particular kinds of economic priorities. As will be expanded below, the elitist succession rite in socialist nations does not just rotate leaders and policies; it also, ironically, enforces a kind of responsiveness to mass demands.

[7] It should be noted that a similar pattern exists in housing starts (DiMaio, 1974), and consumer goods production and agriculture (see Bunce, 1980a and 1980b). The reason for the priming of agriculture is that higher expenditures benefit the rural population directly and the consumers who must pay for the goods.

TABLE 5-10
Growth Rates in Selected Personal Income and Public Consumption
Indicators in the Soviet Bloc (Percent)

	Succession[a]	Post-Succession[b]
German Democratic Republic (Disposable income growth, 1971-1976)	5.6	3.8
Poland (Average annual growth in real wages, 1956-1975)	7.4	1.8
Czechoslovakia (Personal consumption in constant prices per capita, 1967-1973)	5.5	4.5
Soviet Union (increases in national income, 1964-1977)	7.1	4.1

[a] Succession is defined as 1972-1974 (the German Democratic Republic), 1957-1959 and 1971-1973 (Poland), 1957-1959 and 1968-1970 (Czechoslovakia), and 1965-1967 (Soviet Union).

[b] Post-Succession is defined as all other years, except succession periods, depending on data availability.

Sources: See the Appendix and Current Digest of the Soviet Press, Vol. 29, No. 48 (December 27, 1978), p. 12.

An Empirical Theory of the Impact of Socialist Successions

The question then becomes, *how* does succession lead to policy change in the communist party states? How can one flesh out what have thus far been essentially correlations between new leaders and new policies?

Of course, part of the answer to this query lies in the arguments presented in Chapter One in support of the hypothesis that socialist successions should affect public policy. There, it was argued that innovation would occur because of a supportive ideology, a centralized power structure, and an issue-oriented succession process. To put this another way, new leaders would innovate because they would want to (ideology); they would have the power to do so (centralization); and it would be in their interest to do so (the mechanics of succession). The picture that emerges from this analysis, then, is one of a succession process, a

TABLE 5-11

Average Annual Growth Rates Under Khrushchev and Brezhnev (Percent)

	Nat'l Income (1960-1978)	Real Income Per Capita (1965-1978)	Monthly Wage Increases: Workers and Employees (1964-1978)	Monthly Wage Increases: Collective Farmers (1964-1978)	Number of Persons Receiving Pension Benefits (1954-1978)
Succession periods (1954-1957, 1965-1968)	7.7	6.2	5.2	10.1	9.1
Post-Succession periods (1958-1964, 1969-1978)	5.6	4.4	3.2	4.6	3.2

Sources: See the Appendix and *Current Digest of the Soviet Press*, Vol. 29, No. 48 (Dec. 27, 1978), p. 12; Vol. 28, No. 50 (Jan. 11, 1977), p. 9; Vol. 27, No. 48 (Dec. 24, 1976), p. 7; Vol. 26, No. 51 (Jan. 15, 1975), p. 12.

decision environment, and an ideology that encourages public policies to change in response to leadership turnover.

While all these factors are important, the real key to the findings would seem to have to do with the succession *process*, for that is what makes innovation both desirable and necessary. In its absence, as is apparent in all the evidence on incrementalism, the power of the leader and the ideology—the other two factors—generally work to sanction small, not large, change. Thus, succession operates as a catalyst, expanding power, opening up the range of acceptable policies, and emphasizing the legitimacy of large shifts in priorities. But how does this transformation work? What is it about succession that encourages policy change?

If I may borrow the language of Western electoral analyses, it can be said that succession changes public policy in socialist systems because of the nature of the campaign for office and decision-making during the honeymoon period. The campaign works to generate policy ideas, whereas decision-making in the honeymoon allows for the implementation of those new ideas. But what is meant in the socialist context by a "campaign" and a "honeymoon"?

When socialist contenders "run" for office, they must demonstrate to the elites around them that they can wield power, that they know the important policy areas and issues, and that they understand well how the system works. This would seem to be their minimal qualifications; it is the least they must have, *if* they are to appeal to and win over the small sophisticated group of officials at the top of the system (Linden, 1966; Conquest, 1967). These officials would not settle for less; they are, after all, professional politicians themselves whose position testifies to their ability to wield power and to comprehend the inner workings of the party and the state. Thus, the qualifications are stringent because of the nature of the "selectorate" and the background of the major contenders for the leader's mantle.

But if everyone at the top is highly qualified, how are the various contenders sorted out? One answer is that some are more qualified than others: some have especially broad experience; some are old enough to have proven their worth, yet not too old so that they would have a short tenure at best; some come from the more dominant nationality; and, finally, only a few combine these traits with being members of the Politburo, the stepping stone to power. Thus, the pool is a very limited one. But, even taking these factors into account, one finds a small potential group—perhaps four or five—who can lay legitimate claim to the office of First Secretary. How are they to be differentiated? How does one win over the others?

Clearly, there are two ways of succeeding in such a situation: one is to win by force and the other is to win by making persuasive appeals. The first mode is, of course, common practice. Leaders at the apex in socialist systems are terribly ambitious and power-hungry; this is natural in a system where a political career is based on professionalism, the exercise of immense power and responsibilities, and tremendous risks. Just as failure can be catastrophic, so success can be euphoric—this is a sure combination for intense power drives and intense competition. Those who have survived and flourished in such an environment, moreover, would seem to be extreme in terms of these characteristics. They would know best how to compete and how to be successful, and they would want the ultimate reward: the office of First Secretary. Their need for power and their ability to manipulate it would seem to be an ingrained habit by the time they had become members of the Politburo.

But, if everyone is highly ambitious and highly conversant with the ways of power, how can one person dominate? Here is where the second strategy comes in. Power is won by both astute manipulations of coalitions *and* by policy appeals. In a highly competitive campaign, contenders fight to line up supporters and one way they form a coalition is to speak to the important issues of the day and offer some solutions to prevailing problems. One way the electorate can differentiate among contenders, then, is to listen to their ideas, and one way candidates can stand out is to present a number of ideas.

Thus, in battling for power, the major competitors use power and policy. They not only "gang up" in a series of shifting coalitions against one another, but they also speak to the major concerns that the party elites have and attempt to assuage their worries about the party and about the polity. This means that succession is a time of power plays and policy-posturings; it is a time of criticizing the status quo, generating new ideas, and proving one's worth. The fact that the mandate is provisional only exacerbates these tendencies; intense conflict and strident policy debates go hand in hand during the struggle for power in socialist systems as contestants seek to prove their worth to the elites around them. He who wins would seem to be the one who wields power most effectively, who is highly qualified, and who best meets the needs of the party and the party's perception of national needs. Both Leonid Brezhnev and Nikita Khrushchev are, of course, good cases in point (Hodnett, 1975).

Losers, by contrast, would seem to be those who did not wield power very well and who did not address the compelling issues of the period. Standing pat and avoiding the major problems that weigh on the elites would not seem to be the best strategy under such conditions; others would jump to the fore and attract supporters with their ideas, while the less issue oriented candidates would have no glue with which to hold their coalitions together. In a sense, then, power and issues go together. Power can be exercised for the sake of issues or vice versa, but desire for one tends to necessitate the manipulation of the other. In this way, socialist campaigns for office are mechanisms of policy innovation. Winners tend to be innovators, and power and policy priorities are both up for grabs in the succession struggle. The competitiveness of the process, its elitist character, its policy orientation, and its lack of an institutionalized mandate, then, are precisely the reasons why such successions are mechanisms of policy innovation. What many scholars see as indicators of instability, I see as indicators of innovation.

But if the system is flung open to new ideas and to new power arrangements during succession, how do the new ideas get translated into actual policies? How does the new leader take hold over the system and put the promises he made into practice? It is precisely on this point that this analysis diverges from most treatments of socialist successions. Many students of socialist systems tend to see succession as a continuous process, often never resolved until years after the new First Secretary is ushered into office (Rush, 1968 and 1974). Thus, for example, scholars have spoken of Khrushchev *and* the Soviet leadership[8]—a clear indication of permanent conflict at the top—and of Brezhnev's continuing search for more power from 1964-1971 (Breslauer, 1978). The picture is, therefore, one of a never-ending struggle; occupying the office of the First Secretary is, it seems, only the beginning of a long battle.

My results, by contrast, indicate that quite a different process may be going on, that in socialist systems there may be something equivalent to a honeymoon period that allows new leaders a grace period within which to enact some of their policy ideas.[9] Both the data presented here and nu-

[8] This, of course, is the title of Carl Linden's book (1966) about Khrushchev. This emphasis on constraints, though, can be carried too far, so that *all* elite behavior and policy outcomes are explained by constraints. For example, see Teresa Rakowska-Harmstone (1976:53), who argues that "The search for a golden mean in trading off solutions, group satisfactions, and authority was evident in Krushchev's 'subjectivism' and rapid policy changes. It is still present now in the compromises adopted by his successors, in their simultaneous emphasis on practical approaches to policy problems, and in their preoccupation with ideological orthodoxy. . . ."

[9] This, for example, is what is implied in works that rely on the mobi-

merous case studies provide strong evidence that policy change is greatest right after succession, and those new policies are precisely the ones advocated by the new First Secretary (Bronson and Krueger, 1971; Volkov, 1972). One can point, for example, to Khrushchev's virgin-lands project, or de-Stalinization, or to Brezhnev's innovations in detente, increased agricultural investment, or more scientific decision-making. These were themes and ideas that came up early; only *later* did they run into difficulties in implementation. Thus, a honeymoon, with its implied cooperative spirit, would seem to operate in socialist contexts. It seems to be a time, in view of the results, when the new leader has the power and desire to make a change. He seems to be allowed a grace period during which he is supposed to earn his mandate.

This notion of a honeymoon clarifies a number of what seem to be ambiguous points about succession. First, the common idea of constant conflict among the leadership stratum does not allow for the possibility that socialist elites want the system to flourish and do not want to place policy and the polity in abeyance for an extended duration while they resolve the succession crisis. It would seem, in view of their long careers in politics and their intense socialization as *apparatchiki*, that putting limits on the succession struggle (and in the conflict and uncertainty it generates) would be top priority (see Brezhnev, 1972, Vol. III: 409-412; Morozow, 1973: 109-117). It makes far more sense, when realizing that power needs work within a sense of polity needs as well (which could affect power, after all) to argue that elites decide on a new leader, and give him an extended opportunity to show what he can do. The honeymoon would, therefore, make sense in the socialist context, and it certainly makes sense, given the results reported in this chapter.

---

lization or totalitarian models of communist high politics. For convenient summaries of this position, see Thornton (1972).

This view of controlled conflict and instability also helps to explain several other anomalies that appeared in the data. The first is that succession is indeed infrequent in socialist states, and one rarely has (except under the infrequent condition of mass unrest) clustered patterns of turnover. The fact that tenure is long and new leaders are never thrown out immediately, except under exceptional circumstances, would seem to reflect the operation of a honeymoon period far more than the existence of an ongoing succession struggle. While I would not say that long tenure indicates low conflict, I would argue that, particularly in the early years when innovation is most frequent, leaders do seem to have a fair amount of power. They seem to have a chance to prove what they can do.[10] Later, of course, failures expand, political debts pile up, opposition grows, compliance falls—the honeymoon ends as it does in the West.

A second pattern in the data which is made more understandable from the vantage point of a honeymoon is the pronounced tendency in *all* countries for social-welfare expenditures (and other areas concerned with mass consumption) to rise after succession (Mieczkowski, 1978; Bunce, 1980a and 1980b). It would seem that such actions tell us a great deal about how socialist leaders look at succession and its impact on the system. What seems to be happening is a concerted effort on the part of the newly installed leadership to buy the support or at least the acquiescence of the masses during a time of instability. The successors seem to feel that they must somehow earn support and quell the potential unrest that might arise in a

[10] This is not to argue, of course, that they have no enemies and no constraints in the early days of the administration. Khrushchev had to deal with Malenkov and Molotov and had to purge the Politburo in 1957, just as Brezhnev had to deal with Polyansky, Shelepin, and Voronov. But, comparatively speaking, both Brezhnev and Khrushchev seemed to be *able* to do more early in their tenure than later in their administration, which suggests the operation of a honeymoon period and some consensus.

time of unusual vulnerability. The honeymoon, therefore, is a respite from battle—a time of policy change, expanded power, and the wooing of the masses.

Such a deal between elites and masses is, of course, not terribly dissimilar from the campaign promises made with abandon by political candidates in the West. One major difference seems to be that in Western elections action is not required, since the votes come in *before* the candidates have to make good on their promises (see Tufte, 1978). In the Second World, by contrast, with the creation of a mandate following (not preceding) the election, action must accompany words, at least for awhile. In this sense, the policy responsiveness of socialist succession can be seen as being perhaps greater than it is in the West. But the purpose of such promises in both instances is roughly similar— to win support and (in the socialist world in particular) to quell potential discontent. For both of these reasons, then, new socialist leaders tend to innovate and to pump money into "people" areas; this is the nature of policy-making during the honeymoon period. At that time, elites band together to enhance stability, to curry the favor of the masses, to reevaluate and reorder priorities, and to give the new leader an opportunity to show his stuff.[11]

Thus, policy change in socialist states occurs for roughly the same reasons it occurs in the West: the campaign and the honeymoon encourage new ideas, and provide sufficient power for their enactment into law. Ambition, power, and desire for change all meet in the honeymoon period, East and West, and innovation becomes the norm. Later in the administration, though, this particular combination of factors begins to disperse: the power of the leader declines, innovation becomes more difficult and risky, and the new leader gets increasingly stuck in his ways.[12] Incre-

[11] There is, as will be evident in the next chapter, some further strong support for this notion of campaign promises in the socialist world. In addition, see Bronson and Krueger (1971).

[12] All of this is to add to the growing evidence on the similarities between

mentalism at that point becomes once again the dominant form of decision-making (Bunce and Echols, 1978). The time for change has passed, and will not in all likelihood rise again until the next succession "crisis."

Thus, new leaders East and West do affect public policy in their honeymoons because they have the desire and the capacity to do so. The desire comes from the campaign process (and, in socialist states, from an activist ideology), and from the fact that they are surrounded by ideas and people who want some action. Capacity, likewise, is enhanced by what is an unusually compliant power structure. Just as bureaucrats, members of Congress, and interest groups line up to give the new executive a chance and to curry his favor in the United States, so the *apparatchiki* find it in their interest and in those of the system to give the new leader a grace period. However, with new policies comes a hardening up of support coalitions, demands for fair shares from other groups, a crystallization of opposition as the new policies create some losers, and the inevitable appearance of some failures as the administration goes about creating a record. Moreover, as conflict increases so does complexity; feelings of newness and optimism evolve into pessimism. The costs of innovation, then, go up and incrementalism becomes the new norm. Thus, innovation withers as power declines, as new ideas become less attractive and less manageable. There seems to be, therefore, a policy cycle East and West, calibrated by succession, and marked by a regularized alternation between innovation and incrementalism.

CONCLUSIONS

In an overview of the problems and premises of political science, Lucien Pye (1968:245) has bemoaned the fact that

----

socialist and capitalist states. For other arguments along this line, see for instance, Bruce and Clawson (1977); Hough (1973); Hough (1975); Bunce and Echols (1978).

"just as we have tended to look at the past rather than to the future, so we have been more interested in analyzing sources and causes than in studying consequences and outcomes." This criticism is certainly a telling one for students of socialist successions; considerable emphasis has been placed by scholars on the process of succession, to the detriment of assessing its impact. Just as in the Western electoral literature, the concern with socialist successions has been with the "selectorate" and the candidate, and not with their effects on public policy. Very few scholars have even tried to answer the question: Does it matter who rules in socialist systems?

In this chapter, I have provided an answer to this query and it is "yes" with respect to budgetary and investment allocations. At the national level, changes in political leaders in socialist countries are usually accompanied by significant changes in public policy priorities, and this impact is steady and strong across time and polity, and even across type of succession. Thus, the impact of leadership changeover is not diminishing as these systems mature, and the circumstances under which the succession began—mass or elite dissatisfaction, Soviet intervention, or the death of the leader—do not seem to matter as far as policy change is concerned.

However, successions which involve a change in leadership have more impact than those where a change of incumbents did not occur. Moreover, successions following longer tenure in office did show disproportionate changes in budgetary and investment policy. Finally, the national/local distinction in succession proved to be helpful, but not crucial; national-level succession does affect policy more than turnovers at the republic level in the Soviet Union, but even in that context leadership turnover was an important political variable. Whatever the variance in the results, though, the conclusion remains that new leaders do put through new priorities.

However, this is not to argue either that socialist systems are in fact leader-dependent or that successions are the crises they have been made out to be. As with the case of Western elections, so in the socialist context policy changes because leaders and structures change, and those changes enhance—but within limits—the malleability of the policy environment and the desire and capacity of leaders to innovate. Leaders may activate those forces, because of ambition and ideological conviction but, in the final analysis, the dynamics of succession and the honeymoon interact to allow, if not force, leaders to do some new things. Thus, leaders do matter more when they are new, but their environments also shape these possibilities and provide incentives for this greater impact, just as their environments dictate incrementalism once succession is resolved.

All of this supports the contention that elites, their succession to office, and the structural variables that shape their policy context are important to study, precisely because the changing of the political guard "makes a difference." I can, therefore, question the rather common charge that policy-making, East and West, is somehow immune to elite control. It depends on one's time frame. The "petrification" school in communist area studies (which is at its base a different normative slant on incrementalism) receives *no* support in this analysis, except as a description of stable leadership periods. Nor do I agree with those who argue for the non-impact of elections and the dominance of incrementalism, even when leaders are in flux. Rather, public policy is cyclical and is calibrated by a "succession connection" (Mayhew, 1974). Thus, if any view is upheld in this analysis, it is that of Lenin, who once remarked (and more than once put into practice): "Politics cannot help but have dominance over economics. To argue otherwise, is to forget the ABC's of Marxism" (quoted in Nove, 1975:631).

SIX

Leadership Change and Policy Innovation: A Case Study of the Impact of Succession on Soviet Postwar Agricultural Policy

Inasmuch as the antithesis between town and country is one of the root causes of the economic and cultural backwardness of the countryside . . . the Russian Communist Party regards the eradication of this antithesis as one of the basic tasks of building communism.
—*V. I. Lenin* (1919)

With the disappearance of kulak bondage, poverty in the rural districts has disappeared. Every peasant, collective farmer, or individual farmer now has the opportunity to enjoy a human existence, if only he wants to work honestly and not be a loafer.
. . .
—*J. Stalin* (1934)

The problems of building communism cannot be successfully solved without the advance of agriculture.
—*N. Khrushchev* (1953)

To more quickly develop agriculture and place it on a strong scientific-technical base is one of the most important and primary tasks of the current period.
—*L. Brezhnev* (1975b, Vol. I)

INTRODUCTION

In the last chapter I found that changes in political leadership seem to have a consistent effect on budgetary allocations and capital investments in socialist nations. However, in the absence of a succession, policy change was found generally to be quite incremental. This pattern—of changes in priorities immediately after succession, which settle into routines until the next executive turnover—led to the conclusion that succession seems to be a mechanism for policy innovation in budgetary and investment allocations and macroeconomic policy in the Soviet bloc. When succession occurs, some kind of change in priorities in these policy areas—generally, to expand public consumption—invariably seems to follow. Conversely, when the leadership stratum is stable, budgetary and investment policy tends to proceed as before, seemingly quarantined against any contamination from the conflictual political environment.

In this chapter I will flesh out this linkage between leadership succession and policy innovation in socialist states by looking at one policy area in detail, tracing its development over time, and linking these developments to changes in political leaders. Specifically, I will examine how Khrushchev's and Brezhnev's rise to power ushered in major changes in agrarian policies in the Soviet Union in the postwar era. It will be argued that, to a large extent, agricultural innovation in the Soviet Union can be seen as being intimately linked to the succession process. In fact, a leader's rise to power in that system in the post-Stalin period seems to depend in part upon the successful exploitation of the agricultural crisis.

This, of course, is precisely why I chose to use agricultural politics as a case study. Numerous scholars have emphasized the central role this issue has played in the Soviet policy process since 1953:

> The importance of agriculture in Soviet politics has been obvious ever since the public recognition of the agricultural crisis soon after Stalin's death. Stalin's first successor, Malenkov, resigned as Premier in February, 1955, confessing incompetence in agricultural leadership. Khrushchev, whose victory over Malenkov was greatly facilitated by the success of his agricultural initiatives, was himself overthrown in October, 1964, after his leadership had been seriously undermined by the 1963 agriculture debacle. Like Khrushchev Brezhnev's first ini-

tiative upon his election as First Secretary was to present a big program to solve the agricultural crisis, and his 1970-1971 rise has been closely linked with the victory of the agricultural lobby in the resource struggle (Hahn, 1972:3).

Indicative of the political importance of agriculture is the fact that, while First Secretaries of the Soviet republics from 1955 to 1970 averaged seven and one-half years in office, agricultural secretaries lasted an average of four and one-half years (see Hodnett and Ogareff, 1973). It is also telling that, of all the Central Committee plenums in the period 1953-1971, more than one-third have been primarily concerned with agriculture (twenty-five out of sixty-one) (see *Spravochnyi tom*, 1973). Thus, agrarian issues are clearly high (along with some other issues, it must be added) on the Soviet policy agenda.

However, while many analyses of policy-making in the Soviet Union have been concerned with agriculture, no one has systematically linked the process of succession to agricultural innovation. Instead, such studies tend to give blow-by-blow accounts of who advocates what when, without any structural or theoretical context. At best, the tie between succession and the nature of policy innovation in agriculture in such analyses enters in almost by accident, by the back door.

This account will be different. While I will draw upon much of the data in these studies (as well as some more original data), I will place this information in an interpretive framework in order to illustrate how the succession process leads to the generation of new policies—specifically, in the case of agriculture. This will mean, among other things, that my interpretation will at times go against the common wisdom. I will, for example, treat policy, not as an accidental byproduct of the power struggle, but rather as *the* arena through which political fortunes are won and lost. Moreover, I will not focus exclusively on elites, but rather decisions and issues and how these change over time. The logic here is that "ultimately, the test of the direction in which the Soviet political system is evolving must be the nature of policies that emerge from that system" (Hough, 1972:35).

In contrast to previous studies, then, the focus here will be as much on public policies and how they change—with agriculture as an example—as on the jousting among principal players. The basic contention will be that the process of succession—how political power is won and maintained—when combined with the nature of the agricultural issue, provides what seems to be an optimal environment for policy innovation. By contrast, the resolution of the succession "crisis" seems to signal a diminution of agricultural innovation as well.

SOVIET AGRICULTURE: THE LEGACY OF STALIN

The death of Stalin in March 1953 ushered in a number of dramatic changes in the style and substance of Soviet high politics. As with the passing of any strong leader of long tenure, the immediate reaction among the elites was fear and confusion. Since policy-making was so dominated by Stalin, the process itself was suspended as the principal elites groped around to define their roles in the post-Stalinist era. This confusion was hardly ameliorated by the lack of an institutionalized succession procedure; not only was the leader gone, but he had left several successors, and no means by which to sort them out.

In the absence of any clear guidelines about how policy was to be made, who was to participate, or what the substance was to be, the major players decided to divide up various responsibilities among themselves. The head of the Party went to Nikita Khrushchev, the state apparatus to Georgi Malenkov, and the Secret Police to its former head, Lavrenti Beria. Policy arenas were also divided up: Khrushchev focused primarily (but not exclusively) on agriculture; Malenkov dominated the dialogue on consumer goods and international affairs; Lazar Kaganovich and Vyacheslav Molotov took on heavy industry; Mikhail Suslov concerned himself with ideology; and, finally, Beria focused primarily on the nationalities question (Rush, 1968; Ploss, 1965).

This arrangement, however, was unstable from the start. When one places a combative and ambitious group of politicians into a fluid power structure and then adds a wide-open policy agenda, the decision process will necessarily be conflict-ridden. Such, of course, was the case in the fall of 1953. As each contender tried to push his pet projects, define his turf, and expand his base of power, policy priorities were challenged and positions turned over at a rapid rate. The climate, then, throughout the later months of 1953 was at once unstable and yet innovative: unstable in the sense that no procedures or rules of the game had emerged from the process, yet innovative in the sense that a number of new approaches and ideas were aired. That the 1953 succession was a "crisis," then, spoke in one sense at least to its capacity to unleash new policies and new leaders on the system. And the power conflicts brought on by the crisis served only to further enhance the prospects for innovation.

Thus, succession "crises" can be seen not just as crises, but also as antechambers for new public policies. In the 1953 case this was clearly evident in the tripartite struggle among Beria, Malenkov, and Khrushchev. The first to founder was Beria, whose access to the Secret Police and fostering of national irredentism frightened his colleagues on the Praesidium (now the Politburo). He was executed in July 1953. The struggle then centered on the two leaders who had been since the late 1940's Stalin's heirs apparent, Malenkov and Khrushchev. This battle settled into a fight over policy priorities; while Khrushchev argued for the necessity of reforms and increased investment in agriculture, Malenkov placed consumer goods and peaceful coexistence at the center of his vision of the post-Stalinist world. Khrushchev eventually won, precisely because he succeeded in convincing the upper reaches of the Party that agriculture was *the* critical issue of the time, and that he had at least some answers to most of the problems in that sector of the economy. Thus, Khrushchev took the initiative, seized upon a key issue, and promised important changes. By contrast, Malenkov was vulnerable on agriculture and failed to capture the hearts and minds of the elites with his policy proposals. It is therefore fair to say that Khrushchev rose to power in part by riding on the back of the agricultural crisis, just as Stalin had ridden industrialization and "socialism in one country" before him.

But how was Khrushchev able to so successfully exploit the agriculture issue? Any attempt to answer this question would have to begin with recognition of the pauperized state of Soviet agriculture in the postwar era in the Soviet Union. The war, of course, had done great damage, but perhaps even more debilitating was the decades-old policy of forcing agriculture to bear the costs of industrialization; not only was investment squeezed from the agricultural sector by extracting surplus product, but its very base had atrophied as a response to the collectivization campaigns. Deportation and death of millions of peasants, destruction of the land and cattle by overzealous party lieutenants and angry peasants (in 1932, for example, grain output and livestock production were below the 1917 level), and class war between kulaks and other peasants had all left a ravaged countryside—an unwilling and flimsy base for the industrialization drive (Strauss, 1969:304-305). In addition, Stalin's commitment to moral (not material) incentives for agricultural production and the establishment of centralized political control in the rural area contributed greatly to the political and economic pressures on the rural areas in the Stalinist era. The result was a widening gap between urban and rural areas, extreme deprivation in the countryside, inefficiency and low productivity, and alienation of the peasants from the regime. The legacy of Stalin, then, in the agricultural sector was a very negative one:

> There can be no question that the long-run effects have been extremely deleterious and extraordinarily difficult and costly to reverse. The relatively poor performance of agricultural enterprises today and the persisting backwardness of the contemporary rural community are direct consequences of both what was done and what was left undone . . . during the Stalinist phase. . . . (Millar, 1971:xi-xii; also see, for a more revisionist view, Millar, 1977).

But while agriculture was indeed in a state of crisis in the postwar period, Stalin was not convinced that organizational problems and deficient investment were the major reasons behind the lag in the agricultural sector. He maintained to the end a belief that coercion, centralization and moral exhortation—rhetoric and repression, rather than rubles—were the keys to increasing agricultural productivity. Thus, Soviet agriculture was being strangled because Stalin saw agriculture as merely the fodder for industrialization, rather than as a sector deserving investment in its own right.

However much Stalin tried to ignore the agriculture issue, it did keep coming up primarily because several of his major lieutenants—Malenkov and Khrushchev—were very interested in the issue, and because agriculture lagged far behind industry in recovering from the war. In 1949 after a series of purges which sought to reaffirm the hard line in political control, economic organization, and cultural affairs, Stalin brought Khrushchev to Moscow as a counterweight to his heir apparent, Georgi Malenkov. When Khrushchev arrived, agriculture was already a hot issue. He himself had done some critiques of agriculture prior to and after the war. Somewhat later, the Zhdanov and anti-Tito purges of 1948 and 1949 took aim at Nikolai Voznesensky, an economist whom Stalin had appointed as postwar director of agricultural recovery. Thus, by 1949 agricultural policy was in some dispute, and its low productivity was widely recognized among the upper reaches of the Party.

From 1949 until Stalin's death, Khrushchev proposed a number of agricultural innovations, including a scheme to merge *kolkhozes* into (nearly) self-sufficient communities, or *agrogorods*. This idea received support from Stalin, until its impracticability became apparent. While Malenkov scored some points as a result, Khrushchev and others did succeed in keeping the agricultural issue alive. Stalin tolerated these ideas, in part because he needed to balance Malenkov and in part because Khrushchev was at least correct in the observation that agriculture was indeed lagging far behind industry, and that the gap was growing larger after the war. In fact, it took until the early 1950's for Soviet agricultural output to reach its 1940 level, and even then grain shortages were widespread.

Thus, the last years of Stalin were years of seeking to resolve the crisis in agriculture; some heavy doses of complacency were coupled with much self-criticism. On the one hand, Malenkov, trying to squelch the issue, could claim in 1952 at the Nineteenth Party Congress that "the grain problem, formerly considered the most acute problem, has thus been solved successfully once and for all" (quoted in Mills, 1970:380; also see Ploss, 1965:53; McCauley, 1976; Millar, 1977). However, on the other hand, a flurry of agricultural decisions, moving from a policy of more investment and higher prices in 1946-1948 to a more centralized, coercive approach from 1948 to 1953, indicated that agriculture was a problem and that the proper stance towards the issue was a matter of some debate. Khrushchev, then, with the tacit cooperation of Stalin and the impetus of a stalled agricultural sector, had created a political issue.

It was no wonder that agriculture came to the fore as a major issue in the months following Stalin's death; it was already on the docket and served conveniently to divide

Khrushchev from Malenkov. The "availability" of the issue, however, was only part of the story; another was that in 1953 agriculture was faring unusually badly, especially in comparison with the record harvest in 1952. While agricultural investment from 1950 to 1953 comprised on the average 14.7 percent of all capital investment in the economy, in 1953 the comparable figure was only 13.6 percent (Khrushchev, 1962, Vol. I:7-84). The result of this decline was readily evident; after two years of increasing output, agricultural productivity in 1953 fell back to the 1940 level. Thus, agriculture jumped rather easily to the top of the policy agenda immediately after Stalin's death.

The final factor that guaranteed a pivotal role for agriculture in the succession had to do with Khrushchev's credentials as a contender for power. Malenkov was rather deficient in agricultural expertise and could not dominate the Party dialogue on this topic. His political experience was largely in the state apparatus in heavy industry, not in agriculture, light industry, or even party affairs. Moreover, he had no ready list of new policies; while he defined problems, he provided few specific solutions. By contrast, Khrushchev had a great deal of experience in agriculture (and in industry as well, which is also important), and had since the middle 1940's developed a number of policy ideas. Khrushchev, it seems, behaved and was seen as an innovator whose ideas and expertise provided a good way out of the agricultural dilemma (and, later, other problems), and eventually out of the succession crisis as well (Fainsod, 1965). His impact, moreover, was enhanced by both the centrality of the issue to the party cadres and by Malenkov's vulnerability—after all, it was Malenkov who declared an end to the grain crisis, just a year before Stalin's departure. Thus, Khrushchev identified himself as a leader who could get the Soviet Union moving again, and he used agriculture as one base of his appeal (Breslauer, 1976).

His first step was at the September 1953 plenum of the Central Committee, a meeting which both Soviet and

American observers agree was one of two major turning points in Soviet agriculture in the postwar era (the other being the 1965 plenum) (Volkov, 1972; Danilov, 1972; Grossman, 1976; Anisimov, 1975; Karcz, 1965).[1] While, like most policy innovations, the dramatic results reflected in fact a great deal of previous ideas and thinking on the subject, this plenum nevertheless ushered in a new approach to Soviet agriculture. Khrushchev, just elected First Secretary of the Party, seasoned his keynote address with pointed criticisms of the agricultural sector. For example, he noted (Khrushchev, 1962, Vol. I:10) that "the rate of growth in agriculture has clearly lagged behind the rate of growth in industry. . . . It is sufficient to say that from 1940-1952 industrial output grew 2.3 times, while agriculture increased by only ten percent." From this rather negative appraisal of agriculture, Khrushchev proceeded to call for a number of measures which were designed to ease the economic burden on the countryside, to make country life more tolerable, and to enhance agricultural productivity. Specifically, he called for: (1) a large increase in agricultural procurement prices; (2) a reduction in *kolkhoz* taxes; (3) increases in collective farm pay; (4) greater economic incentives for over-production; (5) stabilization of delivery quotas; (6) expansion of acreage farmed (especially the corn crop); (7) an increase in agricultural investment, both in absolute terms and in the share contributed by the state (as opposed to the *kolkhozes*); and, finally, (8) the expansion of educational, cultural, and mechanical facilities in the countryside. However, in addition to pumping up peasant

---

[1] However, Volkov (1975) has argued that many of the ideas Khrushchev presented in 1953 were the culmination of previous work done by a number of committees in the Central Committee from 1949 to 1953. Given what is known about the origins of new policies in the West (that even the most striking deviations from past practices have in fact simmered a long time in various private and public arenas), Volkov's point is well taken. However, this does not diminish the fact that Khrushchev was responsible for placing these ideas squarely on the public agenda.

income and expanding their resources and access to education and culture, Khrushchev also proposed, as he was to do later in other sectors of the polity, greater Party control over the agricultural sector. It was his view that the Party should provide more economic incentives to peasants to produce more, and that the Party should more directly participate in and furnish expertise to agrarian decision-making. In his words, "we need to move agricultural decision-making closer to production" (Khrushchev, 1962, Vol. I:73). Thus, Khrushchev remained true to the policy proposals he had suggested throughout his career; that is, greater local Party control, more investment, and the use of economic as well as moral incentives.

All of Khrushchev's proposals at the plenum were ratified by the Central Committee. In one week, Soviet agriculture was transformed from the captive mistress of industrialization to its partner. If all these innovations were not enough, Khrushchev also pushed, from the September plenum through March 1954, a program to expand productivity by enlarging acreage under cultivation to include the so-called virgin land areas (*tselinnyi krai*) of North Kazakhstan, Siberia, the Urals, and the North Caucusus (McCauley, 1976; Mills, 1970; Cleary, 1965; Durgin, 1962). When he first proposed this idea, it was a small program acceptable to local leaders in Kazakhstan as well as to his colleagues (with the exception of Molotov, the ringleader of the heavy industry lobby). However, after discussing its potential with a number of leaders and experts throughout the fall and early winter, Khrushchev became more and more committed to a policy of "upturning the virgin soil" on a gigantic scale.

Why he became more radical in his goals is not hard to answer. First, Khrushchev—the moderate tone of his speech in September notwithstanding—was most likely very worried about the state of Soviet agriculture. His experiences from 1938 (when he became First Secretary of the Ukraine) to 1953 had driven home to him the frailty of

Soviet agriculture. When the enormity of the 1953 agricultural crisis became apparent after the September plenum, Khrushchev must have become even more desperate to find some solution to the seemingly capricious nature of agricultural production. One can cite other factors that influenced Khrushchev's decision as well, such as his career-long willingness to experiment with new policy approaches, and the advice of some experts at the time that such a program was indeed plausible. But perhaps the best explanation is that Khrushchev was in a hurry, and the innovations of September would take too much time to transform agriculture into a productive sector of the economy. Khrushchev wanted quick results that would demonstrate his competence, expand his coalition of support, and make Malenkov's initiatives pale by comparison.[2]

Thus, throughout the fall and winter Khrushchev expanded his projections about the size of the virgin lands project and simultaneously tried to force a recalcitrant Kazakh party apparatus to go along. They resisted Khrushchev because his grandiose plans would place tremendous pressures on them, would most likely fail to provide adequate resources to fulfill objectives, and would interfere unnecessarily with internal Kazakh affairs. Following a number of purges after which he installed his own men, Pyotr Ponomarenko and Leonid Brezhnev, to lead the Kazakhstan party apparatus, Khrushchev eventually won the battle. In January 1954, addressing a series of agricultural conferences that just "happened" to convene sequentially in Moscow, Khrushchev began escalating the scope of his program. In February alone, he gave four speeches on agriculture—to the Komsomol, the Machine Tractor Station Conference, a *kolkhoz* association, and, finally, a plenum of the Central Committee. By the February/March

---

[2] It is interesting to note the similarity here between Presidents and First Secretaries: they need fast results and are often drawn to policies that will achieve this. See, for example, Adam Yarmolinsky (1969) and Schon (1971:123-158).

plenum, the virgin lands program was finally approved, and Khrushchev's aggressive use of this policy had finally paid off. The result was, what Roy Laird (1965:106) has called, "the most significant departure in Soviet agricultural policy since collectivization." In 1955, Malenkov submitted his resignation; he had lost out to a more innovative and more widely experienced contender, who had found salient issues that appealed to the Party faithful, and who had bested him in terms of other qualifications as well.[3]

Of course, Khrushchev's troubles were not over with the departure of Malenkov; he still had the "anti-Party" group with which to contend. In the coming years he introduced a number of new policies in a variety of arenas which sought to challenge the pretenders to his throne, expand his coalition of support, and realize his own policy objectives. Whatever their inspiration, though, the new policies of the Khrushchev era, which seemed clustered at the beginning and at the end of his rule, were numerous, reflecting both the conditional nature of his power base and his penchant for experimentation. One can point, for example, to innovations in foreign policy, such as peaceful coexistence (which was Malenkov's idea initially); rapprochement with Tito; traveling abroad to the United States, China, Czechoslovakia, and Austria; de-Stalinization; polycentrism (with its attendant externalities); and expanded relations with

---

[3] It is, of course, difficult to explain leaders' motivations for particular actions, and I will not presume to do so here. However, I do think that the issue of whether leaders treat issues as a football or as deeply held ideological concerns is something that is too often treated as an either/or proposition. In many cases—such as the case study here—leaders do manipulate issues, but their stance is often consonant with long-held beliefs. For examples of the degree to which leaders *choose* which issues to manipulate in accordance with their ideology and prevailing conditions, see Tilton (1979), Putnam (1973 and 1971), Blackmer (1975), and Brown (1971). The general point seems to be that leaders do have ideologies and do learn and adjust those ideologies to the needs—broadly defined—of the moment (i.e., power, structural forces, coalitional considerations, and the like).

Third World nations. Social welfare benefits, liberalization in the arts, the 1958 educational reform, increases in national disposable income, the many administrative reforms of the Party and the state, and the dramatic expansion of urban housing are all examples of the innovative thrust of domestic policy-making during the Khrushchev years (Breslauer, 1976; Osborn, 1970; Bunce, 1980a and 1980b; DiMaio, 1974). Khrushchev was a leader who indeed made a difference.

But at some points in time he seemed to make more of a difference than in other periods, and this is abundantly clear in the case of agricultural policy. There is ample evidence that agricultural innovations followed a succession cycle, increasing when Khrushchev was building his mandate and tapering off once he became dominant in 1958 after the defeat of the anti-Party group. To take the virgin-lands program as one example, from 1954 to 1958 the program surpassed all expectations in its scope and success (see Table 6-1). In the first three years, ninety million acres (an area about three times the size of England) were ploughed up, of which about three-fourths could be farmed to advantage. All told, the virgin-lands policy by 1961 had expanded the total crop land of the USSR by 30 percent (including increases in Kazakhstan of 300 percent and in the RSFSR of 40 percent). Several hundred completely new rural settlements went up, millions of workers "went East," and Kazakhstan surpassed the Ukraine—the Russian "breadbasket"—as second only to the RSFSR in grain production (McCauley, 1976:82; Strauss, 1969:188-189). Moreover, Soviet grain production as a whole dramatically increased during this period, with grain increases averaging 8.3 percent per year, a growth rate far outstripping the previous annual average in the postwar era of 2.3 percent. The virgin lands, it has been calculated, contributed some 70 percent to this rise in output. Thus, while there were a number of snags—particularly with housing, and the planting, harvesting, storage, and transport of grain—the program in its early years was clearly a success. The virgin lands program, then, was doing precisely what it was supposed to do: providing that "extra" that would cushion Soviet agriculture from its oscillating yields. Agricultural autarky in the Soviet Union by the mid-1950's, therefore, seemed to be for the first time a possibility.

TABLE 6-1
Indicators of Soviet Agricultural Performance

	Crop Production (1913 = 100)	Livestock Production (millions of metric tons)	Grain (millions of metric tons)	Of Which Virgin Lands	Gross Agricultural Production (billions of rubles, 1973 prices)
1950	151	118	81.2	—	48.9
1951	133	126	78.7	—	45.6
1952	148	129	92.2	—	49.2
1953	148	141	82.5	26.9	51.0
1954	153	153	85.6	37.2	53.6
1955	175	160	103.7	27.7	59.6
1956	201	177	125.0	63.2	67.6
1957	198	196	102.6	38.1	69.1
1958	227	205	134.7	58.4	76.5
1959	215	221	119.5	54.6	76.9
1960	226	219	125.5	58.1	78.7
1961	230	229	130.8	—	81.0
1962	229	235	140.2	—	81.9
1963	209	221	107.5	—	75.8
1964	270	217	152.1	—	86.8

Sources: Strauss (1969:303-304): Durgin (1962:237-254); Narodnoe Khoziaistvo SSSR za 60 let: iubeleinyi statisticheskii ezhegodnik (1977:272-273).

A similar picture of optimism and innovation can be presented with respect to other areas of agriculture in the early Khrushchev years. For example, in their survey of rural income in the Soviet Union, David Bronson and Constance Kreuger (1971:221-222) concluded that "the most rapid growth (in farm incomes) occurred immediately following the accession to power of new regimes." Thus, from 1954 to 1955 farm wages went up 70 percent, and by 1958 they

had in fact doubled. These increases reflected the new policies announced in September 1953: higher wages, higher
procurement prices (which increased threefold from 1953
to 1958), economic incentives for overproduction, more
sensitivity to regional crop limitations, and, finally, larger
investment and supply inputs from the state. In addition
to this veritable "revolution in peasant income," one can
point to a dramatic increase in the number of trained specialists in the countryside: a fourfold expansion from 1953
to 1963, again more dramatic in the early years immediately
following Stalin's death (Denisov, 1971). There was also
remarkable growth in Soviet agricultural investment, which
comprised one-fifth of all investment from 1953 to 1958
as compared with a mere one-eighth of all investment from
1948 to 1953 (Dibb, 1969).

Thus, it is fair to say that the dramatic innovations announced in September 1953 and the February/March
plenum of the following year were indeed implemented
with dramatic effects. Just as Khrushchev had promised,
agricultural output increased, state investment in agriculture was expanded, the economic life of the peasantry became far more bearable, and the local party organs became
more involved in agricultural policy-making. In the early
years, Nikita Khrushchev was a grandiose politician with
rather grandiose results.

Unfortunately for the peasantry and eventually for
Khrushchev himself, by 1958 the success story was clouded
over by falling yields, declining investment, and a slowdown
in the socio-economic transformation of the countryside
(Gubenko, 1975; Tiurina, 1972). To take the virgin-lands
policy first, one can readily see from Table 6-1 that the
early successes indeed withered away, culminating in a dis-
astrous crop in 1963. The growth rate in agricultural output from 1958 to 1964, for example, was one-fourth the
rate reported in the previous six years (Brezhnev, 1970,
Vol. I:318). In fact, if one calculates gross farm output in
per-capita terms, agricultural productivity in the last years

of Khrushchev's rule never again reached the high reported for 1958. As I. M. Volkov (1973:50), a Soviet expert on agriculture, has summarized, "the second half of the fifties and the first half of the sixties in particular marked a seamy side of life for agriculture, reflecting the implementation of measures which underestimated the needs of the kolkhozes and the sovkhozes."

What went wrong? One can point to a number of factors, most of which Soviet analysts themselves have readily admitted. First, the virgin lands gave declining yields because of decreasing inputs, overcultivation, the use of high-yield wheat which depleted the soil, huge personnel turnover, *shablon* (or administrative stereo-typing and rigidity), and the natural decline one expects when new lands lose their virginity. In his desire for success, Khrushchev, against the advice of many experts, refused to leave enough land fallow. In dry land areas, the usual practice is to leave about 40 percent fallow a year; in Khrushchev's time, however, 15 percent was more the norm. The result was the beginning of a dust bowl. In addition, Khrushchev failed to recognize the inevitable capriciousness of dry-land farming and based his expectations for future yields on the bumper crop of 1958, a crop that even surpassed in yield the outputs characteristic of a highly developed monoculture like Manitoba (Durgin, 1962; Cleary, 1965; McCauley, 1976:66-80). These unrealistic goals diverted rubles from European Russia to the virgin lands in order to fulfill the plan. Thus, safer bets were, essentially, abandoned for long shots in the virgin lands.

But all of this would not have been so detrimental had not Khrushchev begun to substitute moral exhortations, Party interference, and administrative reorganizations for monetary incentives in agriculture. From 1958 to 1964 there were five major agricultural reorganizations; the Machine Tractor Stations were sold (at too high a price and with inadequate supplies for upkeep) to collective farms, thus beginning a decline once again into poverty for many farms; procurement prices remained steady, and some even declined (as in 1958, for example, in response to a bumper crop); delivery quotas were increased; and the government failed to modernize the agricultural sector through fertilizer, irrigation, and machine supplies. Finally, as Brezhnev and Volkov have reiterated a number of times in their diagnoses of the problems in this period, the political climate—combining pressure to produce with a seeming endless supply of "subjective" decisions from Moscow with inadequate resources—thoroughly demoralized Party and state officials (Volkov, 1973; Brezhnev, 1970, Vol. I:68-70). All of this meant essentially that both peasants and cadres were asked to produce more with much less, substituting their grit for rubles. It would seem that Stalin had indeed returned from his grave.

But the issue then remains: why did Khrushchev change his strategy? One common interpretation of this change is that by Werner Hahn (1972:30), who argues that Khrushchev's

> reliance on innovations in techniques and organization, rather than new investment to aid agricultural production was not entirely voluntary. While he was able to force through his ideas on crops, agrotechniques, and reorganization . . . , he was much less successful when proposing more investment in agriculture (which had to come from industry and defense).

However, this explanation of a deficit of power correlating with policy retreats does not jell with the successes of 1953 to 1958, when, supposedly, Khrushchev was merely building his mandate. After 1958 and the defeat of the anti-Party, Khrushchev was, purportedly, more powerful and, therefore, should have been freer than ever to increase agricultural investment. Yet, he did not do so and in fact did quite the opposite: clearly, another explanation is needed.

One interpretation that seems to fit the data better is to argue that Khrushchev, like chief executives in the West, was a victim of his successes as well as of his failures. Khrushchev talked big in 1953 and 1954, and by 1956 and 1957 had in fact delivered much of what he had promised. Given that most Soviet elites have been trained to emphasize heavy industry and essentially guarantee only that agriculture survives, there is most likely a tendency to look for any indicator of success in agriculture as an excuse to abandon it for more "important" policy arenas. Thus, as Brezhnev was to find out in 1967, so Khrushchev learned that agricultural investment is hard to increase if no compelling case can be made for a pressing "need" or "crisis" in the policy area.

This interpretation is further buttressed by the argument that power is for most leaders a fixed sum. Taking advantage of the openness of the system for change in 1953 and 1954, Khrushchev had put through his agricultural innovations by eliciting support from a number of quarters. Similarly, his defeat of the anti-Party group had in all likelihood entailed a number of deals and favors as well. Thus, while Khrushchev seemed to be sitting on top of the system in 1958, uniquely free of agricultural woes and demands from the anti-Party opposition, he was, it would appear, severely constrained by the very debts he had contracted to expand his power. Ironically, he seems to have won only by forfeiting some of his power.

Moreover, by 1957-1958 the climate for bold change had passed, leaving a desire for consolidation among the ruling elite in its wake. Khrushchev seems to have increasingly reverted to symbolic and administrative innovations and abandoned monetary incentives in the later years of his administration, precisely because the time for such change was gone. The succession crisis was over, and as a result Khrushchev had lost much of his capability to change agriculture:

In domestic affairs Khrushchev suffered the fate of many essentially conservative transitional figures who undertake to build a bridge from the old to the new. As the limits within which he was prepared to tolerate change became apparent, his reputation as an innovator dimmed. His early accomplishments and bold initiatives tended to be taken for granted and forgotten, while he found himself increasingly measured by the expectations that he had aroused and failed to fulfill (Fainsod, 1965:132).

Thus, just as was argued in the quantitative analysis in Chapter Five, it can be suggested here that what Khrushchev lost in his later years in office was the *power* to change policy. As a result, agricultural policy, just as was the case for budgetary and investment priorities, tends to change the most early in the administration, when chief executives are new and powerful, and to become routinized soon after, as the administration ages, conflict hardens, and new coalitions become harder to form.

It is also reasonable to suggest that the spirit became weak as well. Khrushchev was a product of Stalinism, and this showed in his career-long concern with moral incentives and the role of the Party as an energizer in policy-making and implementation. Moreover, he had risen through the ranks by virtue of his propensity to experiment with new approaches and policies which did not involve changes in investment outlays and hence threats to pre-existing coalitions. But in the case of his early initiatives in agriculture, he had gone against these lessons of his past and used money instead of moral exhortations and structural rearrangements as a stimulus for higher agricultural productivity. It is no wonder, then, given the inevitable monetary constraints, that when the expanded inputs did not produce a commensurate rise in outputs, Khrushchev turned increasingly back to more familiar and less costly policy ploys. This line of argument would explain, for instance, why he consistently came up with new alternatives throughout his tenure, from Lysenkoism to massive corn planting to an expansion of chemical fertilizer production, which would spur productivity without threatening other economic sectors and the powerful interests formed around those sectors (see, for example, Khrushchev, 1964, Vol. 8:454-455). Khrushchev was not just cheap; he valued highly the power of new techniques, ideas, and approaches. Just as the virgin lands program had given him fast, but essentially declining, results, so might other approaches have similar dramatic, if diminishing, returns. Thus, Khrushchev's policy style, along with pressure from other elites and the natural withering away of power and innovation over the course of an administration, explain why 1953-1954 represented the height of agricultural innovation and investment levels during his term of office.

It is, of course, one of the great ironies of power politics in socialist states that the very issues on which the leader rode into power often become the very issues which signal his downfall. By 1964 Khrushchev had suffered a number of policy failures and defeats, and was criticized for his penchant for disrupting "politics as usual." Clearly, one important indictment was the 1963 grain debacle which forced the Soviets to buy grain abroad. This hurt because of the commitment to autarky, and because of Khrushchev's dramatization of the agricultural issue and his expertise in that area. Thus, failures in agriculture provided at least one reason for the Central Committee's vote of no confidence in the fall of 1964.

However, before one too readily criticizes Khrushchev for his handling of agriculture in the twilight of his years in office, one would do well to remember the epitaph written by Jerczy Karcz:

> Suffice it to say that Khrushchev's preoccupation with agriculture, harmful as it was in many respects, has nevertheless succeeded in placing the farm problem squarely on the nation's agenda of unfinished business.

. . . It is in this sense, perhaps, that he has partially determined the course that his successors are now following (Karcz, 1965:134; Volkov, 1975).[4]

As will be clear below, the next succession crisis was every bit as permeated with the agriculture issue as was the battle for Stalin's mantle, and the pattern of innovation followed a similar cycle of dramatic change followed by marginal adjustments later on in the administration.

The Khrushchev Succession

While agriculture was, of course, a major issue that foreshadowed the downfall of Khrushchev in the autumn of 1964, it would be too simplified to assert that the 1963 drought was the only reason. Rather, this crisis was merely indicative of any number of problems that were "cropping up" in that sector. As Leonid Brezhnev has pointed out, all the statistics by 1964 pointed to a general agricultural crisis; from 1960 to 1965 the average annual increase in output had plummeted to less than 2 percent a year, investment was down to only 7.5 percent of all economic investment, and more and more inputs were needed to produce the same level of output. Lysenko, Khrushchev's favored geneticist, was unmasked as a fraud, the morale of party cadres was seen to be very low, and the virgin lands program was in ruins (Nove, 1970; Kulakov, 1975). With regard to the last indicator, D. A. Kunaev (1972:23-24), First Secretary of the Kazakhstan Central Committee in that period, argued (contrary to Khrushchev's glowing projections) that the virgin lands project really petered out after the highpoint of 1956-1958:

---

[4] This conclusion of Khrushchev as an agenda-setter and Brezhnev as the "doer" is remarkably similar (for similar reasons) to the roles of Kennedy and Johnson in policy regarding poverty. Major innovations do seem to require two such stages to develop, East and West.

Until the October 1964 plenum of the Central Committee of the Communist Party of the Soviet Union, the rate of growth of agriculture in Kazakhstan was slow. Among other things, there was insufficient attention paid to objective economic laws, the material needs of the workers, and there were serious deficiencies in agricultural equipment and supplies. Insufficient capital investment and material technical resources were directed to the agriculture sector. . . . However, after the March 1965 plenum, there was a turning point in agriculture, which opened up the possibility of utilizing our vast resources.

If one transgression stands out in all of these exercises in *samokritika*, it is the related charges of subjectivism and *kampaneishchina* (Brezhnev, 1970, Vol. I:68-71). L. Ia. Florient'iev (1975), recounting Khrushchev's sins, makes what is a fairly typical appraisal of agriculture under Khrushchev:

The March 1965 plenum of the Central Committee of the Communist Party of the Soviet Union signified the beginning of the modern stage in the development of agriculture. This plenum listed the reasons for deficiencies in agriculture, including among them subjectivism and voluntarism in leadership and most of all insufficient heed paid to the laws of socialist principles of material incentives . . . insufficient planning, financing, and pricing in agriculture, intolerable administrative practices, and groundless interference by the leadership organs which resulted in irresponsible . . . work.

Brezhnev has echoed much the same point any number of times throughout his term of office. For example, in 1965 he called "for an end to subjectivism" (Brezhnev, 1970, Vol. I:68-71), and in 1976, at the Twenty-Fifth Party Congress, he argued (1976:7) that "the Leninist style of work is alien to subjectivism and is imbued with a scientific approach to the resolution of all social problems." Thus, Khrushchev was deemed guilty on a number of counts: his administrative techniques, investment practices, policy priorities, and, ultimately, of course, his overall performance in office. And one area where all of these deficiencies were well represented was agriculture.

These criticisms, of course, prefigured the agricultural innovations introduced by Khrushchev's successors—Leonid Brezhnev, who succeeded his mentor as head of the Party, and Aleksei Kosygin, who became head of the state apparatus. Just as with the 1953 crisis, so in 1964 the succession was followed immediately by dramatic shifts in agricultural policy. The first changes involved retraction of several of Khrushchev's innovations: the Ministry of Agriculture under V. Matskevich was restored to full administrative powers, and the 1962 bifurcation of the Party apparatus into agricultural and industrial sectors was rescinded (see Brown, 1975). In addition, Lysenko's influence was reduced sharply.

However, the real innovations came in a package of reforms at the March 1965 plenum of the Central Committee, a meeting which numerous Soviet analysts have paired with the September 1953 plenum as the most important statements about agricultural policy in the postwar era (Voss, 1975:168-170). As Khrushchev did in 1953, Brezhnev allied himself quickly and completely in 1965 with the agricultural lobby and gave the keynote address at the March plenum. The thrust of his proposals was that agricultural investment must increase, rational planning must replace "subjectivism," the economic viability of the *kolkhozes* and *sovkhozes* must be guaranteed, and further investments must be devoted to the fertilizer production, land reclamation, further linkages between industry and agriculture, and mechanization of farm production (Anisimov, 1975; Bush, 1974; Brezhnev, 1974:97-98). Thus, Brezhnev's message was that the agricultural sector needed more money, more stable expectations about inputs and performance, and modernization in its techniques and supplies. The irony is that many of these ideas echo those presented by Khrushchev a decade before; however, Brezhnev seems more inclined (for whatever reason) to stick with them throughout his term of office.

Despite these similarities, though, Brezhnev did reveal in 1965 some new thinking about agriculture. For example, he did not promise fast results; rather, he took (in his favorite words) a "business like approach" (*praktichnyi podkhod*), emphasizing that: "the problems in agriculture are such that in one or two or even five years the problems will not be solved" (Brezhnev, 1972, Vol. III:245; Brezhnev, 1973). Second, Brezhnev took a clear stand on economic incentives: "We must orient ourselves toward an increasingly direct dependence between the pay of the individual workers and the end result of their activity" (Brezhnev, 1975a:1). This commitment led to some important policy results: procurement quotas were lowered in 1965 and remained stable until 1970 (when they were raised a small amount and again held fairly steady up to the present); investment in agriculture from 1966 to 1970 by the state was to equal all previous investment from 1945 (this in fact was not quite realized); cancellation of *kolkhoz* debts (which had been primarily incurred through the sale of Machine Tractor Stations); reduction in the prices of tractors and trucks; increases in pension benefits; and, finally, raises in wages through premium prices paid for overproduction, the introduction of a guaranteed wage, sharp increases in the percentage of profits retained by the farms, and the loosening up of restrictions on private plot farming (Bronson and Krueger, 1971; Volkov, 1975; Clarke, 1968; Maier, 1974; Brezhnev, 1970, Vol. I:431 and 1972, Vol. II:208).

Clearly, in introducing these ideas, Brezhnev was taking the position that agriculture needs a secure economic base, that "throwing money at agricultural problems" in fact makes a lot of sense. Thus, Brezhnev in 1965 and consistently since then has reiterated the point that the peasants will not produce unless they have the incentive to do so. This, as Erich Strauss (1969:296) notes, is Brezhnev's greatest innovation in agriculture: "By abandoning the policy of massive exploitation of the peasantry, the Soviet authorities have removed the biggest single obstacle to a permanent solution of the agricultural difficulties."

The 1965 plenum also introduced a phrase—the creation of a scientific-technical base—that was to underline many of the agricultural innovations of the Brezhnev era, and to separate his approach from his predecessor's. Since he became First Secretary, Brezhnev has repeated a number of times the need for rational (methodical and well informed) decision-making (Brezhnev, 1970, Vol. I:71; Cocks, 1977). In agriculture, this has meant the modernization of the countryside (all the way from increasing the availability of experts, schools, and cultural activities to the expansion of agricultural think tanks that work by contract for collective farms); decentralization of agricultural planning; and the proliferation of inter-*kolkhoz* associations and agro-industrial complexes. The rural areas have in fact become more attractive and more self-sufficient, along with becoming more efficient and effective economic units. While progress has been slow, the point remains that Brezhnev has since the 1965 plenum sought to pull agriculture into the modern world (Barkaiskas, 1973).

Finally, any list of the innovations introduced at the 1965 plenum would be incomplete if agricultural investment priorities were not noted. While there were few direct attacks on the goals of the virgin lands project in 1965 (Brezhnev, after all, had been Khrushchev's lieutenant in Kazakhstan), it has been clear that Brezhnev has reordered priorities to give more weight to the non-*chernozem* (non-black earth) areas of the Soviet Union, including Belorussia, the Baltic republics, and North and West Russia (Mills, 1976). In addition, Brezhnev has expanded fallow land, stabilized personnel, sought better equipment and living conditions, and supported measures to reduce the dust-bowl problems developing in the virgin lands. However, he did not abandon Khrushchev's general policy, because, like most leaders, he resisted throwing away previous investment and exposing his own role and that of many of his colleagues in the virgin lands program. Brezhnev felt that the margin of difference allowed by the virgin lands cultivation (providing some 10 percent of total grain purchases in a given year) was necessary, if agricultural autarky was to be achieved, and he—like his predecessors—has been committed to autarky. Thus, Brezhnev's virgin lands policy was similar to Khrushchev's and to that of the agricultural experts prior to the escalation of Khrushchev's demands in 1954 (Brezhnev, 1974 and 1976a:503-505).

As for other agricultural priorities, Brezhnev expanded some of Khrushchev's ideas and rejected others. For example, he built on Khrushchev's last-minute effort to expand the chemicals industry, but abandoned Khrushchev's obsession with corn. In addition, he emphasized livestock production, making it profitable for the first time in years, and invested heavily in irrigation. Brezhnev has also been far more sensitive in his agricultural policies to regional variations in output; thus, poorer farms were allowed lower targets for productivity than their richer counterparts (Bush, 1974; Nove, 1970). Therefore, it seems fair to conclude that, while Khrushchev's solutions involved administrative techniques and extensive farming, Brezhnev approached agricultural innovation as an issue of money and intensive techniques. In the agricultural sphere, they were, despite all their collaboration in the past, very different leaders.

Thus, the 1965 agricultural plenum involved a number of innovations in Soviet agricultural policy. Moreover, the pattern of these innovations, as they related to the ongoing succession struggle, was remarkably similar to the one just chronicled for Khrushchev's rise to power. First, the succession struggle began in a climate of debate about the premises and promises of the existing agricultural system. Next, a policy entrepreneur, Leonid Brezhnev, with access to power through the Party apparatus and credentials in agricultural decision-making (as well as in *many* other arenas) adopted agriculture as a base for his coalition.[5] Rather than passively sitting back, however, Brezhnev quickly made a number of innovative proposals, thereby linking himself with "change" and separating himself from his predecessors as well as from his colleagues. Then, given a chance to show what he could do—a honeymoon period, if you will—Brezhnev, like Khrushchev in his honeymoon, introduced and implemented numerous innovations with the seeming consent of his colleagues in the Politburo.

In the final stage, Brezhnev emerged as "prime inter pares" in part on the basis of his performance in one of his chosen sectors of evaluation, agriculture. However, as with Khrushchev, Brezhnev did have to continue his struggle for power throughout his tenure, as indicated by a continuing series of policy setbacks, changes, and challenges from other rivals from 1964 up to the early 1970's. Unlike Khrushchev, though, Brezhnev avoided changing his tactics or area of issues; instead, he kept working on his original plan. But, just as with his predecessor, so Brezhnev's assault on agriculture in later years never equalled the innovations of the first years of his administration. Never again was policy debate so open, his colleagues so divided and compliant, his desire to make a mark so strong, the linkage between power and policy so tight, and the crises in agriculture policy so apparent. This is precisely why in the statistical analysis (see Chapter Five) and in this case study, one sees innovations bunched at the beginning of new administrations. It is precisely at that point when power and capability, bold policy initiatives and ambition, meet to form new policy priorities.[6]

---

[5] It is abundantly clear, for example, in *Kursom Martovskogo plenuma* (Golikov, 1975) that Brezhnev is credited with being the father of the agricultural innovations announced in 1965.

[6] This entire scenario not only fits the data, but also fits in with many

The diminution of innovation in agricultural policy following the honeymoon period that was outlined for the
Khrushchev era was in fact repeated in the Brezhnev period. Both leaders retreated to some extent from their active posture in the agriculture arena once they introduced
their reform packages. After the avalanche of proposals by
Brezhnev in March 1965, the following years epitomized
Keith Bush's (1974:151) appraisal of Brezhnevian agriculture as "consistent policy consistently implemented." The
thrust of Brezhnev's policies has been to improve life in the
countryside, in the words of the Twenty-Third Congress
(and the two Congresses since), "to reduce the gap between
city and country" and to guard against any decrease in
agricultural investment. His enemies on these policies have
been numerous: GOSPLAN has been singled out several
times for resisting agricultural investment; Kosygin seems
to have wanted excess funds diverted to consumer goods;
Voronov pushed for and lost out on new organizational
techniques (the *zveno* system, or each farm divided into
small work teams) in the countryside and reducing investment in animal husbandry; Shelepin and Shelest fought
against high agricultural investment (and the former
pushed for and never really won higher investment in consumer goods); and, finally, Podgorny fought for and lost
a share of the agricultural limelight. While Brezhnev has
at times seemed to have gone over to heavy industry and
to have lost some important battles in agriculture, his commitment to this area has not in fact waned since 1965. In
1966, for example, Brezhnev's investment priorities came
under attack, in part because the 1965 plenum had been
noticeably vague about the painful investment trade-offs
that the new agricultural policy would involve, and because
the 1964 harvest had turned out to be a bumper crop.
However, he consistently defended the investment levels,

---

theories about policy innovation and the linkage between power and policy
(see, for instance, Walker [1974]; Schon [1970]; Wilson [1966]).

especially after the demotion of Podgorny in late 1965 (see Hahn, 1972:166-235).

Another indication of Brezhnev's continuing commitment to agriculture can be seen in investment levels in agriculture called for in the Five Year Plans and the way in which the media and Brezhnev's speeches have reported successes and failures in agricultural policy. For example, one can point to the fact that, in contrast to the past, agricultural investment has grown faster than total economic investment in *both* the Eighth (1966-1970) and Ninth (1971-1975) Five Year Plans. Or, to cite another case, whenever investment has lagged in the agricultural sector, Brezhnev has pointed this out in a critical tone (Florient'iev, 1975; Brezhnev, 1975; Brezhnev, 1970, Vol. I:1). When agricultural investment is on target, though, it is not unusual to see V. Garbuzov, the Soviet budget director, thank Brezhnev for his support of that policy area (see *Pravda*, Dec. 21, 1973). Thus, Brezhnev is a leader who has based much of his power on the issue of agriculture.

It is clear that Brezhnev takes a particular interest in and assumes special responsibility for agriculture. In March 1975, a Pravda editorial reminded its readers that the basic lines of the successful agricultural policy that had been pursued in recent years had been laid down a decade ago at the March plenum of the Central Committee in 1965 when the principal speech was delivered by Brezhnev (Brown, 1975:209).

It is, therefore, fair to say that Brezhnev, unlike his mentor, has stuck consistently with the reforms and ideas he outlined when he first became head of the Party in 1964. It is no wonder, then, that a recent collection of articles published in the Soviet Union (Golikov, 1975) on agriculture could be entitled *Following the Course of the March Plenum* (*Kursom Martovskogo plenuma*) and would overflow with references to Brezhnev's contributions to the vitality of the agricultural sector in the Soviet Union.

Part of the key to understanding Brezhnev's approach to the agricultural problem, though, lies in his repeated calls for *sblizhenie*, or reducing socio-economic distinctions between the city and the countryside, and the *kolkhoz* and the *sovkhoz*. In 1966 at the Twenty-Third Congress, Brezhnev stressed in his opening address that:

> A critical aspect of the Five Year Plan is that it provides new and serious measures, which allow for greater reduction in the differences in the standard of living in the city and country and simultaneously raising the standard of living of the whole country. The existence of such measures, we feel, will soon erase the difference between city and country, between mental and physical labor. The political implication of these measures is that they will strengthen the unbreakable union between the working class and the peasantry (Brezhnev, 1972, Vol. 2:334; Monov, 1972; Brezhnev, 1976b).

Ten years later, at the Twenty-Fifth Congress, the same goal was articulated, again indicating the consistency of this goal orientation. Thus, given these patterns, one can characterize Brezhnev's agricultural policies as a flurry of innovations in 1965 and 1966, followed by a consistent commitment (with some successes) to see that these changes are fully carried through. The pattern of large change followed by routinization, then, that I found in the quantitative analysis seems to appear once again when the focus is on more programmatic measures of changes in agrarian policy after Brezhnev's accession to power.

The results of Brezhnev's support for the agrarian sector and his commitment to *sblizhenie* have indeed been impressive. From 1965 to 1975, for example, the average monthly pay of collective farmers increased 80 percent and is now nine-tenths the pay of state farm workers. The latter in turn now earn 80 percent of the average wage of industrial and office personnel. These improvements are a function of a number of policies; introduction of a minimum wage for *kolkhozniki* (implemented in 1966 and 1968 and increased in 1974 and 1976); the ratification of income allowances for children of poor families (1974); increases in the purchase price of agricultural produce (in 1970, for example, it was 1.4 times the rate of 1964); and several large increases in social-insurance benefits paid by the state to collective and state farmers (1965 and 1971, for instance) (Simush, 1977; Bunce, 1980a and 1980b). However, the most important contributing factor seems to have been the cumulative effects of differential wage increases (see Chapter Five).

One can in addition point to a number of other changes in the countryside during Brezhnev's tenure as General Secretary. His commitment to decentralized agricultural decision-making has been strong, as revealed in the shift of *sovkhozy* to full self-reliance (*polnyi rashchet*). In addition, the number of *kolkhozy* has declined sharply, while the number of *sovkhozy* has expanded, reflecting Brezhnev's commitment to the abolition of collective farms (Bryan, 1974). The modernization of the rural areas has also been striking; one can cite, for example, the near complete electrification of collective farms; progress in land reclamation, irrigation, and chemicalization (particularly since 1974, the Tenth Anniversary of the virgin lands project); the growth of agro-industrial complexes; unconditional rights of ruralities to passports (passed in 1974); and, finally, the growing access among rural dwellers to secondary and higher educational institutions. Many of these policies are examples of what could be called incremental, yet cumulative innovation—Brezhnev's call for "a realistic complex program" has been the picture of moderation. The results, however, have been the picture of innovation.

Before getting too carried away by Brezhnev's record on agriculture, though, it should be noted that: (1) he has had a number of setbacks; and (2) Soviet agriculture is still inefficient and often ineffective. While in 1965 and 1970, Brezhnev enjoyed major agricultural successes, he has never yet reached either planned investment levels of agricultural output, as stipulated in the Eighth or Ninth Five Year Plans (even though, annually in the 1970's, fixed capital investment was increasing as a proportion of total investment). He has also had his share of agricultural debacles (Seidenstecker, 1974). Consistency in inputs and intentions, then, do not necessarily lead to consistency in outputs. Even in his pet project, animal husbandry, Brezhnev's record is mixed (Klatt, 1976).

Perhaps the most serious indictment of the progress in Soviet agriculture, though, is its inefficiency. No matter how rosy the picture of Soviet agriculture under Brezhnev is, the fact remains that from 1965 to 1974 there has been a doubling of agricultural inputs but only a 50 percent increase in outputs. Moreover, the ratio seems to be getting worse over time; from 1956 to 1970 the return on rubles invested per input was 1.32, while from 1961 to 1965 it was .45. From 1966 to 1968 it fell further to .42. Soviet agriculture, therefore, is expensive to maintain, and this is evident in the huge subsidies the leaders are willing to pay in order to achieve autarky (Feiwel, 1972:622-623; Bush, 1974). Thus, agriculture under Brezhnev has been more productive, but less efficient, and far more responsive to rural needs. Brezhnev's innovations, then, have been won at a very high price.

COMPARING KHRUSHCHEV AND BREZHNEV AS INNOVATORS

Thus, it is fair to say, in view of the discussion above, that agriculture was an important issue in both the 1953 and 1964 successions in the Soviet Union. On the face of it, the two leaders—Khrushchev and Brezhnev—seemed very different in how they approached agriculture. Khrushchev was unwilling to substitute money for moral incentives. He thought flamboyant goals and rhetoric would spur productivity, and he felt that administrative reorganization and unclear role expectations would enhance creativity and outputs. By contrast, Brezhnev learned in Kazakhstan and later in Moscow that such gimmicks lead to rising frustrations and uneven productivity. Thus, he reacted to "hurrah planning" by cloaking major changes in conservative rhetoric, by building slowly but surely an economic base for the agricultural sector, and by emphasizing "rational" decision-making, and a consistent, complete agricultural program. Most of all, though, he took a strong stand on the need for increased agricultural investment, and he stuck to it. In these ways, Khrushchev and Brezhnev took on the agricultural issue in very different ways, each reacting to the problems bequeathed by their predecessors, to the "Zeitgeist" of the party, and to their previous political experiences.

Yet, despite these contrasts, in one important way, they were very similar: they addressed the agricultural issue over the course of their terms with a parallel patterned response. Both Khrushchev and Brezhnev began their administrations with a number of innovative proposals and then spent their tenure trying to put them through. Both leaders used agriculture (and other issues) to expand their power and to win their respective struggles for power. In the two cases, the succession crisis was foreshadowed by debates on the agricultural sector—its performance in 1953 *and* 1964 was considered substandard. While Soviet agriculture has a habit (as is evident from the discussion so far) of foundering every few years, bold initiatives in that sector are rare, except right after succession. Failure in agriculture, then, does not ensure action, except, for the most part, during the course of a succession struggle. Thus, as the agricultural case indicates, there seem to be several preconditions for a crisis to lead to policy innovation in socialist systems: decision-makers must recognize and publicize the crisis, and they must see the exploitation of such failures as advantageous to their careers. Crises in and of themselves are not necessarily forcing actions; they are only if coupled with political ambitions, with the needs of leaders to create issues and innovative proposals. In this sense, it may be misleading to treat innovation as a natural response to crisis, or to assume that leaders respond objectively to failures in performance. They respond when it is in their interest to do so and in ways that reflect a mixture of their own policy concerns, their power needs, and the prevailing state of the system.[7] For both Khrushchev and Brezhnev, such was the case with agriculture, particularly in the period immediately following succession. They chose to exploit the issue, whereas others around them did not, and they used it to win their respective succession struggles.

Agriculture was high on their list of policy priorities, both because it was a sector in trouble and because of their career backgrounds. Both men had strong ties to the country in their childhood, and spent a great deal of time there in their Party work. This made them aware, not just of rural economic problems, but also political ones—the peasants were hostile to the regime and Party penetration in the countryside was spotty at best. These problems were magnified by the dubious status of agriculture in the Soviet economy, which became obvious by the postwar era. Thus, the career backgrounds of both Khrushchev and Brezhnev evidenced a long-time concern with agriculture and a fair amount of expertise in rural affairs (see Morozow, 1973). This, of course, made them aware of the issue and its implications, and gave them an aura of authority when they eventually addressed the agricultural problems in their bids for power.

In addition to these rather personal factors, one can point to several external considerations that worked to accentuate the importance of the agriculture issue, particularly during succession crises. One is the fear—a legacy of Lenin, Stalin,

---

[7] It is, of course, the case that succession is a dependent as well as an independent variable; that is, succession occurs often in response to poor policy performance, which necessitates change after succession (a developmental sequence). However, as shall be noted below, succession is critical because of the power and policy dynamics it generates.

and the Civil War—that the agricultural sector would somehow hold back the progress of the urban areas and stall the
drive to communism. For instance, when Brezhnev and
Khrushchev pushed for agricultural development, they
usually emphasized its vital contribution to the ultimate
power and modernization of the country as a whole. In
between the lines, one can at times see a hint of fear, that
at some point the exploitation of agriculture would go too
far and there would be heavy economic and political costs
to pay. Agricultural development was, therefore, both a
political and an economic issue—if the Soviet Union was
to be really modern *and* politically stable, it had to have a
viable agricultural sector. This logic would seem to be particularly compelling during a succession crisis, when the
polity is perceived as delicate and when the discussion turns
to larger and longer-range issues than is usually the case.
At this time, concerns about economic dislocation and re-
bellion in the countryside would be particularly salient to
the elite stratum. Thus, agriculture lends itself to the kind
of concerns that dominate elite dialogue during succession,
and Khrushchev and Brezhnev both realized this very
quickly.

Agriculture was in many ways, then, an obvious issue to
invigorate elite debate during succession: it was in a state
of crisis, it had political and economic significance going
back to the Bolshevik days, and, finally, it was an arena in
which major contenders could feel comfortable battling it
out. However, the real turning point in transforming agricultural policy into a succession issue came when both
Khrushchev and Brezhnev realized that poor agricultural
performance was in many ways an ideal topic for debate
because it would play to *their* strengths and their opponents'
weaknesses. Every contender had experience, for example,
in heavy industry; moreover, that sector was hardly in its
death throes. There was, therefore, little incentive to come
up with new approaches, when the old ones seemed to
work just fine. Agriculture, by contrast, was something in

which both Khrushchev and Brezhnev could claim expertise. Thus, the "crisis" in Soviet agriculture and the political perspectives of Brezhnev and Khrushchev worked together to make agriculture a potent weapon in their struggle for power in the Soviet system.

Given the extent to which agriculture seems to be a natural issue during succession, the next question concerns the tie between the dynamics of elite changeover and agricultural innovation. What is it about succession that encouraged both Khrushchev and Brezhnev, not just to discuss agriculture, but also to introduce major changes in agriculture policy right at the beginning of the crisis? Clearly, the most obvious answer is that they did so because they felt that it would enhance their power, and they had the power to act on those ambitions. Again, the key seems to be the will and the way; policy innovation occurs because leaders want change and have the power to translate those goals into real policies.

If one dwells on the succession process for a moment, one can see how leaders develop both the desire and the power to enact major changes, to take, in this case, the agricultural issue and transform it into dramatic policy initiatives. As noted in Chapter Five, the "selectorate" in socialist successions is a group of sophisticated, experienced people, most of whom want to expand their power and yet do not want to endanger the stability of the system or their position within it through incessant internal bickering. The most logical solution to this dilemma would seem to be to choose a government which is headed by a leader who appeals to other elites in the system; whose career combines the party and state experience and expertise in industry, agriculture, domestic and foreign politics; who is not too old; and who is of a dominant nationality (read Russian) (Hodnett, 1975). After appointment, it would seem logical that the new leader would then be given a grace period— or what was called a honeymoon in the last chapter—in which to prove himself and to provide some breathing space for the Party after the turmoil of the succession. The newly selected leader, working with the advantage of the power that is implied in a honeymoon period and yet constrained by a conditional mandate, would be primarily concerned with using his newly won freedom to expand that mandate, and thereby solidify this position. He would have to act fast, while his power was still strong and his enemies quiescent. One obvious thing to do at this time would be for the new First Secretary to take advantage of the honeymoon and become a policy entrepreneur, focusing on issues that are salient, playing to his own unique expertise and to an area that separates him from the previous leader and the challengers around him. Moreover, by focusing on a few policies and being innovative, the newly installed leader would demonstrate to his colleagues that he *is* a leader and has a series of issues around which he can build a coalition of support. Nothing, it seems, would be gained by taking an ambiguous or moderate approach to the issues of the day; this would not demonstrate leadership potential to upper-level party cadres, and would leave a policy vacuum. Counter-elites would then try to create mandates of their own and coalitions of support through a variety of policy initiatives and thereby challenge the capacity of the leader to lead.

Thus, there are considerable pressures—of time, of fleeting power, of a radical ideology, of the tradition of leader dominance, and of competition and conflict—that push the new leader to introduce radical policy initiatives during the honeymoon period. While the risks are great—indeed, Khrushchev raised expectations only to have his policies compared unfavorably with his rhetoric—inaction would seem to be a sure cause of demotion. He who hesitates would seem to be lost in such an environment, and this is why innovation—in agriculture and budgetary and investment policy—is immediate in socialist succession struggles.

But why does the tendency to innovate seem to wither away with the aging of the administration? I would suggest that this pattern can be explained by adopting the same arguments for the socialist case that were used to explain the results in the American case study; that is, the notions of diminishing returns and routinization of policy priorities. In order to put through their proposals in 1953 and 1965, respectively, Khrushchev and Brezhnev probably expended a great deal of their resources. Moreover, as they moved through their terms in office, they perhaps incurred even more debts. Thus, coalitions for change become harder to form as an administration develops, not just because leaders get stuck in their ways, but also because their freedom to form coalitions narrows considerably. As for routinization, leaders do get stuck in their ways—Brezhnev in 1980 was not that different in his goals from 1965, and the same could be said of Khrushchev as well over the course of his administration. The fact that leaders are consistent, then, means that priorities will change little within administrations—commitments, values, and goals are the product of long experience and do not fluctuate that much as the political environment changes. Incrementalism is not just the result of conflict and complexity; it is also the outcome of a leader's standing by his principles, his priorities, and his coalition of support.

If these two arguments are combined—diminishing returns and routinization—with the very real increases in constraints on policy change that occur when the honeymoon ends, it is easy to see why agricultural innovation follows a succession-related cycle of development. As with the American case study, then, I have found what seems to be a regularized and predictable alternation between incremental decision-making during periods of leadership stability and innovative decision-making during changes of leadership. When power and desire for change are strong, innovation occurs; when the spirit is not willing and the flesh is weak, incrementalism comes to the fore.

Thus, innovation—in agriculture and in budgetary and investment decisions—seems to be intimately connected

with leadership succession in the Soviet bloc. The honeymoon period, the provisional mandate, the nature of the
"selectorate," and the lack of an "inheritance" effect (Anderson, 1967:341)[8]—all explain why both Khrushchev and
Brezhnev engaged in extensive agricultural innovations in
their first year or so in office. Such behavior worked to
expand their power and to realize some important personal
policy objectives as well. In this sense, socialist successions—
because they are "unstable," "elite-centered," and policy-
relevant processes—are indeed at times and in certain policy areas mechanisms of innovation. This is particularly the
case in the early years of the new administration, when
power and the generation of new policy proposals are so
closely linked. Just as elections in the West seem to encourage policy reevaluation and innovation, so in the Second World "the succession crisis" works to generate policy
evaluation and policy change.

CONCLUSIONS

In this case study and in the previous chapter, I have challenged some of the common wisdom concerning power and
policy in the Soviet Union (and Eastern Europe). Certainly
the role of succession that emerges from this analysis is not
terribly akin to the widespread argument that "one of the
greatest sources of strain in the Soviet system is the succession problem" (Fainsod, 1970:592). Rather, I would contend that the succession process works as a mechanism
through which prevailing policy priorities and leadership
performance are evaluated, and through which new policy
ideas are generated and sometimes implemented. In this
sense, the approach to succession in the communist party
states cannot be reduced to simply a dysfunctional process.

    [8] This term refers to the extent to which leaders must "inherit" or stick
with the priorities of their predecessors. Compare, for example, Khrushchev's five major reorganizations of the Soviet bureaucracy with Nixon's
repeated frustrations in dismantling the Office of Economic Opportunity.

Just as incrementalism assures some stability in the policy process—and this occurs East as well as West—so the succession rite is functional as well in that it provides for periodic readjustments in power, policy, and personnel. The "instability" of succession, then, is another term for its potential for creating new policies through new personnel and through a fresh look at current priorities. It complements, then, the stability of incrementalism.

Once succession is reexamined from this perspective of its functional aspects, one finds that a number of hitherto "problematic" characteristics may in fact be sources of strength as far as the overall policy process is concerned. For example, many scholars berate the high intra-elite conflict generated by succession, arguing that this exposes the system to "instability" (Rush, 1974; Hodgson, 1976). However, this study indicates that conflict can play (but not always) a more positive role, similar to Morton Deutsch's understanding of this process; that is, conflict can "prevent the ossification of social systems by exerting pressures for innovation and creativity; it [can] prevent habitual accommodations from freezing into rigid molds and hence impoverishing the ability to react creatively to novel circumstances" (Coser, 1968:232).[9] One effect of "instability," therefore, is to allow for creativity (also see Assael, 1969).

Relatedly, one can question the assumption that widespread ambition (which in turn produces conflict) undermines meaningful policy discourse. The usual argument in communist area studies is that high ambition leads to too much conflict and encourages contenders to sacrifice public policy on the altar of power (Rush, 1974; Hodgson, 1976). The problem with this argument is that: (1) it assumes ambition to be a negative force, an idea that reflects American cultural biases more than empirical realities. Ambition may in fact upgrade policy discussion by forcing elites to

[9] A Marxist view of social change, for example, emphasizes the tie between conflict and creativity (see Neal, 1965:1-11).

compete with one another by using the currency of new policies to prove their competence. (2) It does not take into account the creative aspects of conflict, or the extent to which conflict may promote social solidarity and the clarification of social norms and public policy. (3) It ignores the fact that many "policy byproducts" of succession are not accidental, but in keeping with the emerging leader's past experiences and preferences. And, finally, (4) it disallows the possibility that even if innovation occurs "for the wrong reason" (i.e., in order to get power), it may still benefit the system by forcing contenders to be responsive to the party cadres and to various significant groups in the system. What I am suggesting is that it may be useful to look at ambition in socialist nations in much the same way that Joseph Schlesinger (1966) has viewed it in the American system, and analysts, such as Anthony Downs (1966:Ch. 13), have treated it in theories of organizational behavior; that is, the notion that "competition is stimulating" (as Franklin Roosevelt used to say, and his staff arrangements seem to validate), and the idea that "the desire to aggrandize breeds innovation" (Downs, 1967:94).

However, this is not to assert that, in the extreme, conflict and high ambition may not deter innovation by immobilizing the decision process. While this is one outcome, it is mitigated in the socialist case by the fact that the elites share certain values (such as the maintenance of the system), are well socialized, have articulate policy orientations, and seem to ascribe (or at least behave as though they do) to the notion of a honeymoon period. The pattern of policy change I have described in the past two chapters would seem to indicate, not total conflict and an immobilized policy process, but rather a policy process that alternates between small and not-so-small change. Thus, the succession process does seem to be rather institutionalized in its impact and seems, therefore, to create a fertile climate for innovation—by sparking conflict and creativity and yet bequeathing adequate power to follow through on some of these ideas.

This study also suggests that one should not be terribly bothered by the "uncertain" climate surrounding succession, a quality that has led scholars to worry a great deal about instability. Crises in public policy—the very stuff of socialist successions—can open up the policy agenda, force action, increase "search" behavior, and at times concentrate power in the hands of the leader (Wilson, 1966; Korten, 1972). While one can see how too much of this may hinder rational policy-making, periodic shakeups and emergencies do make some sense. Certainly Khrushchev's approach to public administration demonstrates the pros (as well as some of the cons) of such a strategy. Crises can regenerate political systems, public policies, and political leaders.[10]

Thus, the case study along with the quantitative analysis would suggest that a revised interpretation of succession and policy-making in socialist systems may be useful. Because "the decision process is organically linked to the succession struggle" (Morton, 1967:19), many policies change along with personnel. In the absence of succession, agriculture and budgetary and investment policies tend to move on as before, seemingly undisturbed by maneuverings among the political leadership.

In support of the conclusions drawn in Chapter Five, I can now state—on the basis of the illustration drawn in this chapter and other policy case studies—that succession does seem to cause policy innovation in socialist systems. It does so precisely because it is an unstable process that pits ambitious contenders against one another. To turn Merle Fainsod (1970:592) on his head, I would therefore conclude that leadership succession is one of the great sources of *strength* in the Soviet political system insofar as it evaluates policy and generates new approaches.

[10] It is also interesting to note, in view of these cross-system parallels, the similarities between American and Soviet responses to crises in public policy. To take the two case studies as examples, there is first an administrative solution (Johnson and Khrushchev) and, then, in desperation, a monetary one (Nixon and Brezhnev).

SEVEN

Conclusion: Policy Cycles and Leadership Succession

A key feature in any political system is the relation between the processes of policy-making and those of acquiring power.
—*Zbigniew Brzezinski and Samuel Huntington* (1963)

The United States has a regular procedure for placing its top political leader [while] the Soviet Union lacks any such system. This is one of the most important ways in which the American political system is more stable and effective than that of the Soviet Union.
—*Zbigniew Brzezinski and Samuel Huntington* (1963)

INTRODUCTION

Political scientists have addressed the issue of leadership succession from several perspectives. Some scholars—indeed, most—have tended to analyze succession as a *dependent* variable, that is, as a process that needs to be explained rather than an event that somehow affects the nature of the political environment (see Rush, 1968 and 1974; Burling, 1974; Polsby and Wildavsky, 1971). Thus, most studies concerned with succession, East and West, have addressed the topic from the perspective of candidate recruitment, campaigns for office, and the like, with little attention paid to the impact of those factors on the system once the succession is over. However, a few scholars have adopted a different approach and have taken their analyses of succession beyond the actual transfer of power; they have examined succession as an independent variable that influences the operation of the political system. In such studies, the primary focus is on succession as a process having systemic impact—the changing of the political guard can work to either de-stabilize or perhaps to further legitimate the polity (Fainsod, 1970:590-591; Rush, 1974:209-242). Thus, the analysis of leadership changeover has been based on two different views of its essential importance; some see it as a struggle for power and some see it as a barometer of political development.

This study diverges from both of these approaches by looking at the impact of leadership changeover on public policy. The guiding concern has been with whether new leaders in socialist and bourgeois democratic nations sponsor new policy priorities, or whether they maintain the existing policy routines. In the course of addressing this issue, I have examined three related questions. First, do new leaders make a difference as far as public policy is concerned? Second, how and under what conditions do succession processes, East and West, work as mechanisms of policy change? Finally, what are the relative effects of leaders and their environments in shaping policy priorities and how does this change as the leadership stratum moves from a state of flux to stability?

The answer to the first question is that new leaders—under socialism and under bourgeois democracy—do matter. This conclusion was drawn from several types of evidence. First, in a quantitative sense, budgetary priorities (and also investments, for the socialist nations) change in the immediate aftermath of succession far more than they do at other times. Moreover, these shifts remained stable within administrations until the next succession. Thus, new leaders have an immediate and enduring effect on budgetary (and investment) allocations, with the first year in office being the time in which new priorities are set which eventually settle into routines until the next election. However, it is not just change which is important, but also the direction of change. New leaders of the left (as defined within their systems and across polities) tend to pump up social-welfare areas more in their honeymoons than do new leaders of the right. The more competitive the system over time and the smaller the size of the particular mandate, though, the more this distinction is blurred. While competition still allows for innovation (in the honeymoon), it also encourages imitation.

The second source of evidence was more indirect and had to do with patterns of change and stasis in other policy areas. In the Western case, I relied on the work of others—case studies and quantitative analyses—to document the presence of a succession cycle in American educational policy and macroeconomic policy in advanced industrial societies (see Lowi, 1963; Bailey and Mosher, 1968; Hibbs, 1977; Cowart, 1978a and 1978b; Cameron, 1978; Frey, 1978; Tufte, 1978). As Stephen Hess (1977) and others (Wilson, 1976; Crossman, 1976) have argued, certain priorities are more likely, given the influence of ideology, and innovations tend to cluster at the beginning of administrations. Thus, new leaders make a difference in the rhythm of policy change and the types of policies that are advocated.[1]

In the case of the Soviet bloc, considerably less secondary literature exists to supplement the findings concerning the responsiveness of budgetary and investment allocations to changes in the First Secretary. Following the lead of the Western studies, I examined the linkage between succession and a variety of social and economic policies: the rate of housing starts; consumer-goods allocations and production; changes in wage levels, public consumption and national income per capita; and finally growth in social benefits. All of these areas showed a clear pattern of growth and stability: new leaders seem to pump up popular areas while succession is in question, and move on to a more diversified approach, once succession is resolved. Thus,

---

[1] It should be noted, though, that the electoral cycle does operate somewhat differently from the budgetary cycle, in that certain priorities in the former are pumped just prior to a reelection campaign, rather in the honeymoon. However, the direction of priorities and their timing in terms of introduction follow the patterns noted in this book.

there is an equivalent to the electoral cycle in the socialist context, a "succession connection" if you will (Mayhew, 1974).

The third source of evidence involved case studies of the evolution of agricultural policies in the Soviet Union during the post-Stalin era and welfare policies in the United States during the 1960's. In both examples, it was clear that major changes, if they occurred at all, tended to be introduced in conjunction with the rise of new chief executives in these two systems. In addition, both policy areas fell into incremental patterns of development in the absence of succession. Thus, in view of the theoretical evidence presented throughout this book concerning the linkage between succession and policy innovation, and the consistency of the results in the case studies and the quantitative assessments, it can be concluded that new leaders in fact do new things and, what is more, certain kinds of things. Just as problematic areas, like welfare in the U.S. and agriculture in the Soviet Union, evoke administrative and then monetary solutions, so certain policy areas are favored at certain times because of ideology and political ambition. Thus, it is reasonable to conclude that succession is a mechanism of policy innovation under "developed socialism" and late capitalism. New leaders do make a difference, setting the new priorities in their honeymoon, which evolve into new routines.

However, the relationship between succession and cycles of policy innovation and incremental change is not as simple as new leaders doing new things. The specifics of the linkage between leadership turnover and policy-making are much more complex and involve an interaction between the campaign experience (how power is won and maintained) and the honeymoon in office, an interaction which enhances the incentives and capacity of new leaders to go in some new directions. In the West, for example, it can be argued that the campaign opens up issues and surrounds the candidate with pressures for action, ranging from demands from articulate groups, other contenders, and from the inner circle surrounding the candidate, all the way to a more amorphous agenda presented by the mass public. The impact of the campaign on the candidate, then, is intense and is far more issue-oriented than public rhetoric would suggest. In the aftermath of succession, this heightened desire for change is amplified by the climate of the new administration: its optimism, its desire to make a mark, and its forward momentum left over from the campaign. If one adds to this the fact that leaders do have some ideological goals, and do feel that they are different from their predecessors', then it is easy to see how the desire for change reaches a high point in the early period of the new administration.

This desire, moreover, is met by unusual power in a comparative sense. The public is very supportive, the new leader has just undergone the heady experience of winning a mandate, and the legislature is unusually compliant. Moreover, the bureaucracy and the staff are supportive—they want the new leader to ally with them and their projects and hence they try to win the favor of the new chief executive. Finally, in this initial period, the new President or Prime Minister is unusually receptive to new ideas; the campaign has left the candidate with many promises and few concrete ideas. Hence, there is great hunger for information, for guidelines on what to do. These ideas, moreover, gravitate easily to the chief executive, since the power structure is clear, centralized, and consensual in the first year in office. Thus, for a variety of reasons—having to do with ambition, consensus, and power—the honeymoon seems to provide a unique antechamber for policy innovation. While constraints operate—ranging from past promises, the inevitable resource limitations, and the entrenched interests which endure from one executive transition to another—the point remains that the honeymoon is a comparatively optimal environment for policy change.

A similar argument can be made with respect to honeymoons in the socialist states. There, an activist ideology, a centralized power structure, and the comparatively long tenure and hence entrenched biases of First Secretaries, which lead to well-defined problems, once succession is underway, all work to facilitate the impact of succession on policy priorities. However, the real key seems to be the nature of socialist successions, which provide provisional mandates, are infused with the big issues of the day, and which are resolved only when one contender manages to convince the other highly competent and experienced elites around him that he in fact can govern by responding to their needs and those of the system. Conflict, then, generates new ideas, and winners are those who form enduring coalitions based on certain notions of how the system should develop. The campaign and the honeymoon are telescoped in socialist systems, but this leads to innovations precisely because the "selectorate" has high standards and can withdraw the mandate at any time. However, amidst conflict, there is some consensus—that the process should not undermine the polity, that the new leader should try out his ideas (ideas which must be popular, since he was elected over others), and that certain problems should be addressed immediately. In this sense, socialist "honeymoons" are like their Western counterparts; there is optimism, the notion of a grace period to prove one's worth, an agenda which is new and which seems to require immediate attention, and an unusual amount of compliance, reflecting the policy consensus and the fact that other elites want to be part of the new ruling coalition and want their interests represented. As in the West, then, succession generates new policies because leaders differ in priorities, and because they operate under certain structural pressures and incentives during their honeymoons. Ambition, then, meets with strong incentives to innovate.

Of course, in both types of polities the strength of the linkage between succession and innovation is affected by certain aspects of the political context. In the Western case, leftism of the party in power, both extremes of party competition, the installation of new parties and new chief executives, and a low turnover rate—all enhance the impact of succession. In socialist states, infrequent turnover and actual changes in leaders (as opposed to Politburo shakeups) provide the optimal conditions under which succession ushers in new priorities. Beyond these factors, though, there seems to be little to choose among socialist successions; impact—and of a certain type—seems to be invariably the case.

All of these conditions, however, are hardly mandatory; innovation seems to be generally as much a phenomenon of succession and the honeymoon as incrementalism is of policy-making at other times. In both political contexts desire and capacity wane as new leaders settle into office. This reflects the consistency of their initial commitments, the inordinate time it takes to see those through, the inevitable development of coalitions cemented around the new policies and pockets of opposition responding to the very fact that decisions imply losers as well as winners, and the degree to which power diffuses as the conflict and complexity embedded in decision-making rise once again. Innovation becomes more costly, and incremental adjustments dominate—for good reason—until the next succession. Thus, in East and West, innovation (but within limits) is a phenomenon of the honeymoon and incrementalism describes policy-making at other times. Both represent understandable responses to changes in the policy environment; that is, to fluctuations in the capacity of and incentives for leaders to alter existing priorities. And those fluctuations seem to be calibrated by the succession cycle.

I would conclude, therefore, from this study that in both socialist and bourgeois democratic states, succession—for many of the same reasons—affects the nature of the policy process and hence the amount of change in priorities that occur. In the absence of succession, policy change is generally small and consistent; in its presence, innovation (but circumscribed, it must be emphasized), not incrementalism, is the more pronounced tendency. I thus have provided some evidence for what has been a perennial assumption in the study of leadership succession: that succession somehow is important beyond the drama that it unfolds. The analysis in this study indicates that succession is indeed something that merits close scrutiny, not just because it determines who rules, but also because it shapes what happens in terms of public policy. It is a mechanism of policy change—East and West.

However, to argue that succession and thereby new leaders matter is not the same thing as arguing that leaders in general matter. As noted throughout this book, "actor dispensability" (Greenstein, 1969:51-55) is a tricky issue, since, even under succession, leaders operate in a particular context that helps to shape what they do. In the final analysis, though, succession can be seen as a process that, when interacting with the honeymoon, alters the policy environment in such a way as to *allow* leaders to exert more control over what happens. But such a structural view is not complete. Given what the case studies revealed, the evidence on the lesser impact of succession which reinstated leaders, and the apparent linkage between ideology and innovation, I would have to conclude that particular leaders do seem to matter when they are in their honeymoons. In this sense, while environment is always important, it is more malleable and more supportive of elite direction and innovation during the honeymoon in office. The existence of a policy cycle, alternating regularly between innovation and incrementalism, tells us that succession produces certain changes in the policy environment as well as in leadership, and that leaders are less dispensable when they are new in office. The key question, then, is not whether leaders matter, but rather *where* they are in their terms and what that tells us about their impact and the degree to which the policy context allows for their influence and for policy change in general.

This basic conclusion, however, leaves us with some un-answered questions. First, how generalizable are the find-ings that I have reported? Second, how firm is the causal connection between succession and policy innovation? Fi-nally, what do the results say about more general issues? In a sense, then, what I am asking is: how powerful are the findings in this study, and what do they tell us about power and policy in advanced industrial societies—of whatever ideological complexion?

GENERALIZABILITY OF THE FINDINGS

The issue of generalizability has reverberated throughout this analysis; I have been concerned in each chapter with being able to speak about succession and policy change in general. I have at times noted a succession cycle in a number of policy areas outside the policy focus of this particular study—for example, changes in macroeconomic and edu-cation policy in the West and fluctuations in the minimum wage, income per capita, and social policy priorities in the socialist world. In addition, I have looked closely at agri-cultural policy in the Soviet Union and welfare policy in the United States in the postwar era and found strong support for the generalizations made on the basis of the more aggregate policy indicators. All of these policies, therefore, seem to share certain patterns in response to the succession cycle.

Thus, I have tried to diversify the policy areas as much as the emphasis on executive turnover would allow.[2] The fact that such a range in policies and programs would be so similar in their patterns of change—and the extent to which these patterns appear in other case studies and em-pirical models of innovation—make it plausible to suggest

[2] Of course, I could look only at those policies which are under the aegis of chief executives; otherwise, I could hardly speak to the policy impact of rotation in that particular office.

that I am speaking in this study to a general phenomenon, general in that it captures what happens to a variety of executive-controlled public policies. Succession seems to induce changes in public policies of all kinds, and its absence seems to encourage incrementalism.

However, even if the focus were only on budgetary change, the findings would still merit attention. Budgets, after all, are important policy documents and are at the same time a tough test of the impact of succession. The salience of budgetary allocations to elites is undeniable—their power and their priorities are reflected directly in the monetary divisions of the budget. As Richard Winters (1976:598) put it, "each new administration draws up a reelection calculus, the central items of which are the expenditure and revenue allocation matrices." Budgets are difficult tests as well because, as noted in Chapter Two, they are very complex, and provoke a great deal of conflict, reflecting the many vested interests that are represented. "Satisficing" and "incrementalism" are, in fact, standard practices with regard to these documents in both socialist and bourgeois democratic states (Bunce and Echols, 1978). I would argue, then, that if *budgets* react to leadership succession, so should other executive-sponsored policies that involve perhaps less conflict and complexity.

Furthermore, it is in some ways misleading to treat budgets as a separate area of decision-making, since they contain so many policies and programs that concern chief executives. So much of what leaders want to do depends on the monetary allocations found in the budget. As noted in Chapters Four and Six, for example, every significant innovation in welfare policy in the United States and in agricultural policy in the Soviet Union since 1950 has involved budgetary, as well as program, change. While I would not contend that this is true for all policies, the point remains that budgets are fairly inclusive and representative documents. As such, they are suggestive (though not necessarily indicative) of policy behavior in general. Thus, elite succession may very well reorder, and indeed does reorder, public policy priorities in many sectors outside of budgets.

Even if elite changes were to affect only the policies discussed in this book, then this would certainly in itself justify the analysis. To find a predictable succession cycle in budgetary and other policies, East and West, is important. Moreover, the other evidence cited throughout this book merely buttress the quantitative and case study findings. The consistency of the results and their theoretical and empirical support all indicate that the linkage between new leaders and new policies may be generalizable—across time, across policy areas, across nation states, and even, surprisingly enough, across system types.

TOWARD A CAUSAL INTERPRETATION

But, in finding a succession related cycle, can it then be concluded that succession "causes" policy innovation? Or can one speak only of correlations between the two variables? I would answer this query by arguing that I have indeed uncovered a causal process. I would argue this because of the strength of the results and the strong theory that supports such an interpretation. The findings of this study have been clear and consistent; succession did appear to be a very good predicter of policy innovation. Not only was there a significant impact, time and again, but it appeared when employing several different kinds of tests and looking at a variety of evidence. Thus, this study established the presence of immediate change that endured throughout each administration, and this occurred in the 1950's as well as in the 1970's; a similar succession cycle operated at the national as well as at the sub-national levels of government; and the relationship between succession and policy change appeared in the aggregate budgetary analysis and in the case studies (see, for example, Ginsberg and Solow,

1974; Hess, 1977; Volkov, 1975; Bronson and Krueger, 1971).

Perhaps the strongest indicator of causality, though, is the similarity of the results for socialist and bourgeois democratic states. Clearly, succession rites are very different, East and West, as is the structure of decision-making, the ideology of the elites, and their career background, yet in terms of the *policy* impact of succession, there is little to choose between socialism and Western democracy. It would seem, therefore, that this study has dealt with a very basic phenomenon, having to do with processes of change and stasis in both systems. I can argue as well that I am not mistaking succession in this study for some other causal agent; succession is after all the only variable the two system types share that would explain the resulting similar patterns of innovation. Thus, there would not seem to be a developmental sequence, or a spurious correlation, operating here; there are no other variables that the United States and the Soviet Union, for example, would both have that could produce over and over again policy innovation—and innovation in predictable directions—in the period right after elite turnover.

It could be argued, though, that "need for a change," rather than succession, is what is causing the changes in policy priorities (Zaltman et al., 1973). The problem with this argument is that poor performance in a policy area such as agriculture in the Soviet Union or welfare in the United States happens quite often, yet the policy is altered primarily only when leaders turn over.[3] Moreover, I have presented numerous examples of innovation in successful areas as well as in less successful ones right after succession. The common ingredient to all this, then, seems to be the

---

[3] This, of course, is a common argument in studies of foreign policy crises—for example, Nixon's withdrawal from Vietnam and Eisenhower's from Korea. It is also important to note how many foreign crises seem to occur in honeymoons (Hess, 1977).

inauguration of a new leader who has the incentives and the capability to reorder priorities. When succession happens, all kinds of policies are revised and reversed, whether they are areas of success or failure.

The fact that in the absence of succession one does not usually see such innovations further supports the case for the causal linkage between succession and policy change. The pervasiveness of incrementalism, when coupled with its predictable disruption after succession, indicates that succession is the key factor in generating policy innovation. That succession seems to be almost prerequisite for policy change to happen, therefore, would seem to prove that, whatever else is going on in the polity, succession works as an agent of change. What else could affect policy in such widely varying circumstances at the same intervals, and in the same way?

However, I am not arguing for a causal relationship between succession and policy innovation simply by process of elimination; I have throughout this study offered a number of theoretical arguments that link leadership succession with policy innovation. In both socialist and bourgeois democratic systems, the power and the capability to change public policy are indeed enhanced during the campaign for office and during the honeymoon period. In this sense, leadership succession does cause policy innovation East and West.

Thus, there do seem to be good theoretical as well as empirical reasons why succession should change public policy priorities. Given this empirical base, one can argue that the relationship between succession and policy change is a causal one. Leadership rotation, when interacting with the politics of the honeymoon period, does produce policy innovation in socialist and bourgeois democratic systems. This is, then, the central finding of this study.

Given this overall conclusion, what are some of the major implications that can and should be drawn from this analysis? What does the conclusion that new leaders make a difference say about the common scholarly wisdom concerning political leaders, their rotation in office, and the policy process in socialist and liberal democratic states?

THE IMPLICATIONS FOR THE STUDY OF LEADERSHIP SUCCESSION

Given the finding that leadership succession does alter policy outputs, what does this say about the role of succession in political systems? The first point that should be made is a heuristic one. In view of the impact of succession, it is clear that leadership rotation should be analyzed more than it is in studies of elite behavior, decision-making, and the determinants of public policy. While the study of elections, for example, certainly plays a central part in the analysis of American politics, the general tendency has been for scholars to treat elections in a limited way, as dependent variables. For instance, Nelson Polsby and Aaron Wildavsky (1971:3) have opened their text on American elections with the following description:

> This book is about the winning of the Presidential office. In spite of the great and lonely eminence of the Presidency, this office exists within a cultural and political tradition that guides and shapes the ways in which the Presidency is won and, later, the ways in which Presidential power is exercised. *But we will not speak further here about the exercise of executive power.* Rather, the task before us is to make plain the context within which the battle for Presidential office is waged, to discuss the strategies of contending parties and, if possible, to explain why some strategies are used by some contestants and other strategies by others.

There is, clearly, no attempt to extend the causal connection—to examine systematically the impact of elections on public policy. Similarly, David Butler and Donald Stokes (1974) boldly entitled their book, *Political Change in Great*

Britain, but dealt only with changes in the electorate over time. Apparently, in their view and that of so many others who study elections, "change" is something only mass publics do and elections are important only insofar as they tell us about voting behavior. Once the contest is over, interest wanes and the systemic or policy impact is left for journalistic speculation.

I would suggest, instead, in view of the findings, that there should be more awareness of the policy impact of succession. This implies that the concept of an election should be expanded beyond the campaign period to include the policy-making process *after* the election. Western elections are much more influential processes than scholars have tended to acknowledge in their analyses, and as such should be receiving far more attention in studies of elite decision-making and policy outputs. This is one political variable that does seem "to work," and its effects should be included in analyses of public policy in bourgeois democratic states.

I do not, of course, need to make this point with respect to successions in socialist systems; the notion of impact there has hardly been overlooked. As Myron Rush (1974:13) has noted:

> Succession is important in communist regimes because power is highly concentrated and controlled at the top and because their politics are highly variable. The ruler is not independent of his circumstances, but greater means are available to him for modifying his circumstances. Moreover, although the politics of a communist state can change radically without a change in the ruler, their consequences for the country may very much depend on who carries them out.

However, this is not to suggest that scholars in communist area studies have been free of biases in their analyses of leadership succession. In contrast to Western studies on the topic, policy change in socialist nations is often assumed, not to remain static, but to change dramatically after a change in incumbents. This is why Merle Fainsod (1970:591; Rush, 1974; Hodgson, 1976), and others have seen socialist successions as destabilizing events; they purportedly expose leaders, policy, and a "vulnerable" political system to extreme change. Thus, succession is for most scholars considered to be a time of stress, not a time of creativity:

> The interest in communist succession crises has been prompted in the past at least by a belief that communist systems were rather fragile. Lacking a consensual infrastructure, the glue which held a communist system together was provided by a combination of coercion and the charismatic authority of the political leader. Consequently, many persons, West and East, have considered succession to be highly dysfunctional . . . and have expected that succession might not only produce changes in policy, but set in motion disequilibrating tendencies which would involve new constituencies and effect changes in the basic nature of the system (Zimmerman, 1976:63).

However, to what extent that impact is really extreme and dysfunctional is a question that is rarely broached, let alone answered, and this is my essential point. The impact of succession deserves more careful scrutiny in both socialist and bourgeois democratic studies; it should not be assumed to be negligible, as in the West, or necessarily dramatic, as in the East, particularly in view of the findings summarized above and presented in Chapters Three through Six. While I found succession to affect public policy in the Soviet bloc, the disturbances were hardly cataclysmic. If anything, I would term these changes *innovative*, and this is a major corrective that students of socialist successions should note.

They should also be more sensitive to the fact that succession "crises" do work, not just to tune the system in terms of its priorities, but also in terms of its legitimacy. Much ado has been made about the lack of responsiveness to mass demands in Soviet-type systems and the elitist insulated nature of the succession process. However, this analysis suggests that it may be more important to look at policy outputs than at succession rites, when examining the issue of responsiveness. New leaders seem to reach out for mass support by producing policies that anyone would construe as being highly popular among the broad masses of people. Raising wages, providing more housing, and pumping up social outlays are hardly priorities that one could term "elitist." Whether this occurs because of beneficence, ideology, power needs, or fear of mass unrest is unclear, but the point remains that succession does usher in priorities that are highly responsive to mass demands. The people do not have to participate in selecting their leaders to benefit from the succession process.

However, I do not want to leave the lessons of this study just with the admonition that succession East and West has important policy consequences. I also want to emphasize that the consequences found were not those predicted by much of the literature. The common wisdom has been that socialist successions are very different from western democratic elections—they have more dramatic effects on public policy. Zbigniew Brzezinski and Samuel Huntington (1963:267) are typical in their observation that:

> Khrushchev had to win the support of the Party and the bureaucratic leaders directly concerned with the specific content and substance of government policy. Kennedy and Nixon, however, had to win the support of large masses of voters, who, unlike institutional leaders, were moved not by specific issues but by general appeals. While real issues of policy were at stake in the Soviet struggle, the differences between Kennedy and his opponents were marginal at best. . . . The American struggle involved many more participants and its implications for both policy and individual power were correspondingly limited.

Yet I found the impact of succession to be similar, East and West, similar in that changing leaders changed policies in parallel ways in both types of systems. Thus, the usual contrast—that succession is very different in socialist than in Western states—was not upheld. In both polities, policy changed but hardly in a de-stabilizing manner. Thus, I would have to conclude that socialist and bourgeois democratic successions are more similar than they appear at first glance—in both types of nations succession and its interaction with the honeymoon functions as a mechanism of policy innovation.

This in turn leads to the argument that leadership succession in socialist and capitalist states is a *regularized* process of policy evaluation and change. It is not a "critical source of weakness in communist polities" (Rush, 1974:327); rather, it seems instead to be a source of system dynamism, a way in which such systems readjust their policy priorities and open the polity to new blood and new priorities. It is a tuning mechanism.[4] Similarly, democratic elections are not merely symbolic events; they are processes that alternate leaders and public policy priorities in a legitimate and regularized manner. In both cases, the fact that the process promotes change and stability in personnel and public policy speaks to the assets of the particular succession rite, not to its liabilities. Policy change, policy reevaluation, and personnel turnover—these are functional to the system and are the natural by-products of the struggle for political power in Washington, London, or Moscow. That the masses are involved more in Washington than in Moscow, that the timing of the process is more predictable in the United States than in the Soviet Union, or that it is easier to narrow down the list of potential successors in the Soviet than in the American case says nothing about whether the process

---

[4] Indeed, the whole assumption that conflict is de-stabilizing is suspect; it can be quite functional to the system (see Coser, 1956; Josephson, 1972; Neal, 1965).

is stable or beneficial to the system. What really counts is that, in both modes of succession, policy is discussed and critiqued and new ideas and some new people have a chance to affect the decision process.

This generalization also speaks against the tendency to treat socialist and capitalist successions as separable and incomparable processes. They are not, as this analysis has shown. In both systems succession involves ambition, conflict, the airing of issues, the eventual victory of one candidate over another, and policy change once the honeymoon interacts with the campaign experience. The essence of the process—its impact and its logic—would seem to be very similar, East and West. There are, indeed, a number of functional equivalencies in succession in different systems that scholars have tended to ignore.

To a great extent, then, I am arguing for new approaches to the study of leadership turnover which emphasize both the pros and cons and the similarities as well as the differences among different modes of succession. While socialist successions are perhaps too elite-centered—which undermines their ability to reevaluate public policy and be responsive to certain needs—they do in fact reorder priorities once in a while, encourage some responsiveness, and force elites to be successful in their pet projects or be purged from office. Similarly, Western elections have their trade-offs as well. While campaigns do not educate the masses or the candidates as well as they should, they do open up the system to some criticism and change. In neither the socialist nor the bourgeois democratic cases, then, can one say that the process is dysfunctional—it has its good points and its weaknesses. Certainly, on the basis of the evidence in this book, it cannot be argued, as is the usual case, that socialist succession rites and their policy effects are all that different from or are inferior to Western electoral practices and impacts. In both systems, succession is a rather routinized way of reevaluating leaders and some policies as well.

Having said all this, we can see that what is needed in

the study of leadership change (and comparative analysis in general) is the greater use of middle-range theory, particularly in communist area studies where grand theory has tended to dominate the dialogue for so long about high politics. It makes little sense, for example, to point to low turnover in the Soviet Union and argue that this "proves" that succession is becoming routinized and will have little policy impact in such systems. Low turnover has a variety of possible consequences, among which are the diminution of political opportunities, long political experience as well as an aging political leadership, frustration among the upwardly mobile elite, comparative continuity of personnel in policy-making, and perhaps a budding policy crisis which reflects the unchanging mobilization of bias in the system. It may also simply reflect a commitment to regularized procedures, the prevailing elite power structure, or a consensus about current policies and performance (see Oliver, 1973). The point, then, is that variables such as the rate of elite turnover, or any variables having to do with succession may mean a lot of things and may affect a variety of aspects of elite behavior, policy outputs, or succession itself. These particular linkages need to be specified, tested, and analyzed—otherwise, the conception of rotation is not very meaningful. One cannot assume or infer the policy impact of succession from the political style of the leader, the level of development of the political or social system, or the nature of the succession rite. One has to test for these relationships.

Thus, succession is a far more complex, influential, and universal process than scholars have generally tended to admit. Therefore, the changing of the political guard should be analyzed in a more extensive, rigorous, and specified fashion across similar and different systems, and its positive as well as negative effects—for the system, the leadership, the mass public, or whatever—should be duly tabulated. Moreover, it should be studied with an eye on the input and output side of the decision-making process. As is the case with many variables in political science, elite succession has been burdened too long with "the fallacy of inputism" (Macridis, 1968:84, quoted in Scharf, 1976:154). Succession is an independent as well as a dependent variable, and in both roles it is a very critical factor for understanding who rules and what difference rulers make.

The Implications For Elite Studies

The findings, of course, are also relevant to the study of political elites and not just to their rotation in office. First, the fact that American and Soviet leaders are innovative in terms of priorities and allocations speaks to the impact of leadership recruitment and political ambition in the two nations. In studies of recruitment in America, the conclusion is usually drawn that:

> American elections appear to be the change process which is least likely to affect the policy outputs of a country. The electoral process is likely to screen out highly abberant personalities and values, and the quest for popular support is likely to induce the prospective leader to adopt an essentially moderate stance (Rosen, 1974:10-11).

Nor are socialist recruitment processes reputed to produce a very innovative leadership stratum:

> As a body primarily oriented towards the maintenance of control for the controller's sake, the Party apparatus tends to attract a particular kind of person—energetic and ambitious, not the most intelligent, not too principled—who is willing to conform in order to share the exercise of power (Daniels, 1971:21).

The stress, then, in analyses of both American and Soviet elite recruitment is on its bias against different or innovative leaders.

This picture, of course, is somewhat at odds with the

findings. Thus, either recruitment is different from what is commonly thought, or I am looking at the wrong aspects, or it has no impact on elite behavior. I think the answer lies in the first two explanations and not in the third. It makes perfect sense that recruitment should effect elites, because it incorporates so many of the forces that affect a candidate's behavior—his or her prior experience, values and goals.[5] All that is missing is the influence of the decision context. But, given its obvious importance, let me pose the issue from the perspective of change, not continuity (as is the usual approach). What is it about recruitment in capitalist and socialist states that might encourage policy innovation?

In the Western case, I would argue that, by treating career socialization as a mechanism of stability, political scientists have too often overlooked the diversity of career experiences of Western chief executives. It has too long been assumed that politicians get ahead through conformity, that long experience breeds stagnation and rigidity, that leaders have few policy goals, and that the acquisition of power is antithetical to the development of new public policies. However, if one pauses over the careers of various chief executives, one finds a rich array of experiences, a long-term commitment to certain issues, and a willingness to take political risks (Heclo, 1973; Brown, 1971; Blondel, 1977). It would be hard—as the case studies demonstrated—to reduce President Johnson's, Nixon's or even Kennedy's policy ventures into welfare reform to simply playing it safe (which was, admittedly, influential, as the case studies demonstrated), or adopting stances with little ideological commitment. Nor could one explain the be-

[5] Of course, I have noted throughout this book that as far as succession is concerned, the situational context is critical in the sense that one can distinguish a honeymoon period and after, but not critical in the sense that different newly-elected elites within a given nation act differently. The findings are very clear in the consistency of impact of succession within states.

havior of Brezhnev or Khrushchev with regards to agricultural reform, detente, or innovations in social policy if
one adopted a model that stressed policy rigidity, policy
ambiguity, and the like, or if one assumed that power and
innovativeness are necessarily negatively related. In all of
these cases, ambition, ideological concerns, and prior experience were not hostile to innovation; in fact, under certain circumstances, they encouraged it, and this linkage
appeared periodically throughout their careers in office.
Thus, I am suggesting that top leaders may be more open
to change than has traditionally been allowed, because their
prior socialization may tolerate it more than is often
thought, and because new ideas can work to *expand* power.

Second, it can be argued that elites can be innovative
precisely because elections may encourage policy innovation, not policy stability. In most analysis of political campaigns in the United States, for example, the emphasis is
placed on the formation of the winning coalition—that is,
the mobilization of the electorate, the lineup of the state,
the use of the media, and the personal issue, and party
appeal of the candidates. The problem with this view is that
it focuses attention away from the candidates' experiences
in the campaign, as they interact with the electorate as well
as with other political influentials in the system. As noted
in previous chapters, while candidates are forming coalitions, they are also forming a picture of what to do once
in office. The American Presidential campaign, with its
prolonged duration and its peculiar concept of the national
constituency of the Presidency, is uniquely adapted to preparing an agenda for the President and encouraging him
to take bold initiatives in public policy (Hess, 1974).

Thus, the campaign for office, just like the socialization
process, may be more conducive to encouraging elites to
introduce new policies than has been noted in traditional
emphases on sources of policy stability in recruitment and
campaigning. The campaign for office does not have to be
at odds with the notion of policy innovation. In fact, the

campaign can link power with policy change—in Europe and America.

In the case of leadership recruitment in the Second World, the conformity of the recruitment process also has been overemphasized to the detriment of any consideration of the impact of ambition or ideology on fostering innovative elite behavior. What Joseph Schlesinger (1966; also see Mezey, 1970) has argued for ambition in the United States has relevance for socialist politics as well, in that ambition can force elites to be responsive to others in the system and to introduce new public policies (Ciboski, 1974). Just as in the analysis of Western politicians, so in communist area studies, the impact of ambition has too often been considered to be negative. Thus, the fact that ambition leads to conflict is stressed, while the positive aspects of conflict, such as the generation of new ideas and the screening and testing of political candidates, are ignored (Deutsch, 1972; Coser, 1956; Brzezinski and Huntington, 1963:42). It can be argued, given their high stress environment, that Soviet elites are ambitious and conflictual and use new ideas and point out policy failings in order to get ahead in the political system. Thus, just as Western elites feel pressure to introduce initiatives in their honeymoon, and feel this will aid reelection, so do socialist elites for similar reasons. Conflict, ambition, and policy innovation can, in fact, vary together in both types of systems (Downs, 1967:198).

I would also challenge, in view of the results, the argument that Soviet elites are moribund because of the long, linear, and intense socialization process they have undergone in the highly bureaucratic Soviet system. As Jerry Hough (1972:39; also see Taubman, 1972) questions, the impact of Soviet elite training may not be as obvious as many scholars would intimate:

Does the fact that all its members are employed in bureaucratic institutions of one sort or another and are almost all required to be members of the Communist

Party ensure that the ideas flowing from them will be conservative rather than innovative? Does the fact that almost all major political actors are senior bureaucrats who supervise state, economic, party, or scientific-educational institutions of one type or another mean that ideas challenging the status quo will be filtered out before they reach political decision-makers?

While the answers to Hough's queries are not fully available, one can look at the rich diversity of the socialization process and the many skills it teaches and conclude that the supposedly conservative bias of Soviet recruitment and socialization is more debatable than at first glance. Certainly, if innovation requires expertise and familiarity with common problems in policy implementation, then the Soviet selection process—with its emphasis on professional politicians—imparts great potential for policy innovation (Kaufman, 1971:99-100; Pressman and Wildavsky, 1973:130-133). This, plus the nature of upward mobility—with its stress on high performance and experience in many geographical sectors and policy areas—would point away from the petrification thesis and would better fit in with the results reported in this study. The point, then, is that Soviet elite socialization can work as a double-edged sword where innovation is concerned: it can encourage conformity and yet at the same time enhance policy expertise and openness to new ideas. This latter effect, of course, is very plausible, given the findings in this study, yet it has received little attention in the scholarly community.

Finally, and this was touched on above, the fact that succession does have a strong impact, East and West, clarifies what has been a rather muddied picture of the nature of elite power in advanced industrial societies. While some analysts weight the effect of centralization and expertise heavily and thus attribute great power to decision-makers in developed societies, others diagnose something called, variously, the "democratic distemper," incrementalism, or, for the socialist world, the petrification model (Crozier et al., 1975; Brzezinski, 1969). Which of these views is correct? Are elites pawns of their environments or masters over it? As I noted earlier, I would suggest that chief executives in industrialized systems—socialist and bourgeois democratic—do seem to have some power, or at least enough to put an individualized stamp on the policy priorities of their administration (Tsurutani and Mullen, 1977). However, this is within certain bounds; there is only so much a new leader can do, and that margin of impact is remarkably similar in the United States, Western Europe and the Soviet bloc.

This issue of the power of chief executives also speaks to the more general literature on the role of elites in the policy-making process in advanced industrial societies. Over the past ten years, as noted throughout this book, there has been a trend away from the rational actor or actress approach—and indeed the "actor" or "actress" approach in general—and towards treating policy as the result of the influence of structural factors and standard patterns of behavior (Allison, 1969). The outcome of this emphasis has been that studies of policy outputs have tended to ignore how variables, such as party competition, economic development, and the like, are actually transformed into constraints on decisions. What governments produce, then, is supposed to reflect bureaucratic behavior; organizations make policies, people do not.

In the past few years, this view of policy-making without policy-makers has been criticized, in particular by students of American state politics. For example, Eric Uslaner and Ronald Weber (1975:131) have noted, ironically, the relative absence of actual decision-making processes in decision-making studies:

> We maintain that the analyses of policy outputs which have dominated previous research have served to obfuscate rather than to clarify the structure of the conversion *process* in state policy-making. In these studies, the concern has been with the *determinants of policy outputs* rather

than with the actual factors which state decision-makers employ in formulating these outputs. Environmental factors—be they economic, social or political—undoubtedly have a great impact on the decision-making process. Previous studies, however, have not attempted to link the environment to the decision-making process in state houses, legislative bodies, and the bureaucracies. The missing element is the decision-maker himself [sic] (also see Hofferbert, 1971).

This analysis suggests that the importance of leaders in Western policy-making has been underestimated, and that Prime Ministers and First Secretaries as well as Presidents are important participants (especially in the honeymoon) in the policy process. Otherwise (but given the qualification noted above), their rotation in office should have little impact, and the setting of new routines in each administration should not occur. The impact of succession on public policy, then, implies at the same time some impact of elites (as well as their changing decision environment).

This generalization is particularly striking, when one remembers how much "actor dispensability" there is supposed to be in budgetary decision-making in particular. Presidents and Prime Ministers are supposed to be prisoners of routine, as:

> Budgeting turns out to be an incremental process, proceeding from an historical base, guided by accepted notions of fair share, in which decisions are fragmented, made in sequence by specialized bodies, and coordinated through repeated attacks on problems and through multiple feedback mechanisms. The roles of the participants, and their perception of each others' powers and desires, fit together to provide a reasonably stable set of criteria on which to base calculations (Wildavsky, 1964:62).

The fact that these "fair shares" are defined differently after each succession suggests that elites do make decisions and do change priorities. In short, they matter to some degree and are central to understanding how decisions are made and what decisions are made—especially during the honeymoon.

In the Soviet case, the scholarly bias against elite impact on decision-making does not exist; in fact, it runs the other way. The error in communist area studies, from the vantage point of the results of this study, may be an overemphasis on actor *in*dispensability—that is, assuming that all policy reflects leadership action and not organizational routines. Certainly, the extent to which I found budgetary allocations and many other policy areas to behave incrementally in the periods between succession (and sometimes even during succession) challenges the simple assumption that policy outputs are a direct product of elite manipulation. Just as in the United States, in socialist nations policy outputs reflect a combination of elite objectives and environmental influences. Thus, to understand policy-making in socialist systems, as in Western democratic states, one needs to take elites and their policy contexts into account, and one needs to recognize that, while all leaders are different, there is a definite limit to their uniqueness (Allison, 1969; Lowi, 1964; Zimmerman, 1973). While this is hardly a heretical notion from an American policy perspective, it can be said to be one from the viewpoint of communist area studies.

Thus, as far as elite analysis is concerned, this study has three basic lessons. The first is that elites are not necessarily Babbitts, void of opinions, unable to exercise authority, unwilling or unable to introduce new public policies. In fact, they may satisfy their ambitions and their ideological commitments by being innovators, rather than conformists. Second, the recruitment and campaign process can work to enhance the competence and the incentives necessary for innovation—expertise, experience, ambition, and conflict are hardly antithetical to policy change. Finally, it should be clear that elites are important in the policy process, but even during the honeymoon they do operate under some constraints. To understand their behavior, then, one needs to know their needs, desires, and constraints, and the pressures and possibilities arising from the policy environment. It makes as little sense to talk of a moribund elite (or, in the Western case, incremental decision-making) as it does to talk of leaders' shaping everything. Depending on one's normative stance, one can say either that petrification alternates with more flexibility, or that incementalism alternates with (albeit circumscribed) innovation. The point is that sometimes elite factors are allowed to dominate (i.e., the honeymoon) but most of the time the decision environment dominates (i.e., between successions). But in most decisions, *both* sets of factors come into play.

The Study of Public Policy

This study also touches on several important issues pertaining to public policy analysis. The first issue has to do with the models that scholars use to interpret the decision process. In recent years, students of bourgeois democratic politics (and, more recently, socialist politics) have explained elite decisions primarily in terms of the incremental model. Thus, elites are said to try to reduce the conflict and complexity in their environment by making marginal adjustments in prevailing priorities. The result of this strategy is small change, and a distaste for the risks involved in large change. Though many admit there are exceptions to this argument, few would disagree that the incremental model is the best prediction of how policy is made and how little it changes over time in the West.

This analysis offers an important qualification to that picture in finding not one but two models operating with a regularized alternation between them. I found within administrations, incrementalism, and between administrations, innovation. New leaders innovate, then, only to become prisoners of their own routines—large change becomes small and consistent change until the next administration. Thus, public policy, East and West—from

budgetary allocations to social and agricultural policies—
follows a *cycle* of development that features small change
with periodic shifts in priorities brought on by leadership
succession. New leaders advocate new policies which become routinized until the next changeover, whereupon a
"new routine" appears.

The question then becomes: how does one interpret this
cycle? At first glance, it would appear to be another example of "exceptions" to incrementalism, similar to, for
instance, the American space program or the distinction
between programmatic and agency-related changes in
budgetary policy over time (Natchez and Bupp, 1973;
Schulman, 1975). From this perspective, I would concur
with John Manley (1970:5) that at times "an abnormal
model of decision-making" may be needed to understand
particular policies:

> The normal incremental mode of policy-making is bro-
> ken in enough instances . . . and these instances are such
> important departures in policy, that more attention is
> due to the reasons why federal institutions take new paths
> in policy-making and do not simply rest content with
> marginal adjustments in the status quo. For basic policy
> decisions that significantly extend the scope of federal
> involvement in American life . . . [and] that transform
> policies . . . and that alter arrangements among governing
> units, a model of "abnormal decision-making" is needed.

However, I would object to this characterization because
of its emphasis on deviance, and the implication that the
policy innovation was unexpected, unpredictable, and dependent upon a unique combination of forces (Wilson,
1966). I would counter this conception with the argument
that in this study, innovation was as predictable as incrementalism, that periodic "large change," to borrow Braybrooke and Lindblom's (1969) terminology, seems to be as
much a routine of public policy as small change. Therefore,
this study does not reject incrementalism, but rather qual-

ifies it. I would argue that incrementalism is only part of the policy process; the other part is the electoral period and the honeymoon that follows it. In that time span, both power and desire to change policy priorities are high. Incrementalism becomes less viable and reasonable, and innovation becomes the more logical strategy. While during an administration, conflict, complexity, and the continuity of political desires and policy coalitions all encourage the continuation of previous priorities, in the wake of succession conflict is low, policy-making is simplified (at least it seems to be to the new incumbents), new desires and pressures arise, policy coalitions are fluid, and the policy environment is more malleable. New leaders, therefore, introduce new policies because they want to, because their environment encourages them to do so, and because no one is really there to stop them. Old leaders, by contrast, get stuck in their ways because they lack the power and the desire to change policy priorities. It, therefore, makes sense to innovate when one is new in office, just as it makes sense to make marginal adjustments when one is in the middle of a term.

Thus, just as there is a succession cycle, so there is a policy cycle; incrementalism and innovation alternate, and to emphasize one without the other is to miss the essential ebb and flow of much of policy development.[6] Incrementalism, therefore, is only a portion of what seems to be a larger process that goes on within administrations, just as innovation describes only that cluster of changes that usually occurs at the beginning of administrations. Together,

---

[6] This alternation seems to resemble what Donald Searing (1972) has called the mechanistic versus the organismic models in the elite literature, the first emphasizing the impact of elites (the "great man" [sic] view) and the second emphasizing the dominance of the system and the veritable lack of elite impact (or what could be called, "the social forces" view). Clearly, the analysis confirms Searing's conclusion and that of Max Weber, for that matter, in that both explanations or models are appropriate to different conditions.

incrementalism and innovation capture in a general sense what seems to be the nature of policy-making, East and West, over time. Such a pattern, moreover, suggests how public policies are readjusted in a world of incrementalism, and how political stability is achieved when the door is thrown open to new policy alternatives. The key is the regularity of the shifts between the poles of stability and innovation: "In any political system a balance must be found between management and leadership, between institutionalization and innovation" (Breslauer, 1973:225). In industrial societies, that balance seems to be provided primarily by the periodic replacement of political leaders.

This notion of policy cycles or rhythms also implies that decision-making, East and West, at the apex of the system is not all that different. While this has been argued before, it has primarily been phrased in terms of leadership constraints (Bruce and Clawson, 1977). Thus, everyone agrees that neither the President of the United States nor the Soviet First Secretary can do exactly what he wants; both are hemmed in by political pressures and time, information and resource constraints. Just as Khrushchev reiterated time and again his reliance on the "collective," so Lyndon Johnson complained often of his inability to dominate the policy process.

While the findings of incrementalism within administrations, East and West, verify the similarity of elite constraints under socialism and bourgeois democracy, the results concerning innovation indicate parallels in freedom, power, and modes of policy change as well. In fact, the process of innovation, which was documented in the case studies of American welfare and Soviet agricultural policy, was remarkably similar in the two systems. In the first stage, a critique of the policy arose in response to poor performance, a fluid power structure, and the emergence of several contenders fighting for the leader's mantle. In the second stage—the honeymoon—new policies were quickly patched together and introduced with a great deal of fanfare. How-

ever, the problems became more intractable than the optimistic rhetoric promised, and the leader began to abandon the cause. A reaction then set in, and the policies were
whittled away—sometimes even to a mere shadow of their
former selves. In the next stage, a new succession battle
occured, and once again the policy area was attacked. This
time, though, the new entrepreneur was less concerned
with immediate results and getting at root causes; instead,
the new leader settled for treating the symptoms with cautious methods and deflated rhetoric. The key, in this second
stage, was to provide "cold cash," not utopian programs.

Thus, just as Johnson and Khrushchev both developed
dramatic new policies in welfare and agriculture, respectively, they tended to oversell these ideas and underfinance
them as well. Their successors, however, refined those policies on the basis of experience and better information,
provided more funds, and if anything undersold their potential. Thus, Nixon's resignation to the necessity of fun-
neling cold cash to welfare was similar to Secretary Brezhnev's reluctant but persistent commitment to more economic
investment in agriculture. From these case studies one can
conclude that leaders will engage in all kinds of activity
before they will spend money; all "new" policies seem to
go through several stages and the entrepreneur who puts
the policy on the agenda is oftentimes not the one to fully
implement it; and, finally, the broad coalitions that are
formed around new policies to coopt support often end up
destroying those very policies by placing them in a cross-
fire between the left and the right. Just as the Family Assistance Plan was not enough for liberals and too much for
conservatives, so Brezhnev's agricultural policies were too
little to satisfy the agricultural lobby and too much for the
proponents of heavy industrial development. In both cases,
the path to innovation and to setbacks was very similar.

It is plausible to conclude, therefore, that both the "routines" of politics and their periodic disturbances—in their
formation and their results—is similar in industrial socie-

ties, whether socialist or liberal democratic. In both systems, incrementalism grows out of conflict and complexity, and innovation grows out of ambition, ideological fervor, political pressures, and executive power. The key to which process operates, moreover, seems to be similar as well: the changing of the political guard. Innovations occur usually when leaders turn over; incrementalism occurs when the leadership stratum is stable. Policy-making in Moscow or Washington is cyclical, then, for many of the same reasons, and alternates between change and stability at much the same points in time. There is indeed little to choose, in terms of this study, between how Presidents, Prime Ministers, and First Secretaries make their decisions.

Conclusion

Thus, in finding the impact of succession on public policy to be strong, consistent, and similar in socialist and capitalist states, this study has touched on a number of important questions. I have found succession to be a powerful mechanism of policy innovation, elites are at times policy entrepreneurs, and there is a cycle in policy development that allows for stability and change. Finally, I have discovered a number of similarities between socialism and Western democracy in this study—in many ways life at the top is not all that different, East and West. However, the most important finding is that new leaders mean new policies and old leaders mean the continuation of old priorities—it is almost as simple as that.

Thus, the study of leadership succession and its impact on policy seems to go to the heart of many issues in political science: from elite recruitment, socialization, and decision-making to broader issues of change and the importance of public policy impacts and outputs. However, while succession touches on all these, I hope that the major effect of this analysis will be to provoke a reevaluation of the importance of leadership succession as a process which can and often does alter what elites do, the policies that result, and how the system performs. The importance of succession is that it affects elites very directly, and, in all political systems, socialist or bourgeois democratic, what affects the elites affects the political system. Who rules does indeed make a difference.

Appendix

Country	Data Sources for Budgets and Investment Allocations
Austria	*United Nations Statistical Yearbook* (New York: United Nations, 1976), 690; 1973, 680; 1971, 676; 1966, 653; 1956, 523.
Britain	*United Nations Statistical Yearbook* (New York: United Nations, 1976), 808; 1973, 680; 1971, 696; 1968, 686; 1966, 631; 1961, 549.
Canada	*Canada Yearbook* (Ottowa: Minister of Industry, Trade and Commerce, 1976), 764; 1975, 789. *Historical Statistics of Canada*, M. C. Urguhart, ed. (Toronto: Macmillan, 1965), 200, 202. *United Nations Statistical Yearbook* (New York: United Nations, 1970), 642; 1965, 604.
German Federal Republic	*Statistisches Jahrbuch für die Bundesrepublic Deutschland* (Bonn, West Germany: Weisbaden Verlag, 1977), 483; 1976, 403; 1973, 410; 1968, 388; 1965, 342-344.
Japan	*Japan Statistical Yearbook* (Tokyo: Bureau of Government Statistics, 1972), 450; 1968, 469; 1963, 423. *United Nations Statistical Yearbook* (New York: United Nations, 1976), 772.
Sweden	*United Nations Statistical Yearbook* (New York: United Nations, 1976), 805; 1973, 697; 1966, 656; 1961, 544.
United States (nations)	*United Nations Statistical Yearbook* (New York: United Nations, 1976), 764; 1971, 696; 1966, 646; 1959, 584.
United States (states)	*Compendium of State Government Finances* (Washington, D.C.: Department of Commerce, Bureau of the Census, 1967), 28-33; 1965, 28-33; 1961, 22-23; 1959, 22.

The Book of the States, 1973-1974 (Lexington, Ky.: The Council of State Governments, 1972), 206-210; 1964-1965, 200-205; 1960-1961, 184.

Communist States in General

Public Expenditures in Communist and Capitalist Nations, Frederic Pryor (Homewood, Ill.: Dorsey, 1968), 318-395.
Sovet ekonomicheskoi vzaimopomoshchi statisticheskii ezhegodnik stran chlenov soveta ekonomicheskoi vzaimopomoshchi (Moskva: Statistika, 1976), 130-159.

Bulgaria

Statisticheski Godishnik na Narodna Republika Bulgariia (Sofia: Bureau of Information, 1976), 86, 346-349; 1973, 200, 234; 1966, 225-227, 318; 1959, 154, 214-215.

Czechoslovakia

Public Expenditures in Communist and Capitalist Nations, Frederic Pryor (Homewood, Ill.: Dorsey, 1968), 336.
Statisticka rocenka Ceskoslovenske Socialisticke Republiky (Praha: Statistical Office, 1973), 161; 1971, 207-208; 1966, 133, 150.

German Democratic Republic

Statistisches Jahrbuch der Deutschen Demokratischen Republik (Berlin: State Statistical Office, 1973), 314, 45; 1966, 413-414; 1961, 51-52

Hungary

Public Expenditures in Communist and Capitalist Nations, Frederic Pryor (Homewood, Ill.: Dorsey, 1968), 355.
Statistical Yearbook of Hungary (Budapest: Central Statistical Office, 1973), 89-91.

Poland

Rocznik Statystyczny (Warsawa: Central Statistical Office, 1973), 135, 566; 1966, 91, 524-526; 1960, 102, 489-491.

Romania

Annuarul Statistic al Republicii Romania (Bucharest: Central Statistical Office, 1971), 582-584; 1969, 564-566; 1962, 549-551.

Soviet Union (republics)

Gosudarstvennyi biudzhet SSSR i biudzhety soiuznykh respublik: statisticheskii sbornik (Moskva: Finansy, 1972), 110-222; 1966, 98-214; 1962, 103-213.

Soviet Union (national)	*Narodnoe khoziaistvo SSSR* (Moskva: Statistika, 1971), 730, 482-483; 1967, 618-619, 886; 1965, 522, 509; 1962, 434, 635; 1959, 540-541.
	Narodnoe khoziaistvo SSSR (Moskva: Statistika, 1972), 481, 326.
	Narodnoe khoziaistvo SSSR za 60 let: Iubeleinyi statisticheskii ezhegodnik (Moskva: Statistika, 1977), 272-273, 653-656.
	The Soviet Financial System, R. W. Davies (Cambridge, England: Cambridge University Press, 1958), 244-248.
Country	*Data Sources for Personal Income, Wages, and Public Consumption*
Czechoslovakia	Holesovsky, Vaclav (1977), "Czechoslovak Economy in the 1970's" in Joint Economic Committee (ed.), *East European Economies Post Helsinki: A Compendium of Papers* (Washington, D.C.: G.P.O.), 98-139.
German Democratic Republic	Keren, Michael (1977), "The Return of the Ancient Regime: The GDR in the 1960's" in Joint Economic Committee (ed.), *East European Economies Post Helsinki: A Compendium of Papers* (Washington, D.C. G.P.O.), 720-765.
Poland	Fallenbuchl, Zbigniew (1977), "The Polish Economy in the 1970's," in Joint Economic Committee (ed.), *East European Economies Post Helsinki: A Compendium of Papers* (Washington, D.C.: G.P.O.), 816-864.
USSR	*Current Digest of the Soviet Press*, Vol. 29, Number 48 (December 27, 1978):12; Vol. 28, Number 50 (January 11, 1977):9; Vol. 27, No. 48 (December 24, 1976):7; Vol. 26, No. 51 (January 15, 1975):12; Vol. 24, No. 3 (January 24, 1973):9.
	Narodnoe khoziaistvo SSSR (Moscow: Statistika, 1975), 563, 604; 1974, 602; 1970, 533; 1967, 887; 1965, 607.

Western
Nations:
Electoral
Statistics

M. C. Urguhart, ed., *Historical Statistics of Canada* (Toronto: MacMillan, 1965), 200-202. *Japan Statistical Yearbook* (Tokyo: Bureau of Government Statistics, 1972), 450; 1968, 469; 1963, 423.
Robin Bidwell, ed., *Bidwell's Guide to Government Ministers* (Cambridge, England: Cass, 1973), 1-54.
F.W.S. Craig, ed., *British Parliamentary Election Statistics* (Chichester, England: Political Reference Publications, 1971), 14-20.
Dolf Sternberger and Gerhard Vogel, eds., *Die Wahl der Parlamente und Andere Staatsorgane: Ein Handbuch* (Berlin: De Gruyer, 1969), 1128-1349.
Japan Almanac (Tokyo: Marnichi, 1976), 63.
Mackie, Thomas and Richard Rose. "Election Data: General Elections in Western Nations during 1973," *European Journal of Political Research*, 2 (September 1974), 293-298.
————. "Election Data: General Elections in Western Nations during 1974," *European Journal of Political Research*, 3 (September 1975), 322-327.
————. "Election Data: General Elections in Western Nations during 1975," *European Journal of Political Research*, 4 (September 1976), 329-332.
————. *The International Almanac of Electoral History* (London: MacMillan, 1974), 65-166.
Statistical Abstract of the United States (Washington, D.C.: Department of Commerce, 1976), 461; 1972, 370; 1966, 377; 1964, 379; 1960, 357.

Socialist
Successions

Hodnett, Grey and Val Ogareff (1973), *Leaders of the Soviet Republics, 1955-1972.* (Canberra, Australia: Australian National University).
Rush, Myron (1974), *How Communist States Change Their Rulers* (Ithaca, New York: Cornell University Press).

References

Aberbach, Joel, and Bert Rockman (1976). "Clashing Beliefs Within the Executive Branch." *American Political Science Review*, 70 (June), 456-468.

"Additional Information Concerning the Agricultural Subsidy" (1974). *Radio Liberty Research Paper* (October 2), 1-3.

Afanas'ev, V. (1965). "Nauchnoe rukovodstvo sotsial'nymi protsessami." *Kommunist* (The Soviet Union), 12 (August), 58-73.

Ahlberg, Clark, and Daniel Moynihan (1972). "Changing Governors and Policies." In Thad Beyle and J. Oliver Williams (eds.). *The American Governor in Behavioral Perspective*. New York: Harper and Row, 95-104.

Akademiia Nauka SSSR (1969). *Kul'turnaiia revoliutsiia v SSSR, 1917-1965*. Moscow: Nauka.

Allison, Graham (1969). "Conceptual Models and the Cuban Missile Crisis." *American Political Science Review*, 63 (September), 689-718.

Altshuler, Alan, ed. (1968). *The Politics of Federal Bureaucracy*. New York: Van Nostrand Reinhold.

Anderson, Charles (1967). *Politics and Economic Change in Latin America*. New York: Van Nostrand Reinhold.

Anderson, James (1970). "Poverty, Unemployment and Economic Development: The Search for National Anti-Poverty Policy." In James Anderson (ed.), *Politics and Economic Policy-Making: Selected Readings*. Reading, Mass.: Addison-Wesley, 150-175.

Andrews, William (ed.) (1969). *European Politics II: The Dynamics of Change*. New York: Van Nostrand Reinhold.

Anichkin, D. (1972). "Demokraty pered vyborami." *S.Sh.A.*, 4 (April), 22-31.

Anisimov, N. (1975). "Agrarnaia politika KPSS na sovremennom etape." *Planovoe khoziaistio* (Moscow), 7 (July), 87-95.

Anton, Thomas (1966). *The Politics of State Expenditure in Illinois*. Urbana, Illinois: The University of Illinois.

——— (1967). "Roles and Symbols in the Determination of State Expenditures." *Midwest Journal of Political Science*, 11 (February), 188-214.

Arian, Alan, and Samuel Barnes (1974). "The Dominant Party

System: A Neglected Model of Democratic Political Stability."
Journal of Politics, 36 (August), 526-614.

Assael, Henry (1969). "Constructive Role of Organizational Conflict." *Administrative Science Quarterly*, 14 (December), 573-583.

Bach, Stanley, and George Sulzner (eds.) (1974). *Perspectives on
the Presidency*. Lexington, Mass.: D. C. Heath and Company.

Baibakov, Nikolai (1975). *O gosudarstvennom plane i razvitiia narodnogo khoziaistva SSSR na 1975 god*. Moscow: Finansy.

———— (1973). "On the State Plan for the Development of the
USSR National Economy in 1973." *Current Digest of the Soviet
Press*, 24 (January), 5.

Bailey, Stephen, and Edith Mosher (1968). *ESEA: The Office of
Education Administers A Law*. Syracuse, New York: Syracuse
University Press.

Barber, James (1972). *The Presidential Character: Predicting Performance in the White House*. Englewood Cliffs, New Jersey:
Prentice-Hall.

Barkaiskas, A. (1973). "O preodelinii kulturno-bytovykh razlichii
mezhdu gorodami i derevnei." *Kommunist* (Moscow), 8 (May),
55-66.

Barsukov, Iu. (1972). "Republikanskaiia partiia nakanune vyborov." *S.Sh.A.*, 6 (June), 30-39.

Baumann, Zygmunt (1971). "Twenty Years After: The Crisis in
Soviet-Type Systems." *Problems of Communism*, 20 (November-
December), 45-53.

Baylis, Thomas (1972). "In Quest of Legitimacy." *Problems of Communism*, 20 (March-April), 56-67.

Beck, Carl (1975). "Patterns and Problems of Governance." In
Carl Beck and Carmelo Meso-Lago (eds.), *Comparative Socialist
Systems: Essays on Politics and Economics*. Pittsburgh, Pennsyl-
vania: Pittsburgh University Press, 123-146.

Beck, Carl, William Jarzabek and Paul Ernandez (1976). "Political
Succession in Eastern Europe." *Studies in Comparative Communism*, 8 (Spring/Summer), 35-61.

———— (ed). (1973). *Comparative Communist Political Leadership*.
New York: David McKay.

Beglov, I. (1971). *S.Sh.A.: Sobstvennosti i vlast'*. Moscow: Nauka.

Beliakov, A., and I. Shvets (1967). "Partinaiia informatsiia." *Kommunist* (Moscow), 8 (April), 108-131.

Bell, Daniel (1970). "Ideology and Soviet Politics." In Richard Cornell (ed.), *The Soviet Political System: A Book of Readings*. Englewood Cliffs, New Jersey: Prentice-Hall, 101-110.

Bennis, Warren (1966). *Changing Organizations*. New York: McGraw-Hill.

———, Kenneth Benne and Robert Chin (eds.) (1969). *The Planning of Change*. New York: Holt, Rinehart and Winston.

Bertsch, Gary, and Thomas Ganschow (eds.) (1976). *Comparative Communism*. San Francisco: W. M. Freeman.

Bibby, John, and Roger Davidson (1967). *On Capital Hill*. New York: Holt, Rinehart and Winston.

Birman, A. (1974). "The USSR State Budget in the Perspective of Economic Development." *Problems of Economics*, 16 (March), 74-87.

Blackmer, Donald I. M. (1975). "Change and Continuity in Postwar Italian Communism." In Donald L. M. Blackmer and Sidney Tarrow (eds.), *Communism in Italy and France*. Princeton, New Jersey: Princeton University Press, 21-68.

Blackwell, Robert (1972). "Career Development in the Soviet Obkom Elite: A Conservative Trend." *Soviet Studies*, 24 (July), 24-40.

Blalock, Hubert (1964). *Causal Inferences in Non-Experimental Research*. New York: Norton.

Blondel, Jean (1977). "Types of Government Leadership in Atlantic Countries." *European Journal of Political Research*, 5, 33-51.

Blumenthal, Richard (1969). "The Bureaucracy: Anti-Poverty and The Community Action Program." In Allan Sindler (ed.), *American Political Institutions and Public Policy*. Boston: Little, Brown and Company, 128-179.

Bora, M., and V. Poltogorygina (eds.) (1969). *Planirovanie i khoziaistvennaia reforma*. Moscow: Mysl'.

Bornstein, Morris (1969). "The Soviet Debate on Agricultural Price and Procurement Reforms." *Soviet Studies*, 21 (July), 2-20.

Boulding, Kenneth (1966). *The Parameters of Politics*. Urbana, Illinois: University of Illinois.

Bowler, N. Kenneth (1974). *The Nixon Guaranteed Income Proposal: Substance and Process in Policy Change*. Cambridge, Massachusetts: Ballinger Press.

Brandt, Willy (1976). *People and Politics*. Boston: Little Brown.

Braybrooke, David (1969). "Types of Decision-Making." In James Rosenau (ed.), *International Politics and Foreign Policy*. New York: Free Press.

Braybrooke, David, and Charles Lindblom (1963). *A Strategy of Decision*. New York: Free Press.

Brecher, Charles (1973). *The Impact of Federal Anti-Poverty Policies*. New York: Praeger.

Brecher, Michael (1966). *Nehru's Mantle: The Politics of Succession in India*. New York: Praeger.

Breslauer, George (1978). "On the Adaptability of Welfare State Authoritarianism in the USSR." In Karl Ryavec (ed.), *The Communist Party and Soviet Society*. Amherst, Massachusetts: University of Massachusetts Press, 208-250.

———— (1976). "Khrushchev Reconsidered." *Problems of Communism*, 25 (September-October), 18-33.

———— (1973). "Between Socialism and Communism: Changing Soviet Perspectives Since Stalin." Unpublished Ph.D. dissertation, the University of Michigan.

Brezhnev, Leonid (1976a). *Leninskim kursom*, Volume V. Moscow: Politizdat.

———— (1976b). "Otchet Tsentral'nogo komiteta KPSS: ocherednye zadachi partii v oblasti vnutrennei i vneshnei politiki." *Pravda*, February 25, 1-5.

———— (1975a). *Leninskim kursom*, Volume IV. Moscow: Politizdat.

———— (1975b). *Ob osnovnykh voprosakh ekonomicheskoi politiki KPSS na sovremennom etape*. Volumes I and II. Moscow: Politizdat.

———— (1974). *Voprosy agrarnoi politiki KPSS: osvoenie tselinykh zemel' Kazakhstana*. Moscow: Politizdat.

———— (1973). "Delo vse partii, vsego naroda." *Pravda*, December 16, 1-2.

———— (1972). *Leninskim kursom*, Volumes II and III. Moscow: Politizdat.

———— (1970). *Leninskim kursom*, Volume I. Moscow: Politizdat.

Bromke, Adam (1972). "A New Political Style." *Problems of Communism*, 11 (October), 1-19.

Brown, Archie (1975). "Political Developments." In Archie Brown and Michael Kaser (eds.), *The Soviet Union Since the Fall of Khrushchev*. London: MacMillan, 218-275.

———— (1971). "Prime Ministerial Power." In Mattei Dogan and

REFERENCES   [265]

Richard Rose (eds.), *European Politics: A Reader*. Boston: Little Brown and Company, 459-481.

Bruce, James, and Robert Clawson (1977). "A Zonal Analysis Model for Comparative Politics." *World Politics*, 29 (January), 177-215.

Brumberg, Abraham (1971). "The Fall of Khrushchev." In John Strong (ed.), *The Soviet Union under Brezhnev and Kosygin*. New York: Van Nostrand Reinhold, 1-15.

Bryan, Paige (1974). "The Program for Land Development in the USSR." *Radio Liberty* (January 25), 1-9.

Brzezinski, Zbigniew (ed.) (1969). *Dilemmas of Change in Soviet Politics*. New York: Columbia University Press.

—— (1967). *Ideology and Power in Soviet Politics*. New York: Praeger.

—— (1967). *The Soviet Bloc*. Cambridge, Massachusetts: Harvard University.

—— (1966). "The Soviet System: Transformation or Degeneration." *Problems of Communism*, 15 (January-February), 3-9.

—— and Samuel Huntington (1963). *Political Power: USA/USSR*. New York: Viking Press.

Bunce, Valerie (1980a). "The Political Consumption Cycle: A Comparative Analysis." *Soviet Studies*, 32 (April), 280-290.

—— (1980b). "The Succession Connection: Policy Cycles and Political Change in the Soviet Union and Eastern Europe." *American Political Science Review* (December), 966-977.

—— (1976). *Elite Succession and Policy Change in Communist and Democratic Systems*. Unpublished Ph.D. dissertation, the University of Michigan.

—— and John Echols (1978). "Power and Policy in Communist Systems: The Problem of Incrementalism." *Journal of Politics*, 40 (September), 911-932.

—— (1975). "Aggregate Data Analysis and the Study of Policy Change in Communist Systems." Paper presented at the American Association for the Advancement of Slavic Studies in Atlanta, Georgia, October 8-11.

Burling, Robbins (1974). *The Passage of Power: Studies in Political Succession*. New York: Academic Press.

Burke, Vincent J., and V. Burke (1974). *Nixon's Good Deed: Welfare Reform*. New York: Columbia University.

Burns, James McGregor (1968). *To Heal and to Build: The Programs of Lyndon Johnson.* New York: McGraw-Hill.

Bush, Keith (1974). "Soviet Agriculture: Ten Years Under New Management." *Radio Liberty Research Paper* (August 21).

—— (1972). "Soviet Capital Investment Since Khrushchev: A Note." *Soviet Studies,* 24 (July), 91-96.

Butenko, A. (1972). "O razvitom sotsialisticheskom obshchestve." *Kommunist* (Moscow), 6 (October), 48-58.

Butler, David, and Donald Stokes (1974). *Political Change in Britain.* New York: St. Martin's Press.

Bychek, N. "Khoziaistvennaia reforma i sovershenstvovanie sistemy pokazatelei narodnokhoziaistvennogo plana." In M. Bora and V. Poltorygina (eds.), *Planirovanie i khoziaistvennaia reforma.* Moscow: Mysl' Press, 101-128.

Byrne, Gary, and Kenneth Pederson (eds.) (1971). *Politics in Western European Democracies: Patterns and Problems.* New York: Wiley.

Cameron, David (1978). "The Expansion of the Public Economy: A Comparative Analysis." *American Political Science Review,* 72 (December), 1243-1261.

——, Stephanie Cameron and Richard Hofferbert (1976). "Non Incrementalism in Public Policy: The Dynamics of Change." Paper presented at the Midwest Political Science Convention in Chicago, Illinois, May 1-3.

Campbell, John Creighton (1977). *Contemporary Japanese Budget Politics.* Berkeley, California: University of California Press.

—— and John Echols (1977). *The Budgetary Process in Cross-National Perspective.* Washington, D.C.: The American Political Science Association.

Caporaso, James, and A. Pelowski (1971). "Economic and Political Integration in Europe: A Quasi-Experimental Analysis." *American Political Science Review,* 65 (June), 418-433.

—— and Leslie Roos (eds.) (1973). *Quasi-Experimental Approaches: Testing Theory and Evaluation Policy.* Evanston, Illinois: Northwestern University Press.

Carlson, Richard (1962). *Executive Succession and Organizational Change: Placebound and Career-bound Superintendents.* Chicago: Midwest Administration Center.

Carter, Jimmy (1978). "Budget Message to Congress." Quoted in *Newsweek* (August 12), 13.

Castles, Francis (1976). "Policy Innovation and Institutional Stability in Sweden." *British Journal of Political Science*, 6 (April), 203-216.

Christoph, James (1975). "High Civil Servants and the Politics of Consensualism in Great Britain." In Mattei Dogan (ed.), *The Mandarins of Western Europe*. New York: John Wiley, 25-62.

Ciboski, Kenneth (1974). "Ambition Theory and Candidate Members of the Politburo." *Journal of Politics*, 36 (February), 172-183.

Clarke, Roger (1968). "Soviet Agricultural Reforms Since Khrushchev." *Soviet Studies*, 20 (October), 159-178.

Cleary, J. W. (1965). "The Virgin Lands." *Survey*, 56 (July), 95-105.

Cnudde, Charles, and Donald McCrone (1969). "Party Competition in the American States." *American Political Science Review*, 62 (March), 858-866.

Cocks, Paul (1977). "Re-Tooling the Directed Society: Administrative Modernization and Developed Socialism." In Jan Triska and Paul Cocks (eds.), *Political Development in Eastern Europe*. New York: Praeger, 53-92.

Connor, Walter (1975). "Generations and Politics." *Problems of Communism*, 24 (September-October), 25-39.

Conquest, Robert (1967). *Power and Policy in the USSR*. New York: Harper and Row.

Cornell, Richard (1970). *The Soviet Political System: A Book of Readings*. Englewood Cliffs, New Jersey: Prentice-Hall.

Corwin, Ronald (1973). "Strategies for Organizational Innovation: An Empirical Comparison." *American Sociological Review*, 37 (August), 441-454.

Coser, Lewis (1968). "Conflict: Social Aspects." In *The International Encyclopedia of the Social Sciences*. New York: MacMillan, 232-236.

——— (1956). *The Functions of Social Conflict*. Glencoe, Illinois: Free Press.

Cowart, Andrew (1978a). "The Economic Policies of European Governments, Part I: Monetary Policy." *British Journal of Political Science*, 9 (July), 285-312.

——— (1978b)."The Economic Policies of European Governments, Part II: Fiscal Policy." *British Journal of Political Science*, 9 (October), 425-440.

Cronin, Thomas (1975). " 'Everybody Believes in Democracy Until He Gets to the White House . . .': An Examination of White House-Departmental Relations." In Aaron Wildavsky (ed.), *Perspectives on the Presidency*. Boston: Little Brown, 362-392.

―――― and Sanford Greenberg (eds.) (1969). *The Presidential Advisory System*. New York: Harper and Row.

Crossman, Richard (1976). *Diaries of a Cabinet Minister*. London: Hamilton.

Crozier, Michel, Samuel Huntington and Joji Watanuki (eds.) (1975). *The Crisis of Democracy*. New York: New York University.

Cyert, Richard, and James March (1965). *A Behavioral Theory of the Firm*. Englewood Cliffs, New Jersey: Prentice-Hall.

Dahl, Robert (1966). "Patterns of Opposition." In Robert Dahl (ed.), *Political Opposition in Western Democracies*. New Haven, Connecticut: Yale University Press.

Dallin, Alexander (1978). *The Twenty-Fifth Congress of the CPSU: Assessment and Context*. Stanford, California: Hoover Institution.

Daniels, R. V. (1971). "Soviet Politics Since Khrushchev." In John Strong (ed.), *The Soviet Union Under Brezhnev and Kosygin*. New York: Van Nostrand Reinhold, 16-25.

Danilov, V. P. (1972). "Problemii istorii Sovetskoe derevnei v 1946-1977gg." In I. M. Volkov (ed.), *Razvitie sel'skogo khoziaistva SSSR v poslevoennye gody (1946-1970)*. Moscow: Nauka, 10-28.

David, Paul (ed.) (1961). *The Presidential Election and Transition 1960-1961*. Washington, D.C.: Brookings Institution.

Davies, R. W. (1958). *The Development of the Soviet Budgetary System*. Cambridge, England: Cambridge University Press.

De Grazia, Alfred (1969). "The Myth of the Presidency." In Aaron Wildavsky (ed.), *The Presidency*. Boston: Little Brown, 49-73.

Demitsov, S., and P. Vasil'ev (1973). *Planirovanie narodnogo khoziaistva*. Moscow: Ekonomika Press.

Denisov, A. (1967). *Sovetskoe gosudarstvo*. Moscow: Moskovskii Universitet.

Denisov, Iu. (1971). "Kadry predsedatelei kolkhozov v 1950-1968gg." *Istoriia SSSR* (Moscow), 1 (January-February), 38-57.

Deutsch, Morton (1972). "Productive and Destructive Conflict." In John Thomas and Warren Bennis (eds.), *Management of*

Change and Conflict. Middlesex, England: Penguin Books, 381-398.

Dibb, Paul (1969). "Soviet Agriculture Since Khrushchev: An Economic Appraisal." Occasional Paper, Number Four, Department of Political Science, Australian National University. Canberra, Australia: Australian National University.

Di Maio, Alfred (1974). *Soviet Urban Housing: Problems and Policies*. New York: Praeger.

Divine, Robert (1974a). *Foreign Policy and U.S. Presidential Elections: 1940, 1948*. New York: Watts.

——— (1974b). *Foreign Policy and U.S. Presidential Elections: 1952, 1960*. New York: Watts.

Doern, G. Bruce (1971). "The Budgetary Process and the Policy Role of the Federal Bureaucracy." In G. Bruce Doern and Peter Aucoin (eds.), *The Structure of Policy-Making in Canada*. Toronto: Macmillan, 79-112.

Dogan, Mattei (ed.) (1975). *The Mandarins of Western Europe*. New York: Wiley.

——— and Richard Rose (eds.) (1971). *European Politics: A Reader*. Boston: Little Brown.

Dolbeare, Kenneth (1974). *Political Change in the United States: A Framework for Analysis*. New York: McGraw-Hill.

Donovan, John (1970a). "Community Action: Poor People Against City Hall." In James Anderson (ed.), *Politics and Economic Policy-Making: Selected Readings*. Reading, Massachusetts: Addison-Wesley, 176-186.

——— (1970b). *The Policy-Makers*. New York: Pegasus.

Doolittle, Frederick, Frank Levy and Michael Wiseman (1977). "The Mirage of Welfare Reform." *Public Interest*, 47 (Spring), 62-87.

Dornberg, John (1974). *Brezhnev: The Masks of Power*. New York: Basic.

Downs, Anthony (1974). "The Successes and Failures of Federal Housing Policy." In Eli Ginsberg and Robert Solow (eds.), *The Great Society*. New York: Basic, 124-145.

——— (1966). *Inside Bureaucracy*. Boston: Little Brown.

——— (1957). *An Economic Theory of Democracy*. New York: Wiley.

Downs, George, and Lawrence Mohr (1975). "Conceptual Issues in the Study of Innovation." Paper presented at the American

Political Science Association Convention in San Francisco, September 2-5.

Drakhovitch, Milorad (ed.) (1965). *Marxism in the Modern World.* Stanford, California: Stanford University Press.

Drew, Elizabeth (1975). "Running." *The New Yorker* (December 1), 54-118.

Durgin, Frank, Jr. (1962). "The Virgin Lands Programme, 1954-1960." *Soviet Studies,* 13 (January), 237-254.

Dye, Thomas (1973). *Politics in the States and Communities.* Englewood Cliffs, New Jersey: Prentice-Hall.

—— (1969). "Executive Power and Public Policy in the States." *Western Political Quarterly,* 27 (December), 926-939.

—— and L. Harmon Zeigler (1972). *The Irony of Democracy.* Belmont, California: Duxbury Press.

Echols, John (1975). "Politics, Budgets and Regional Equality in Communist and Capitalist Systems." *Comparative Political Studies,* 8 (October), 259-292.

Eckstein, Harry (1958). *The English Health Service: Its Origin, Structure and Achievement.* Cambridge, Massachusetts: Harvard University Press.

Edelman, Murray (1964). *The Symbolic Uses of Politics.* Urbana, Illinois: University of Illinois Press.

Edinger, Lewis (1970). "Political Change in Germany: The Federal Republic After the 1969 Election." *Comparative Politics,* 2 (July), 549-578.

Edwards, George (1976). "Presidential Influence in the House: Presidential Prestige as a Source of Power." *American Political Science Review,* 70 (March), 101-113.

Eugin-Wadekin, Karl (1975). "Income Distribution in Soviet Agriculture." *Soviet Studies,* 37 (January), 3-26.

Evans, Alfred (1977). "Developed Socialism in Soviet Ideology." *Soviet Studies,* 29 (July), 409-428.

Evans, Rowland, and Robert Novak (1971). *Nixon in the White House: The Frustration of Power.* New York: Random House.

Fainsod, Merle (1970). *How Russia Is Ruled.* Cambridge, Massachusetts: Harvard University Press.

—— (1965). "Khrushchevism." In Milorad Drakhovitch (ed.), *Marxism in the Modern World.* Stanford, California: Stanford University Press, 88-122.

"Family Income Supplements with Caveats" (1974). *Radio Liberty* (September 27).

Feiwal, George (1972). *The Soviet Quest for Economic Efficiency: Issues, Controversies and Reforms.* New York: Praeger.

Fenno, Richard (1959). *The President's Cabinet.* Cambridge, Massachusetts: Harvard University Press.

Finansy SSSR (1972). *Gosudarstvennyi biudzhet SSSR i biudzhety soiuznykh respublik; statisticheskii sbornik.* Moscow: Finansy.

—— (1966). *Gosudarstvennyi biudzhet SSSR i biudzhety soiuznykh respublik: statisticheskii sbornik.* Moscow: Finansy.

—— (1962). *Gosudarstvennyi biudzhet SSSR i biudzhety soiuznykh respublik: statisticheskii sbornik.* Moscow: Finansy.

—— (1966). *The Soviet Financial System.* Moscow: Progress Publishers.

Florient'iev, L. (1975). "Ekonomicheskaiia politika partii v derevnei na sovremennom etape." In *Problemy istorii sovremennoi sovetskoe derevnei.* Moscow: Nauka, 8-22.

Frey, Bruno (1978). "Political Economic Models and Cycles." *Journal of Public Economy,* 9, 203-220.

Fried, Robert (1976). "Party and Policy in West German Cities." *American Political Science Review,* 70 (March), 11-24.

—— (1971). "Communism, Urban Budgets and the Two Italies: A Case Study in Comparative Urban Budgets." *Journal of Politics,* 33 (November), 1008-1051.

Gallik, Daniel (ed.) (1968). *The Soviet Financial System.* Washington, D.C.: U.S. Department of Commerce.

Garbuzov, V. F. (1971). *O gosudarstvennom biudzhete SSSR na 1972 god i ob ispolnenii gosudarstvennogo biudzheta SSSR na 1971 god.* Moscow: Politizdat.

Gawthrop, Lewis (1969). *Bureaucratic Behavior in the Executive Branch.* New York: Free Press.

George, Alexander (1974). "Assessing Presidential Character." *World Politics,* 26 (June), 234-282.

Ginsberg, Benjamin (1976). "Elections and Public Policy." *American Political Science Review,* 70 (March), 41-49.

Ginsberg, Eli and Robert Solow (1974). "Some Lessons of the 1960's." *Public Interest,* 37 (Winter), 211-223.

Glazer, Nathan (1975). "Reform Work, Not Welfare." *Public Interest,* 40 (Summer), 3-10.

Glazer, Nathan (1969). "On Task-Forcing." *Public Interest*, 15 (September), 40-49.

Golan, Galia (1971). *The Czechoslovakia Reform Movement: Communism in Crisis, 1962-1968.* Cambridge, England: Cambridge University Press.

Golikov, V. A. (ed.) (1975). *Kursom Martovskogo plenum.* Moscow: Politizdat.

———— (ed.) (1972). *Sel'skoe khoziaistvo SSSR na sovremennom etape.* Moscow: Politizdat.

Gordon, Kermit (1969). "The Budget Director." In Thomas Crown and Sanford Greenberg (eds.), *The Presidential Advisory System.* New York: Harper and Row, 58-67.

Gordon, Michael (1972). "Civil Servants, Politicians and the British Policy Process." *Comparative Politics*, 4 (December), 149-161.

Gorskaiia, A. (1975). "Leninskii stil' i metody khoziaistvennogo rukovodstva." *Planovoe khoziaistvo* (Moscow), 11 (Noiabr), 93-102.

Gouldner, Alvin (1954). *Patterns of Industrial Bureaucracy.* Glencoe, Illinois: Free Press.

Greenstein, Fred (1969). *Personality and Politics.* Chicago: Markham.

Gross, Bertram (1969). "Timing the Offspring." In Edward Schneier (ed.), *Policy-Making in American Government.* New York: Basic Books, 29-41.

Grossman, Gregory (1976). "An Economy at Middle Age." *Problems of Communism*, 25 (March-April), 18-33.

Grusky, Oscar (1964). "Administrative Succession in Formal Organizations." *Social Forces*, 39 (October), 105-115.

Gubenko, M. P. (1975). "Sravnitel'naiia kharakteristika tendentsii i osobennostei razvitiia sel'sko-khoziaistvennogo proizvodstva RSFSR v 1961-1965 i 1966-1970." In *Problemy istorii sovremennoi sovetskoi derevnei.* Moscow: Nauka, 179-196.

Gunther, Klaus (1970). *Der Kanzlerwechsel in der Bundesrepublik: Adenauer, Erhard, Kiesinger.* Hanover, Federal Republic of Germany: Verlag für Literatur und Zeitgeschehen.

Gvishiani, Dj. (1972). *Organizatsiia i upravlenie.* Moscow: Nauka.

Hage, Jerald, and Robert Dewar (1973). "Elite Values and Organizational Structure in Predicting Innovation." *Administrative Science Quarterly*, 18 (September), 279-290.

Hahn, Werner (1972). *The Politics of Soviet Agriculture*. Baltimore: Johns Hopkins.

Handler, Joel (1972). *Reforming the Poor*. New York: Basic.

—— and Ellen Jane Hollingsworth (1971). *The Deserving Poor: A Study of Welfare Administration*. Chicago: Markham.

Hanson, Robert, and Robert Crew (1973). "The Policy Impact of Reapportionment." *Law and Society Review*, 8 (Fall), 69-94.

Haveman, Robert, and Julius Margolis (eds.) (1970). *Public Expenditures and Policy Analysis*. Chicago: Markham.

Headey, Bruce (1974). *British Cabinet Ministers: The Roles of Politicians in Executive Office*. London: Allen and Unwin.

Heclo, Hugh (1974). *Modern Social Policies in Britain and Sweden: From Relief to Income Maintenance*. New Haven, Connecticut: Yale University Press.

—— (1973). "Presidential and Prime Minister Selection." In Donald Matthews (ed.), *Perspectives on Presidential Selection*. Washington, D.C.: Brookings Institution, 19-48.

—— and Aaron Wildavsky (1974). *The Private Governance of Public Money*. London: Macmillan.

Heisler, Martin (ed.) (1974). *Politics in Europe*. New York: McKay.

Hendel, Samuel (ed.) (1973). *The Soviet Crucible*. North Scituate, Massachusetts: Duxbury.

Henry, Laurin (1960). *Presidential Transitions*. Washington, D.C.: Brookings Institution.

—— (1969). "Presidential Transitions: The 1968-1969 Experience in Perspective." *Public Administration Review*, 29 (September/October), 471-482.

Hermann, Charles (1963). "Crisis and Organizational Viability." *Administrative Science Quarterly*, 8 (June), 61-82.

Hershey, Marjorie Randon (1977). "A Social Learning Theory of Innovation and Change in Political Campaigning." Paper presented at the American Political Science Association Convention in Washington, D.C., September 1-4.

Hess, Stephen (1977). "Portrait of a President." *Woodrow Wilson Quarterly*, 1 (Winter), 43-48.

—— (1976). *Organizing the Presidency*. Washington, D.C.: Brookings Institution.

—— (1974). *The Presidential Campaign: The Leadership Selection Process Since Watergate*. Washington, D.C.: Brookings Institution.

Hibbs, Douglas (1977). "Political Parties and Macro-Economic

Policy." *American Political Science Review*, 71 (December), 1467-1487.

Hill, Ronald (1973). "Patterns of Deputy Selection to Local Soviets." *Slavic Review*, 25 (October), 196-212.

Hockin, Thomas (1971). "Apex of Power." In Thomas Hockin (ed.), *The Prime Minister and Political Leadership in Canada*. Scarborough, Ontario: Prentice-Hall, 35-68.

Hodgson, John (1976). "The Problem of Succession." In Paul Cocks, Robert V. Daniells and Nancy Whittier Heer (eds.), *The Dynamics of Soviet Politics*. Cambridge, Massachusetts: Harvard University Press, 96-116.

Hodnett, Grey (1975). "Succession Contingencies in the Soviet Union." *Problems of Communism*, 24 (March-April), 1-21.

——— and Val Ogareff (1973). *Leaders of the Soviet Republics, 1955-1972*. Canberra, Australia: Australian National University.

Hofferbert, Richard (1970). "Elite Influence in State Policy Formation." *Polity*, 7 (Spring), 81-95.

Hoffman, Erik (1973). "Soviet Meta-Policy: Information Processing in the CPSU." *Journal of Comparative Administration*, 5 (August), 200-232.

Holt, Robert, and John Turner (1969). "Change in British Politics: Labour in Parliament and Government." In William Andrews (ed.), *European Politics, II: The Dynamics of Change*. New York: Van Nostrand Reinhold, 101-148.

Holtzman, Franklyn (1974). *Financial Checks on Soviet Defense Expenditures*. Lexington, Massachusetts: D. C. Heath.

Hoover, Herbert (1928). "Address of Acceptance of the Republican Nomination for President." Washington, D.C.: Republican National Committee.

Hough, Jerry (1977). *The Soviet Union and Social Science Theory*. Cambridge, Massachusetts: Harvard University Press.

——— (1976). "The Brezhnev Era: The Man and the System." *Problems of Communism*, 25 (March-April), 1-17.

——— (1975). "The Soviet Experiment and the Measurement of Power." *Journal of Politics*, 37 (August), 665-710.

——— (1973). "The Bureaucratic Model and the Nature of the Soviet System." *Journal of Comparative Administration*, 5 (August), 134-168.

——— (1972). "The Soviet System: Pluralism or Petrification." *Problems of Communism*, 12 (March-April), 25-45.

———— (1969). *The Soviet Prefects*. Cambridge, Massachusetts: Harvard University Press.

Hunter, Holland (1972). "Soviet Economic Statistics." In Vladimir Treml and John Hardt (eds.), *Soviet Economic Statistics*. Durham, North Carolina: Duke University Press, 3-20.

Huntington, Samuel, and Zbigniew Brzezinski (1963). *Political Power: USA/USSR*. New York: Viking Press.

Inglehart, Ronald and Avram Hockstein (1972). "Alignment and Dealignment of the Electorate in France and the United States." *Comparative Political Studies*, 5 (October), 343-372.

Jackson, John (1972). "Politics and the Budgetary Process." *Social Science Research*, 1 (April), 35-60.

Jancar, Barbara (1971). *Czechoslovakia and the Absolute Monopoly of Power: A Study of Political Power in a Communist State*. New York: Praeger.

Jewell, Malcolm (1972). "The Governor as Legislative Leader." In Thad Beyle and J. Oliver Williams (eds.), *The American Governor in Behavioral Perspective*. New York: Harper and Row, 127-140.

———— (1969). *The State Legislature: Politics and Practice*. New York: Random House.

Johannes, John (1972). "Congress and the Initiation of Legislation." *Public Policy*, 20 (Spring), 281-310.

Johnson, Chalmers (ed.) (1969). *Change in Communist Systems*. Stanford, California: Stanford University Press.

Johnson, Lyndon (1971). *The Vantage Point: Perspectives on the Presidency, 1963-1969*. New York: Holt, Rinehart and Winston.

———— (1964). "The State of the Union." *The New York Times* (January 9), 28-29.

Johnson, Richard (1974). *Managing the White House*. New York: Harper and Row.

Joint Economic Committee (ed.) (1977). *The East European Economies Post-Helsinki*. Washington, D.C.: Government Printing Office.

———— (1966). *New Directions in the Soviet Economy*. Washington, D.C.: Government Printing Office.

Jones, E. Terrance (1974). "Political Change and Spending Shifts in the American States." *American Politics Quarterly*, 2 (April), 159-178.

Jones, George (1971). "The Prime Minister's Power." In Gary Byrne and Kenneth Pederson (eds.), *Politics in Western European Democracies: Patterns and Problems*. New York: John Wiley, 275-291.

Josephson, Eric (1972). "Irrational Leadership in Formal Organizations." In Glenn Paige (ed.), *Political Leadership*. New York: Free Press, 132-145.

Jowitt, Kenneth (1975). "Inclusion and Mobilization in European Leninist Regimes." *World Politics*, 28 (October), 69-96.

Juviler, Peter, and Henry Morton (eds.) (1967). *Soviet Policy-Making*. New York: Praeger.

Kaim-Caudle, P. R. (1973). *Comparative Social Policy and Social Security*. New York: Dunellen.

Kaimuk, V. (1977). "Changes in the Condition and Structure of Rural Population Employment During the Process of Urbanization in the Countryside." *Current Digest of the Soviet Press*, 28 (January 5), 5.

Kanet, Roger (ed.) (1971). *The Behavioral Revolution in Communist Studies*. New York: Free Press.

Karcz, Jerczy (1971). "From Stalin to Brezhnev: Soviet Agricultural Policy in Historical Perspective." In James Millar (ed.), *The Rural Community: A Symposium*. Urbana, Illinois: University of Illinois, 36-70.

——— (1965). "The New Soviet Agricultural Programme." *Soviet Studies*, 17 (October), 129-161.

Karliuk, I. (1974). "Economic Problems in the Development of Agriculture." *Problems of Economics*, 17 (May), 3-21.

Katz, Abraham (1972). *The Politics of Economic Reform in the Soviet Union*. New York: Praeger.

Kaufman, Herbert (1971). *The Limits of Organizational Change*. University, Alabama: University of Alabama Press.

Kearns, Doris (1976). *Lyndon Johnson and the American Dream*. New York: Harper and Row.

Keech, William, and Donald Matthews (1976). *The Party's Choice*. Washington, D.C.: Brookings Institution.

Keefe, William, and Morris Ogul (1970). "Political Parties and Economic Policy." In James Anderson (ed.), *Politics and Eco-*

nomic Policy-Making: Selected Readings. Reading, Massachusetts: Addison-Wesley.

Kelley, Donald (1974). "Toward a Model of Soviet Decision-Making: A Research Note." *American Political Science Review*, 68 (June), 701-706.

Keren, Michael (1973). "The New Economic System in the GDR: An Obituary." *Soviet Studies*, 24 (April), 573-582.

Key, V. O. (1949). *Southern Politics in State and Nation.* New York: Knopf.

Khristorandov, U. (1976). "Na osnove kompleksnogo ekonomicheskogo i sotsial'nogo planirovaniia." *Partiinaia zhizn'*, 2 (January), 19-25.

Khromov, S. (1972). "XXIV s'ezd KPSS i nekotorye voprosy sotsial'nogo razvitiia sovetskogo obshchestva." *Istoriia SSSR* (Moscow), 3 (May-June), 3-19.

Khrushchev, Nikita (1962). *Stroitel'stvo kommunizma v SSSR i razvitie sel'skogo khoziaistva.* Vols. I-IV. Moscow: Politizdat.

――― (1964). *Stroitel'stvo kommunizma v SSSR i razvitie sel'skogo khoziaistva.* Vols. V-VIII. Moscow: Politizdat.

King, Anthony (1969). "Political Parties in Western Democracies." *Polity*, 2 (Winter), 111-141.

Kirchheimer, Otto (1966). "The Transformation of West European Party Systems." In Joseph La Palombara and Myron Weiner (eds.), *Political Parties and Political Development.* Princeton, New Jersey: Princeton University Press, 177-200.

Klatt, W. (1976). "Reflections on the 1975 Harvest." *Soviet Studies*, 28 (October), 485-498.

Klein, Rudolph (1976). "The Politics of Public Expenditure: American Theory and British Practice." *British Journal of Political Science*, 6 (October), 401-432.

Kommunisticheskaia partiia Sovetskogo Soiuza v resoliutsiakh i resheniakh s"ezdov, konferentsii i plenumov Ts. K., 1969-1972 (1973). Moscow: Politizdat.

Kommunisticheskaia partiia Sovetskogo Soiuza v resoliutsiakh i resheniakh s"ezdov, konferentsii i plenumov Ts. K., 1966-1968 (1972). Moscow: Politizdat.

Korbonski, Andrzej (1976). "Leadership Succession and Political Change in Eastern Europe." *Studies in Comparative Communism*, 8 (Spring/Summer), 3-22.

Korten, David (1972). "Situational Determinants of Leadership

Structure." In Glenn Paige (ed.), *Political Leadership*. New York: Free Press, 146-164.

Koval, N. S. (ed.) (1973). *Planirovanie narodnogo khoziaistva SSSR*. Moscow: Vysshaia Shkola.

KPSS: Spravochnik (1971). Moscow: Politizdat.

Krutogolov, M. (1958). *Vybory v SSSR i v burzhuaznykh stranakh*. Moscow: Politizdat.

Kukushkin, M. (ed.) (1975). *Razvitoi sotsializma proizvodstva material'nykh blag*. Leningrad: Lenizdat.

Kulakov, F. (1975). "Desiatiletie istoricheskogo plenuma." In V. Golikov (ed.), *Kursom Martovskogo plenuma*. Moscow: Politizdat, 15-29.

—— (1970). "Toward a New Upswing in Soviet Agriculture." *Current Digest of the Soviet Press*, 22 (July 14), 9.

Kunaev. D. (1972). "Gody krutogo pod"ema." In V. A. Golikov, et al. (eds.), *Sel'skogo khoziaistvo SSSR na sovremennom etape*. Moscow: Politizdat, 23-48.

Laird, Roy (1970). *The Soviet Paradigm: An Experiment in Creating a Mono-Hierarchal Polity*. New York: Free Press.

—— (1965). "Agriculture Under Khrushchev." *Survey*, 56 (July), 105-117.

—— and Edward Crowley (eds.) (1965). *Soviet Agriculture: The Permanent Crisis*. New York: Praeger.

Lampman, Robert (1974). "What Does It Do for the Poor? A New Test for National Policy." *Public Interest*, 34 (Winter), 66-82.

Lander, Louise (1967). *War on Poverty*. New York: Facts on File.

Leichter, Howard (1979). *A Comparative Approach to Policy Analysis: Health Care in Four Nations*. Cambridge, England: Cambridge University Press.

—— (1977). "Comparative Public Policy: Problems and Prospects." *Policy Studies Journal*, 5 (Summer), 83-96.

Lemishev, N. (1970). "Normativy kapital'nykh vlozhenii i sel'skoe khoziastvo."*Voprosy ekonomiki*, 3 (March), 111-120.

Lenin, V. I. (1919). "The Present Situation and the Immediate Tasks of Soviet Power." In *Lenin: Collected Works*. Volume 29 (1965). Moscow: Progress Publishers, 456-459.

Levitan, Sar (1969). *The Great Society's Poor Law*. Baltimore: Johns Hopkins University Press.

Lewin, Moshe (1968). *Russian Peasants and Soviet Power*. Evanston, Illinois: Northwestern University Press.

Lewis, Carol Weiss (1976). "The Budgetary Process in Soviet Cities." New York: Columbia Graduate School of Business.

Liebman, Lance (1974). "Social Intervention in a Democracy." *Public Interest*, 34 (Winter), 17-30.

Lijphart, Arend (1970). "Comparative Politics and the Comparative Method." *American Political Science Review*, 65 (September), 682-693.

Lindblom, Charles (1965). *The Intelligence of Democracy*. New York: Free Press.

Linden, Carl (1966). *Khrushchev and the Soviet Leadership*. Baltimore: Johns Hopkins University Press.

Lockard, Duane (1966). "The State Legislator." In Alex Heard (ed.), *State Legislatures in American Politics*. Englewood Cliffs, New Jersey: Prentice-Hall, 98-125.

Long, Norton (1962). *The Polity*. Chicago: Rand McNally.

Lowenthal, Richard (1974). "On 'Established' Communist Party Regimes." *Studies in Comparative Communism*, 7 (Winter), 335-358.

———— and Boris Meissner (eds.) (1968). *Sowjetische Innenpolitik: Triebkrafte und Tendenzen*. Stuttgart, The Federal Republic of Germany: Kohlhammer.

Lowi, Theodore (1964). "American Business, Public Policy, Case Studies and Political Theory." *World Politics*, 6 (July), 677-715.

———— (1963). "Towards Functionalism in Political Science: The Case of Innovation in Party Systems." *American Political Science Review*, 62 (March), 570-583.

Lowry, Stephen (1976). "A Model for Predicting Successions in Communist Systems: The Case of the Soviet Union." *Studies in Comparative Communism*, 8 (Spring/Summer), 145-151.

Ludz, Peter (1973). "Continuity and Change Since Ulbricht." *Problems of Communism*, 22 (March-April), 56-58.

Macridis, Roy (1968). "Comparative Politics and the Study of Government: The Search for Focus." *Comparative Politics*, 1 (October), 79-90.

Madison, Bernice (1968). *Social Welfare in the Soviet Union*. Stanford, California: Stanford University Press.

Maier, V. (1974). "Rost' narodnogo blagosostoianiia v usloviakh razvitogo sotsializma." *Kommunist* (Moscow), 9 (June), 62-75.

Manley, John (1970). "The Family Assistance Plan: An Essay on Incremental and Non-Incremental Policy-Making." Paper presented at the American Political Science Association Convention in Washington, D.C., September 1-5.

Marmor, Theodore, and Martin Rein (1973). "Reforming the 'Welfare Mess': The Fate of FAP, 1969-1972." In Allan Sindler (ed.), *Policy and Politics in America: Six Case Studies*. Boston: Little, Brown, 2-29.

Marris, Peter, and Martin Rein (1969). *Dilemmas of Social Reform: Poverty and Community Action in the United States*. New York: Atherton Press.

Materialy XXIV s"ezda KPSS (1974). Moscow: Politizdat.

Matiukha, I. (1973). "The Rise in Living Standards of the Working People in the USSR." *Problems of Economics*, 16 (September), 60-71.

Matthews, Donald (ed.) (1973). *Perspectives on Presidential Selection*. Washington, D.C.: Brookings Institution.

Mayhew, David (1974). *Congress: The Electoral Connection*. New Haven, Connecticut: Yale University Press.

McCauley, Martin (1976). *Khrushchev and the Development of Soviet Agriculture*. New York: Holmes and Meier.

McCally, Sarah (1966). "The Governor and His Legislative Party." *American Political Science Review*, 60 (December), 923-942.

Meso-Lago, Carmelo, and Carl Beck (eds.) (1975). *Comparative Socialist Systems*. Pittsburgh, Pennsylvania: University of Pittsburgh Press.

Meyer, Alfred G. (1969). "The Comparative Study of Communist Political Systems." In Frederic Fleron (ed.), *Communist Studies and the Social Sciences*. Chicago: Rand McNally, 188-197.

Mezey, Michael (1970). "Ambition Theory and the Office of Congressman." *Journal of Politics*, 32 (August), 574-595.

Mieczkowski, Bogdan (1978). "The Relationship Between Changes in Consumption and Politics in Poland." *Soviet Studies*, 30 (April), 262-269.

Milius, Pauline (1976). *The State of Welfare*. Washington, D.C.: Brookings Institution.

Millar, James (1977). "The Prospects for Soviet Agriculture." *Problems of Communism*, 26 (May-June), 1-16.

—— (ed.) (1971). *The Soviet Rural Community: A Symposium.* Urbana, Illinois: University of Illinois Press.

Miller, Robert (1976). "The Future of the Soviet Kolkhoz." *Problems of Communism*, 25 (March-April), 18-33.

Miller, S. M., and Martin Rein (1969). "Participation, Poverty and Administration." *Public Administration Review*, 29 (January/February), 15-24.

Mills, Richard (1976). "The Virgin Lands Since Khrushchev: Choices and Decisions in Soviet Policy-Making." In Paul Cocks, Robert V. Daniels and Nancy Whittier Heer (eds.), *The Dynamics of Soviet Politics.* Cambridge, Massachusetts: Harvard University Press, 179-192.

—— (1970). "The Virgin Lands Since Khrushchev: Choices and Decisions in Soviet Policy-Making." *Slavic Review*, 29 (March), 58-69.

Milnor, Andrew (1969). *Elections and Political Stability.* Boston: Little, Brown.

Moe, Ronald (ed.) (1971). *Congress and the Presidency.* Pacific Palisades, California: Goodyear.

—— and Steven Tell (1970). "Congress as Policy-Makers: A Necessary Reappraisal." *Political Science Quarterly*, 85 (September), 443-470.

Monov, A. (1972). "Agriculture During the Current Five Year Plan." *Problems of Economics*, 15 (November), 3-19.

Morozow, Michael (1973). *Leonid Breschnew.* Stuttgart, The Federal Republic of Germany: Kohlhammer Press.

Morrison, Denton (1970). *The Significance Test Controversy: A Reader.* Chicago: Aldine.

Morton, Henry (1967). "The Structure of Decision-Making in the USSR." In Peter Juviler and Henry Morton (eds.), *Soviet Policy-Making.* New York: Praeger, 3-28.

Moses, Joel (1974). *Regional Party Leadership and Policy-Making in the USSR.* New York: Praeger.

Moynihan, Daniel (1973). *The Politics of a Guaranteed Income: The Nixon Administration and the Family Assistance Plan.* New York: Random House.

—— (1969). *Maximum Feasible Misunderstanding.* New York: Free Press.

—— (1965). "The Professionalization of Reform." *Public Interest*, 32 (Fall), 6-16.

Mueller, John (1975). "Presidential Popularity from Truman to Johnson." In Norman Thomas (ed.), *The Presidency in Contemporary Context*. New York: Dodd and Mead, 83-105.

Nagle, John (1977). *System and Succession: The Social Bases of Political Elite Recruitment*. Austin, Texas: University of Texas Press.

Narodnoe khoziaistvo, 1922-1972: Iubileinyi statisticheskii ezhegodnik (1972). Moscow: Statistika.

Narodnoe obrazovanie nauka i kul'tura v SSSR: Statisticheskii sbornik (1971). Moscow: Statistika.

Natchez, Peter, and Irvin Bupp (1973). "Policy and Priority in the Budgetary Process." *American Political Science Review*, 67 (September), 951-963.

Neal, Marie Augusta (1965). *Values and Interests in Social Change*. Englewood Cliffs, New Jersey: Prentice-Hall.

Neustadt, Richard (1976). *Presidential Power: The Politics of Leadership with Reflections on Johnson and Nixon*. New York: John Wiley.

————— (1960). *Presidential Power*. New York: John Wiley.

Nixon, Richard (1969). "Address of the President on Nationwide Radio and Television: Welfare Reform." (August 8). Mimeographed Edition. Washington, D.C.: Office of the White House Press Secretary.

Nove, Alec (1975). "Is There a Ruling Class in the USSR?" *Soviet Studies*, 27 (October), 631-634.

————— (1970). "Soviet Agriculture Under Brezhnev." *Slavic Review*, 29 (September), 379-410.

————— and John Newth (1967). *The Soviet Middle East*. New York: Praeger.

"Novyi etap v razvitii sel'skogo khoziaistva SSSR i iuridicheskaia nauka." (1977). *Sovetskoe gosudarstvo i pravo* (Moscow), 1 (January), 3-10.

Oliver, James (1973). "Turnover and Family Circles in Soviet Administration." *Slavic Review*, 32 (September), 527-545.

"On the State Plan for the Development of the USSR National Economy in 1975" (1975). *Current Digest of the Soviet Press*, 26 (January), 7-11.

Orlov, V. (1975). "Prezident i Kongress." *S.Sh.A.* (Moscow), 59 (Noiabr), 96-101.

Osborn, Robert (1970). *Soviet Social Policies*. Homewood, Illinois: Dorsey Press.

Paige, Glenn (ed.) (1972). *Political Leadership*. New York: Free Press.

Paletz, David (1972). "Perspectives on the Presidency." In Norman Thomas and Hans Baade (eds.), *The Institutionalized Presidency*. Dobbs Ferry, New York: Oceana Publishers, 3-19.

"The Party Leads the People to New Accomplishments" (1975). *Current Digest of the Soviet Press*, 36 (January), 3.

Pechatnov, V. (1974). "V poiskakh teorii partiinoi sistemy." *S.Sh.A.* (Moscow), 59 (Noiabr), 100-102.

Pichotin, M. I. (1971). *Sovetskoe biudzhetnoe pravo*. Moscow: Iuridicheskaia Literatura.

Pilisuk, Marc, and Phyllis Pilisuk (eds.) (1976). *How We Lost the War on Poverty*. New Brunswick, New Jersey: Transaction.

Piven, Francis Fox, and Richard Cloward (1976). "The Relief of Welfare." In Marc Pilisuk and Phyllis Pilisuk (eds.), *How We Lost the War on Poverty*. New Brunswick, New Jersey: Transaction, 269-291.

Platky, Leon (1977). "Aid to Families with Dependent Children." *Social Security Bulletin* (October), 17-22.

Ploss, Sidney (1971). "The Rise of Brezhnev." In Sidney Ploss (ed.), *The Soviet Political Process: Aims, Techniques and Examples of Analysis*. Waltham, Massachusetts: Ginn and Company, 271-295.

Ploss, Sidney (1965). *Conflict and Decision-Making in Soviet Russia*. Princeton, New Jersey: Princeton University Press.

Plotnik, Robert, and Felicity Skidmore (1975). *Progress on Poverty*. New York: Academic Press.

Polsby, Nelson (1968). "The Institutionalization of the House of Representatives." *American Political Science Review*, 62 (March), 109-133.

—— and Aaron Wildavsky (1971). *Presidential Elections*. New York: Charles Scribner's Sons.

Potekhin, L., I. and N. Itin (1962). *Planirovanie raskhodov na sotsial'no-kulturnye meropriiatiia*. Moscow: Finansy.

Pressman, Jeffrey, and Aaron Wildavsky (1973). *Implementation*. Berkeley, California: University of California Press.

Prewitt, Kenneth, and Alan Stone (1973). *The Ruling Elites: Elite*

Theory, Power and American Democracy. New York: Harper & Row.

Price, James (1976). "The Effects of Turnover in Organizations." *Organization and Administrative Science,* 7 (Fall), 61-88.

Problemy istorii sovremennoi sovetskoi derevnei (1975). Moscow: Nauka.

Pryor, Frederic (1968). *Public Expenditures in Communist and Capitalist Nations.* Homewood, Illinois: Dorsey.

Przeworski, Adam, and Henry Teune (1970). *The Logic of Comparative Social Inquiry.* New York: John Wiley.

Putnam, Robert (1976). *The Comparative Study of Political Leadership.* Englewood Cliffs, New Jersey: Prentice-Hall.

———— (1973). "The Political Attitudes of Senior Civil Servants in Europe." *British Journal of Political Research,* 3 (July), 257-290.

———— (1971). "Studying Elite Political Culture: The Case of Ideology." *American Political Science Review,* 65 (September), 651-681.

Pye, Lucien (1968). "Description, Analysis and Sensitivity to Change." In Austin Ranney (ed.), *Political Science and Public Policy.* Chicago: Markham, 239-262.

Rakowska-Harmstone, Teresa (1976). "Toward a Theory of Soviet Leadership Maintenance." In Paul Cocks, Robert V. Daniels and Nancy Whittier Heer (eds.), *The Dynamics of Soviet Politics.* Cambridge, Massachusetts: Harvard University Press, 51-76.

Rein, Martin, and Hugh Heclo (1973). "What Welfare Crisis—A Comparison Among the United States, Britain and Sweden." *Public Interest,* 33 (Fall), 61-83.

Report of the Central Committee of the CPSU: The Twenty-Fourth Party Congress (1971). Moscow: Political Literature.

Resheniia partii i pravitel'stva po sel'skomu khoziaistvu (1965-1972) (1973). Moscow: Kolos.

Rigby, T. H. (1970). "The Soviet Elite: Toward a Self-Stabilizing Oligarchy." *Soviet Studies,* 22 (October), 167-191.

Rimlinger, Gaston (1971). *Welfare Policy and Industrialization in Europe, America, and Russia.* New York: John Wiley.

Rose, Douglas (1973). "National and Local Forces in State Politics: The Implications of a Multi-Level Policy Analysis." *American Political Science Review,* 67 (December), 1162-1173.

Rose, Richard (1973). "Comparing Public Policy: An Overview." *European Journal of Political Research,* 1 (April), 67-94.

—— (1969). *Policy-Making in Britain*. New York: Free Press.

Rosen, David (1974). "Leadership Change and Foreign Policy." Paper presented at the American Political Science Convention in Chicago, Illinois, September 2-5.

Rush, Myron (1974). *How Communist States Change Their Leaders*. Ithaca, New York: Cornell University Press.

—— (1968). *Political Succession in the USSR*. New York: Columbia University Press.

Sartori, Giovanni (1968). "European Political Parties: The Case of Polarized Pluralism." In Robert Dahl and Dean Neubauer (eds.), *Modern Political Analysis*. Englewood Cliffs, New Jersey: Prentice-Hall, 114-149.

Sayre, Wallace, and Herbert Kaufman (1960). *Governing New York City*. New York: Russell Sage Foundation.

Scharf, Bradley (1976). "Environmental Determinants and Communist Leadership Behavior." *Studies in Comparative Communism*, 9 (Spring/Summer), 152-161.

Schlesinger, Arthur (1969). "The Dynamics of Decision." In Aaron Wildavsky (ed.), *The Presidency*. Boston: Little, Brown, 133-150.

Schlesinger, Joseph (1975). "The Primary Goals of Political Parties: A Clarification of Positive Theory." *American Political Science Review*, 69 (September), 840-849.

—— (1966). *Ambition and Politics*. Chicago: Rand McNally.

Schneier, Edward (ed.) (1972). *Policy-Making in American Government*. New York: Basic Books.

Schon, Donald (1971). *Beyond the Stable State*. London: Temple Smith.

Schroeder, Gertrude (1971). "Soviet Economic Reforms at an Impasse." *Problems of Communism*, 11 (July-August), 36-46.

Schulman, Paul (1975). "Non-Incremental Policy-Making: Notes Towards an Alternative Paradigm." *American Political Science Review*, 69 (December), 1354-1370.

Searing, Donald (1972). "Models and Images of Man and Society in Leadership Theory." In Glenn Paige (ed.), *Political Leadership*. New York: Free Press, 19-44.

Seidenstecher, Gerthaud (1974). "Der Sowjetische Staatsaushaltsplan 1974." *Berichte* (Köln, Federal Republic of Germany) 13, 11-15.

Seidman, Harold (1970). *Politics, Position and Power*. New York: Oxford University Press.

Seligman, Lester (1971). "Recruiting Political Elites." New York: General Learning Press.

Semin, S. (1970). "Further Development in the Urbanization of Rural Life." *Current Digest of the Soviet Press*, 22 (November 24), 9-10.

Semin, V. (1971). "Virgin Land Farms Need Scientific Aid." *Current Digest of the Soviet Press*, 22 (January 19), 8.

Sergeev, S. (1972). *Kapital'nye vlozheniia v sel'skom khoziaistve: planirovanie i effektivnost'*. Moscow: Ekonomika.

Shapko, V. I. (1968). *Obosnovanie V. I. Leninym i printsipov gosudarstvennogo rukovodstva*. Moscow: Politizdat.

Sharkansky, Ira (1970). *The Routines of Politics*. New York: Van Nostrand Reinhold.

Shaw, Earl, and John Pierce (eds.) (1970). *Readings in the American Political System*. Lexington, Massachusetts: D.C. Heath.

Shevardnadze, A. (1974). "Vyzykatel'nost'." *Pravda* (May 1), 2.

Simush, P. (1977). "Social Changes in the Countryside." *Current Digest of the Soviet Press*, 49 (January 3), 5-6.

Sindler, Allan (ed.) (1969). *American Political Institutions and Public Policy: Five Contemporary Studies*. Boston: Little, Brown.

Sitarian, S. (1968). *Khoziaistvennaia reforma i biudzhet*. Moscow: Finansy.

Skidmore, Felicity (1975). "Growth in Social Programs, 1964-1974." In Robert Plotnick and Felicity Skidmore (eds.), *Progress on Poverty*. New York: Academic Press, 79-108.

Skilling, H. Gordon, and William Franklyn Griffith (eds.) (1971). *Interest Groups in Soviet Politics*. Princeton, New Jersey: Princeton University Press.

Skocpol, Theda (1979). *States and Social Revolutions*. Cambridge, England: Cambridge University Press.

Skolnick, Alfred, and Sophie Doles (1971). "Social Welfare Expenditures 1968-1969." In James G. Scoville (ed.), *Perspectives on Poverty and Income Distribution*. Lexington, Massachusetts: D.C. Heath, 254-267.

"Some Aspects of the Farm Situation" (1970). *Current Digest of the Soviet Press*, 22 (November 12), 8-10.

Sorenson, Theodore (1963). *Decision-Making in the White House*. New York: Columbia University Press.

The Soviet Financial System (1966). Moscow: Progress.

Spigler, Jancu (1973). *Economic Reform in Romanian Industry.* London: Oxford University Press.

Spravochni tom k vos'mu izdaniyu KPSS v resoliutsiakh i resheniakh s"ezdov, konferentsii i plenumov Ts. K. (1973). Moscow: Politizdat.

Stalin, Iosef (1934). *Foundations of Leninism.* Moscow: Cooperative Publication Society of Foreign Workers in the USSR.

Stanley, David (1965). *Changing Administrations.* Washington, D.C.: Brookings Institution.

Steiner, Gilbert (1974). "Reform Follows Reality: The Growth of Welfare." *Public Interest*, 34 (Winter), 47-65.

—— (1971). *The State of Welfare.* Washington, D.C.: Brookings Institution.

—— (1966). *Social Insecurity: The Politics of Welfare.* Chicago: Rand McNally.

Stimson, James (1976). "Public Support for American Presidents: A Cyclical Model." *Public Opinion Quarterly*, 38 (Spring), 1-21.

Strauss, Erich (1969). *Soviet Agriculture in Perspective: A Study of Its Successes and Failures.* New York: Praeger.

Strong, John (ed.) (1971). *The Soviet Union under Brezhnev and Kosygin.* New York: Van Nostrand Reinhold.

Suleiman, Ezra (1978). *Elites in French Society: The Politics of Survival.* Princeton, New Jersey: Princeton University Press.

Sullivan, Gerald (1972). "Incremental Budgeting in the American States." *Journal of Politics*, 34 (May), 639-647.

Sundquist, James (ed.) (1969). *On Fighting Poverty: Perspectives From Experience.* New York: Basic Books.

—— (1968). *Politics and Policy: The Eisenhower, Kennedy and Johnson Years.* Washington, D.C.: Brookings Institution.

Suslov, Mikhail (1970). "On the Tested Lenin's Course." *Current Digest of the Soviet Press*, 25 (July), 1-2.

Swearer, Howard (1964). *The Politics of Succession in the Soviet Union.* Boston: Little, Brown.

Taubman, William (1972). "The Change to Change in Communist Systems: Modernization and Soviet Politics." Paper presented at the American Political Science Association Convention in Washington, D.C., September 1-4.

Thomas, John, and Warren Bennis (eds.) (1972). *Management of Change and Conflict*. Middlesex, England: Penguin.

Thomas, Norman (1975). "Policy Formulation for Education: The Johnson Administration." In Norman Thomas (ed.), *The Presidency in Contemporary Context*. New York: Dodd and Mead, 318-330.

—— (1977). *The Presidency Reappraised*. New York: Praeger.

—— and Hans Baade (eds.) (1972). *The Institutionalized Presidency*. New York: Oceana.

—— and Harold Wolman (1969). "Policy Formulation in the Institutionalized Presidency: The Johnson Task Forces." In Thomas Cronin and Sanford Greenberg (eds.), *The Presidential Advisory System*. New York: Harper & Row, 124-143.

Thompson, Victor (1969). *Bureaucracy and Innovation*. University, Alabama: University of Alabama Press.

—— (1965). "Bureaucracy and Innovation." *Administrative Science Quarterly*, 15 (June), 4-20.

Thornton, Richard (1972). "The Structure of Communist Politics." *World Politics*, 24 (July), 498-517.

Tilton, Timothy (1979). "A Swedish Road to Socialism: Ernst Wigforss and the Ideological Foundations of Swedish Social Democracy." *American Political Science Review*, 73 (June), 505-520.

Torpornin, B. N. (1976). "Gosudarstvo i demokratiia razvitogo sotsializma." In Torpornin (ed.), *Sotsializm i demokratiia*. Moscow: Iuridicheskaiia, 15-44.

Trepczynski, Stanislaw, and Michael Sandowski (1971). *Socialism and National Development*. Warsaw, Poland: Interpress.

Tsurutani, Taketsugu (1973). *The Politics of National Development: Political Leadership in Transitional Societies*. New York: Chandler.

—— and William Mullen (1977). "A Cross-National Comparison of Chief Executives." Paper presented at the American Political Science Association Convention in Washington, D.C., September 1-4.

XXIV s'ezd KPSS i razvitie Marksistka-Leninskoi teorii (1971). Moscow: Politizdat.

Tufte, Edward (1978). *Political Control of the Economy*. Princeton, New Jersey: Princeton University Press.

—— (1974). *Data Analysis for Politics and Policy*. Englewood Cliffs, New Jersey: Prentice-Hall.

Tulebaev, T. (1969). *Biudzhetnoe planirovanie v soiuznoi respublike.* Moscow: Finansy.
—— (1963). *Voprosy teorii i praktiki planirovaniia biudzhetov v soiuznykh respublik.* Moscow: Iuridicheskaia.

Uslaner, Eric, and Ronald Weber (1975). "The Politics of Redistribution: Towards a Model of the Policy-Making Process in the American States." *American Politics Quarterly*, 3 (April), 130-170.
Usoskin, V. (1973). "Biudzhet: Nekotorye ekonomicheskie i politicheskie aspekty." *S.Sh.A.* (Moscow), 38 (February), 35-46.

Volkov, I. (1975). "Novy etap v razvitii sel'skogo khoziaistva SSSR." *Istoriia SSSR* (Moscow), 22 (March-April), 3-21.
—— (1973). "Nekotoreye voprosy istorii sel'skogo khoziaistva i krest'ianstva v poslevoennye gody." *Istoriia SSSR* (Moscow), 20 (January-February), 3-19.
—— (1972). *Razvitie sel'skogo khoziaistva SSSR v poslevoennye gody (1946-1970).* Moscow: Nauka.
Voss, A. (1975). "Gody bol'shikh peremen." In V. A. Golikov (ed.), *Kursom Martovskog plenuma.* Moscow: Politizdat, 168-185.

Wadekin, Karl-Eugen (1975). "Income Distribution in Soviet Agriculture." *Soviet Studies*, 27 (January), 3-26.
Walker, Jack (1974). "The Diffusion of Knowledge and Policy Change: Toward a Theory of Agenda Setting." Paper presented at the American Convention in Chicago, Illinois, August 29-September 2.
Watson, Goodwin (1971). "Resistance to Change." In Gerald Zaltman (ed.), *Processes and Phenomena of Social Change.* New York: Wiley Interscience, 117-132.
Welsh, William (1975). "Some Issues of Research Design and Measurements: Study of Public Policy in Socialist Systems." Paper presented at the American Association for the Advancement of Slavic Studies Convention in Atlanta, Georgia, October 8-11.
Wesson, Robert (1976). "The Problem of Soviet Leadership." In Gary Bertsch and Thomas Ganschow (eds.), *Comparative Communism.* San Francisco, California: W. H. Freeman, 180-189.
Wildavsky, Aaron (1975). *Budgeting: A Comparative Theory of the Budgetary Process.* Boston: Little, Brown.

Wildavsky, Aaron (1974). *The Politics of the Budgetary Process.*
Second Edition. Boston: Little, Brown.
—— (1969). *The Presidency.* Boston: Little, Brown.
—— (1964). *The Politics of the Budgetary Process.* Boston: Little,
Brown.
—— and Naomi Caiden (1974). *Planning and Budgeting in Poor
Countries.* New York: Wiley.
Wilensky, Harold (1967). *Organizational Intelligence: Knowledge and
Policy in Government and Industry.* New York: Basic Books.
Wiles, Peter (1969). *Communist International Economics.* New York:
Praeger.
Wills, Garry (1970). *Nixon Agonistes: The Crisis of a Self-Made Man.*
Boston: Houghton and Mifflin.
Wilson, Harold (1976). *The Governance of Britain.* New York: Har-
per & Row.
Wilson, James (1968). "The Bureaucracy Problem." In Alan Alt-
schuler (ed.), *The Politics of the Federal Bureaucracy.* New York:
Dodd and Mead, 26-31.
—— (1966). "Innovation in Organizations: Notes Towards a
Theory." In James Thompson (ed.), *Approaches to Organiza-
tional Design.* Pittsburgh, Pennsylvania: University of Pitts-
burgh Press, 193-218.
Winters, Richard (1976). "Party Control and Policy Change."
American Journal of Political Science, 20 (November), 597-636.
Witcover, Jules (1977). *Marathon: The Pursuit of the Presidency,
1972-1976.* New York: Viking.
Witte, Edwin (1962). *The Development of the Social Security Act.*
Madison, Wisconsin: University of Wisconsin Press.

Yarmolinsky, Adam (1969). "Ideas into Programs." In Thomas
Cronin and Sanford Greenberg (eds.), *The Presidential Advisory System,* New York: Harper & Row, 91-100.
Yevdokimov, V. (1974). *Kontrol' za ispolneniem gosudarstvennogo
biudzheta SSSR.* Moscow: Ekonomika.

Zabota partii o blage naroda (1974). Moscow: Politizdat.
Zaltman, Gerald, Robert Duncan and Jonny Holbeck (1973). *In-
novations and Organizations.* New York: Wiley.
Zentner, Joseph (1972). "Presidential Transitions and the Per-
petuation of Programs: The Johnson-Nixon Experience."
Western Political Quarterly, 25 (March), 5-15.

Zielinski, Janusz (1973). *Economic Reforms in Polish Industry.* London: Oxford University Press.

Zimmerman, William (1976). "The Tito Succession and the Evolution of Yugoslav Politics." *Studies in Comparative Communism,* 9 (Spring/Summer), 62-79.

——— (1973). "Issue Area and Foreign Policy Process: A Research Note in Search of a General Theory." *American Political Science Review,* 67 (December), 1204-1212.

Zolutukhin, V. (1972). "Ot 'praimeriz' k natsional'nym s"ezdam." *S.Sh.A.* (Moscow), 32 (August), 55-62.

Zorin, V. (1972). "Pervye itogi vyborov." *S.Sh.A.* (Moscow), 32 (December), 55-60.

Index

Adenauer, Konrad, 63-70, 80
agricultural policy (Soviet Union),
56-68, 108-211; cycles in, 211-
18; importance of, 180-87, 203-
07, 213-14; investment in, 194,
204-05; 1953 plenum, 187-89;
1965 plenum, 188, 201-07; performance, 30, 184-97, 200-02,
210-11; reorganization, 195-96;
rural income, 188-90, 193-94,
209-10, 224; virgin lands, 30,
189-91, 192-96, 200-01, 205.
See also capital investments, Stalin, Khrushchev, Brezhnev.
ambition theory, 104-06, 109,
131, 174-78, 214-16, 218-21,
225-29, 240-41, 245-46

behavioralism, *see* elite theory
Beria, Lavrenti, 182-83
Brandt, Willy, 63-70, 80
Brezhnev, Leonid, 143-67, 206-
18; agricultural policy, 206-18,
254; budgetary priorities, 143-
48, 165-67; capital investment
priorities, 143-48, 165-67; compared with Khrushchev, 211-
18; honeymoon, 167-74, 200-
05; ideology and style, 201-04,
211-14; rise to power, 50, 169-
72, 206-11; social and economic
policies, 163-64, 165-67, 209-
10, 224
budgetary allocations, 40-41, 52n,
53n, 61-87, 140-55, 165-67; in
American states, 40-41, 69-87;
in capitalist states, 40-41, 61-68,
223-24; data reliability, 42-45;
generalizability of results, 230-

32; role in succession, 48-50,
64-75; role of chief executive,
48-51, 231-32; in Soviet bloc,
40-41, 140-48, 165-67, 223-25;
in Soviet republics, 40-41, 148-
55; theory of decision process
(capitalist states), 46-49, 68-72,
248-49; theory of decision process (socialist states), 45-51, 148-
53, 248-49. *See also* incrementalism, innovation.
bureaucracy (United States), 24,
117-19, 136-37

Cabinet, 24-25, 33n, 45n; in Britain, 8, 24-25; in Germany, 25;
in the U.S., 24-25, 136
capital investments (socialist
states), 31, 41n, 46, 140; impact
of succession, 143-48, 223-25.
See also Brezhnev, Khrushchev,
and Stalin.
Carter, Jimmy, 12-13, 25n
Central Committee of the Communist Party of the Soviet
Union, 8
chief executives, *see* elite theory
conflict model (in Soviet area
studies), 172n, 181-82, 197-99;
critique of, 218-21, 245-46
Congress, 8, 25, 70, 135-36
corporation, 3, 5, 85

decision-making, *see* conflict
model, corporatism, elite theory, incrementalism, innovation
de-Stalinization, 30, 50, 191-92

Economic Opportunity Act, *see*
welfare policy

Library of Congress Cataloging in Publication Data

Bunce, Valerie, 1949-
  Do new leaders make a difference?

  Includes index.
  1. Heads of state—Succession.   2. Leadership.
3. Policy sciences.   4. Soviet Union—Politics and
government—1945-   .   5. United States—Politics and
government—1945-   .   I. Title.
JF285.B85   351.003   81-2124
ISBN 0-691-07631-6   AACR2
ISBN 0-691-02205-4 (pbk.)